TRAVELING
ON YOUR
OWN

D0830620

250 GREAT
IDEAS FOR GROUP AND
SOLO VACATIONS

ELEANOR BERMAN

CLARKSON POTTER/PUBLISHERS • NEW YORK

TO MY SINGULAR DAUGHTER TERRY

(though she is no longer single)

With thanks for the diligent research
that helped make this book a reality

Published by Clarkson N. Potter, Inc., distributed by Crown Publishers, Inc., 201 East 50th Street, New York, New York 10022

CLARKSON N. POTTER, POTTER and colophon are trademarks of Clarkson N. Potter, Inc.

Manufactured in the United States of America

Library of Congress Cataloging-in-Publication Data
Berman, Eleanor
Traveling on your own : 250 great ideas for singular vacations by Eleanor Berman.
p. cm.
1. Travel. I. Title.
G151.B483 1990
910—dc20 89-16280
CIP

ISBN 0-517-57454-3

CONTENTS

ACKNOWLEDGMENTS

I want to thank the many tour organizers, groups, and learning programs that provided information and references to be used in this book, as well as the people who agreed to be interviewed about their vacation experiences. My appreciation also to the tourist offices who provided suggestions, the food writers who helped with restaurant recommendations, and my travel-writer friends who contributed their valuable opinions and expertise.

Finally, a special thank-you to my editor, Shirley Wohl, for her encouragement and ever-available moral support; editorial assistant Sharon Naftal; and all the rest of the wonderful, helpful staff at Clarkson Potter.

INTRODUCTION

THE FIRST TIME I TRAVELED BY MYSELF, I WAS newly divorced and scared to death. I never dreamed at that point that travel writing was to become my profession, almost forcing me to become adept at getting around on my own. I was just a travel lover determined that lack of a companion was not going to keep me at home. Happily, I discovered that the excitement of my first solo trip—a visit to San Francisco—overcame my qualms. I did meet people along the way—not every day or for every meal, but enough to keep me from feeling totally alone. And I had a wonderful time.

That was a long time ago, but I still remember my initial fear and I have special empathy when someone asks me plaintively, "But where can I go alone?"

Having now traveled extensively for both business and pleasure, I've learned that there are many happy answers to that question; that, in fact, solo travel can have some special advantages simply because you can tailor it exactly to your own tastes.

The purpose of this book is to point out some of the myriad possibilities for rewarding solo vacations, as well as offer some of the know-how that makes for more confident travel on your own. My aim is to help you discover that you don't always need to start out with a traveling companion to have a wonderful time—that *alone* need not mean lonely.

No one asked or paid to be included in this book. I chose programs and tours strictly because they represented a wide range of activities that seemed to offer an opportunity for comfortable and exciting singular vacations. I tried to stay with those that have been around long enough to have a proven record. The basic information was provided by the operator of each program, as were the names of most of the references quoted. The comments were requested because the trips I could experience personally (you will find my remarks under **E.B.**) were necessarily limited, and wherever possible, I wanted to hear from travelers who could give firsthand reports.

The best way to ensure that any vacation is successful is to gather as much information as possible before you make a choice, but that is doubly true when you are planning a trip alone, without a companion to help cushion disappointments. Use the listings in this book as a guide and a starting point, to be followed up by research with travel agents, friends, and specialized magazines. If you're considering a particular group trip or activity, ask for current information and *references* and phone direct to clear up unanswered questions before signing on. You might follow my example, and ask for names of past solo participants who can tell you whether they felt comfortable as part of such a group.

I've tried to give the cons as well as the pros for some of these trips, in the hopes that they will be of value to you in making a choice. Inevitably, these are personal assessments, and my tastes may not always match your own.

The pages that follow present only a sampling of trips, and I may have omitted some equally rewarding possibilities for solo travel. If you know of any, please write to me care of Clarkson N. Potter and share them for a future edition.

If this book gives you new ideas, encourages you to overcome your fears of traveling by yourself, and helps you to make the right choices for *you*—my mission will be accomplished.

TRAVELING
ON YOUR
OWN

1

ON YOUR OWN: THE REWARDS

NOT VERY LONG AGO IN NEW YORK CITY, A LECture was held that packed the auditorium. The topic: vacations for singles.

The turnout was not surprising. We are living in a world where the number of single people has nearly doubled since 1960; the 25-to-39 age group has nearly tripled. According to a 1987 Quirk's Marketing Research Review, there are close to 77 million unmarried people in America, meaning that approximately 43.1 percent of the population is single, widowed, or divorced. And many people who travel alone are not even counted in these statistics. They may be separated from, or simply unable to coordinate travel dates with, their partners. It has been estimated that solo travelers make up half of today's travel market.

Yet information for those who want to plan a vacation alone has been hard to come by. Most people know about Club Med and some of the tours designed for single travelers. But there is also a world of exciting travel to be enjoyed on your own that is not labeled "For singles only."

Many people are at a loss when it comes to finding these vacations because information is scattered. The occasional lecture or article may not be available when you really need it. Few guidebooks look at things from the point of view of a single traveler. Travel agents also are limited by this lack of reference material.

The aim of *Traveling on Your Own* is to fill that gap, to bring together in one sourcebook the wide range of rewarding vacations that can be enjoyed without a traveling companion.

Today no one, young or old, needs to stay at home for lack of company. The exciting possibilities for travel are as varied as the ages, budgets, and interests of those millions of singles. And while that old stickler, the single supplement, still makes it more expensive to travel alone, for those who need to economize there are more ways than ever to match up with compatible roommates to share the costs, whether on tours or cruises or for independent travel.

One chapter ahead will include the growing range of programs exclusively for singles, but most of the options in this book are not limited by marital status. They are choices based on personal interests, places and programs where you can feel equally comfortable on your own or with a partner. Many of them include family-style meals, eliminating the need to eat alone, a prospect that is not welcome to many travelers. The chapters are divided into various categories of vacation experiences from shaping up your body to stretching your mind, active adventure to relaxing in the sun. There is something here for everyone, from travelers in their 20s to adventure-seekers over age 60.

Many of these ideas can be found in other guides. The difference here is that the information was compiled with the single traveler in mind, *single* in this case meaning simply traveling alone.

The data supplied by the organizer of each trip is supplemented wherever possible by firsthand accounts from past solo travelers—including myself. If there are no reports, it is because no references were made available. Big tour companies and cruise lines in particular were generally unwilling to give out names of past clients.

Exact prices change rapidly, so the trips here are designated by general price categories as follows:

I = $100 a day or less including meals
M = $100 to $150 daily
E = Between $150 and $200 daily
EE = Over $200 per day

Transportation is not included in these estimates except for tours or unless it is specifically mentioned.

One thing should be stressed from the start. This is *not* a book about how to find Mr. or Ms. Right on your vacation. Cupid is notoriously unreliable about where and when he aims his arrows, and there is no surer way to doom your trip than to base its success on whether or not you meet someone special.

The trips here encourage you to look at solo travel not as a way to find someone else, but as a time to find *yourself*. That's the secret of a truly singular vacation.

Certainly there are challenges in traveling by yourself. Dining alone is a big one, and successful solo travel requires more advance research, more careful planning, and more resourcefulness than a trip for two. All these topics will be covered in the pages ahead.

But what stops most people from traveling alone is less logistics than attitude. If you've never traveled by yourself, it may seem frightening. It's easy to feel nervous, shy, self-conscious, and even self-pitying when you seem to be one in a world of twos. The tendency is to imagine that people will look at you and say, "Poor thing—all alone."

In truth, traveling alone says nothing about you whatever except that you have a spirit of independence and adventure. Who's to say you don't have a wonderful friend at home who can't get away for this particular trip?

Furthermore, rather than feeling sorry for you, many of the couples you are envying may be *jealous* of your spirit and your freedom. Travel shared can be wonderful—but it can sometimes pose its own problems. Neither friends nor lovers are always in harmony in their enthusiasms or energy levels. If she loves Gothic cathedrals but he'd rather scuba dive, tensions can loom. Nothing is more frustrating than a companion who wants to use up all of your free time shopping—unless it is a travel mate who taps a foot impatiently every time *you* want to browse in a store. Travel partners sometimes lack your stamina, or, even worse, may keep up a pace that wears you out.

So, travel with a partner means compromises. Solo travel, on the other hand, can be the ultimate self-indulgence, the chance to tailor a vacation strictly to your own tastes, energies, and timetable, to go where you please, do exactly what you want when you want, and meet interesting new people of all ages and both sexes, married and single, in the process.

Without the insulation of a partner, you may find you are more open to experiencing a new environment. You notice more, impressions are more vivid, you can take time to linger—and reactions are completely your own, uncolored by someone else's opinions.

By yourself, you can feel freer to broaden your horizons and try out new roles, to live out a few fantasies perhaps, like riding a horse or rafting a river or painting a sunset, things you might hesitate to attempt in front of the folks back home.

Because there is far more incentive to seek out other people when you are by yourself, you tend to become more outgoing, to seek out new friends—and to find them.

What's more, many travelers who set out a bit shaky about traveling solo return feeling very good about themselves, with a stronger sense of competence, self-assurance, and independence for having proved that they can make it on their own.

Traveling alone has its challenges, yes—but it can also be a wonderful opportunity. In the pages ahead you'll find a world of ideas for rewarding solo adventures. Make the most of them by selecting those that are uniquely right for you.

MAKING CHOICES

In planning a successful solo vacation, the first and most important tip to keep in mind is a simple one: Know yourself.

There are literally thousands of possibilities for vacations, from tennis camps and museum tours to cruising the Nile or trekking in Nepal. One of the pitfalls of planning a trip alone is the temptation to choose what you think other single people are doing, rather than doing the research to find something suited to your own tastes.

Yes, lots of people go on rafting trips by themselves, but if you hate camping and would be terrified by swirling rapids, it makes little sense to head for a river. Remember that the greatest advantage to traveling by yourself is the freedom to do exactly what you like best.

And while trips for "singles" may seem more comfortable than being a single among couples, it is a mistake to limit yourself only to this category. Consider these trips, certainly, but if you sign up for a trip solely for single company and discover that all you have in common with your fellow passengers is your marital status, the trip will be a washout.

The first question to ask yourself, then, is what *you* want from your vacation. Here are some points to consider:

- Do you need to relax and wind down or do you want a pick-me-up, a totally new adventure to spice up your life?
- What kind of physical shape are you in—and how much physical challenge do you want on your trip?
- Do you want to expand your present hobbies or interests or develop a new one?
- Is there some particular area you want to visit? If so, do you prefer seeing a little bit of a lot of places or spending time getting to know one destination in depth?
- Are you seeking a warm climate?
- How important is the quality of the food and lodging?
- Will you be happier making arrangements on your own and moving at your own pace or would you rather be part of a group?

The more carefully you analyze what you are hoping for, the more likely you are to find it. Suppose, for example, that you want to visit the south of France. Your goals are to see the countryside, get some exercise, meet other people ages 30 to 40, and sample gourmet food. There are many luxury tours that could supply the gourmet part of the formula, but they would provide little exercise, and probably attract an older clientele. An upscale biking or hiking trip might fill all of the requirements. What remains then is to research who offers such trips in the area and contact each with the right questions.

If you have the same destination in mind, but want a less strenuous trip, you might look into a learning vacation, perhaps one that stresses cooking, a foreign language, architecture, or art. For a younger scene, there are tours geared to those under 35, as well as camping trips and youth hostel tours.

When your sights are set on sunshine, beware. A Caribbean island or the Mexican Riviera can hold perils for single travelers. Romantic resorts naturally attract loving couples, and there is nothing more depressing than feeling like odd man out in a lovers' hideaway. Look for other possibilities instead. Depending on your tastes, a trip to the Yucatán ruins, a tennis camp in Florida, or painting lessons in Mexico are warm-weather options that should offer companions whose enthusiasms match your own. Windjammer sailing cruises attract lots of active, sociable people in the Caribbean, or you could check into a sunny spa resort that tends to draw many solo participants, married and single alike.

Should you join a group or take off on your own? A lot depends on your travel experience and your disposition. Do you dislike regimentation and prefer setting your own pace? Are you content to amuse yourself at home on occasion with solo walks, shopping expeditions, or museum visits? Are you able to talk to strangers? Are you willing to spend time and effort researching and planning your trip? Most of all, are you an optimist, ready to make the most of what you have rather than pining about what is missing? If the answers are yes, don't be afraid to try a trip by yourself; often it is the most rewarding way to go.

A good way to test the waters is to join a group for a tour, then afterward spend extra time in a city on your own. Or you might break up a solo city visit with short group tours to nearby attractions.

Browse through all of the categories of vacations included in this book. You should find enough ideas to get you happily to almost any part of the world that intrigues you, and inspiration to try some new travel experiences as well. The key to traveling happily on your own is to do it in the way that will be most comfortable and enjoyable for *you*.

2

LEARN A SPORT

SPORTS ARE THE PERFECT VACATION ICEBREAKER when you are alone, particularly when you are learning new techniques with other people. Whether you improve your old game or pick up a new one, you'll also be adding a valuable dimension to your life when you get home. On a sports vacation, everyone is a winner.

Which sports are offered? Almost any you can name. From tennis and golf to fly-fishing and scuba diving, if you want to learn it, you can find someone to teach you on your vacation. You can learn to cross-country ski, canoe, ride a horse, climb a mountain—or even live out your fantasy of being a major leaguer at a spring training baseball camp.

A few caveats from the pros who run sports camps before you set out on any learn-a-sport vacation: Try to avoid blisters. If you buy new shoes for the trip, leave plenty of time to break them in at home before you go. And be prepared for hours out-of-doors by bringing protection—sunscreen, sunglasses or a visor, and a protective hat.

The final bit of advice: Start an exercise routine at home, stressing aerobics, for about a month before you go. Beginner or expert, you'll get more out of sports instruction if you build up your stamina in advance.

Here's a survey of the sporting vacation world.

TENNIS

Tennis camp is by far the most popular sports vacation. Since there is a wide variation in facilities and rates, your first decision in choosing a tennis camp should be based on its ambience—resort versus campus dormitory–style living. This is often a matter of budget as well as preference, since resorts are obviously more expensive. Often locations with group dining are more sociable for single participants.

Your next decision depends on how intensive an instructional program you prefer. Finally, the season will make a difference. Decide whether you want to head for the mountains or the sunshine—or maybe let tennis camp solve the problem of planning a Caribbean vacation on your own.

While the lodgings and atmosphere may vary, the essential teaching programs all are much like the 5½-day All-American Sports tennis week I spent at the Topnotch resort in Stowe, Vermont.

The instruction began late Sunday afternoon with an orientation session and a few minutes of individual play with an instructor who graded and divided us by ability into groups of four. Then we spent about an hour learning the right way to volley at the net.

During the next 5 days, we moved on to forehand, backhand, serve, overhead, and short strokes, with special drills devised to work on each stroke. Each day began with about 15 minutes of warm-up exercises. One morning we were videotaped and got to see firsthand what we were doing right and wrong. Instructors rotated courts every half hour, the system preferred by All-American so that you get a variety of points of view. Other camps favor consistency and have the same pro stay with the group for the week.

On the third day we saw a sample of a common phenomenon that the pros called the "Wednesday Wall." One of the beginners, feeling tired and overwhelmed, was discouraged and ready to quit. It's a common feeling anytime you let yourself in for a lot of unaccustomed exercise, but it passes if you keep going. The staff reassured our unhappy campmate, and after a good night's sleep, she was back for more—and glad she had returned.

The pros were excellent—outgoing, encouraging, and fun as well as fine teachers. The last day we got an honest but upbeat evaluation sheet, with tips as to what to watch out for at home. At the bottom was a "Peanuts" cartoon that really summed up the easygoing attitude of this camp. It pictured Sally saying to Charlie Brown, "What kind of a report card do you call this? I didn't even get any grades. All it says is 'Good Hustle.'"

Will tennis camp work miracles on a mediocre tennis game? Unfortunately, you can't radically change your game in 5 days and most camps don't try. Instead they work on improving your existing strokes. With such concentrated practice, you do see encouraging improvement—and at the same time meet many people who share your interest in the sport.

Below is a listing of a variety of tennis camps. One caveat when you choose: Be sure there are ample indoor courts so your vacation won't be washed out if it rains.

ALL-AMERICAN SPORTS, 116 Radio Circle, Mount Kisco, NY 10549; 800-223-2442 or 914-666-0096. Year round. (EE)

Years in business: 20
Age range: 30–55
Most common age: 35–45
Percent alone: Varies

Number in program and male/female ratio vary widely by location, season, and chance year round. Special weeks available for singles, beginners, advanced, "40s plus," women, doubles strategy, and parent/child. No single supplement for off-season singles weeks or Amherst College programs.

All-American, a pioneer in tennis camp vacations, has programs at a number of top resorts, including Sonesta Sanibel Harbour Resort, Amelia Island Plantation, Boca Raton Resort and Club, and Grand Cypress Resort, Florida; Topnotch at Stowe, and Sugarbush, Vermont; Jiminy Peak, Massachusetts, and Windham Ridge, New York. Locations outside the continental United States are at Half Moon Bay, Jamaica; Palmas del Mar, Puerto Rico; and the Radisson Puerto Plata in the Dominican Republic. Others are added periodically. Guests choose 2 or 4 hours of instruction daily at U.S. resorts, get a 3-hour program in the islands. Programs are for 3, 5, or 7 days.

Traditionally, the most intense program (as well as the youngest and most heavily single group) is the summer adult camp program at Amherst College in Massachusetts, with 5 hours of instruction daily. Intensive programs are also available at Sugarbush and Windham Ridge. (Note that All-American has had financial problems, so check that all these offerings remain on their roster.)

COMMENTS:

E. B.: *All-American has been doing this for a long time, and they do it very well. Be prepared for a lot of tennis, even if you choose just two hours of instruction. What with playing with fellow campers in the afternoon, practicing my serve, working on strokes with the ball machine, and taking part in friendly tournaments, four hours of tennis was the average every day.*

Topnotch is exactly that, a beautiful setting in the Green Mountains and a first-class resort. But our "40 plus" group was on its own after the day's lessons ended, and many couples chose to eat at area restaurants rather than in the dining room. It was harder getting to know people well than if one were in a group that shares meals. All-American's singles weeks might be a better choice. The average age for singles is in the 30s, but 40s are not unusual. Everyone gathers for cocktails late in the day, and almost naturally stays together for dinner. There is no predicting male/female ratio. One recent group had the unusual problem of 12 males and 2 females. This time, the guys were grumbling.

COMMENTS FROM PAST SINGLES WEEK PARTICIPANTS:

Female, 20s: *It was very social, with an equal number of men and women. Ages were from early 20s to late 40s. We all went out to dinner and the bars together, and one day went off for a hike, with a picnic lunch in the woods. The program was very well run. The people were interesting, from all over the U.S. and Canada. The accommodations were wonderful.*

Male, 30s: *The group was diverse and interesting. We played a lot of tennis and the instruction was excellent. The group was about evenly divided male and female and the age was 20s and 30s. It was very easy to meet people, a very good experience.*

TOTAL TENNIS, Box 1106, Wall Street Station, New York, NY 10268; 800-221-6496; 718-636-6141. (I)

Years in business: 11
Most common age: 30–45
Number of participants: 60
Age range: 20–60
Percent alone: 50
Male/female ratio: 50/50

June to August. Rooms shares arranged on request, but singles, when available, are only $10 extra.

This program is conducted on the campus of the Williston-Northampton School in Easthampton, Massachusetts. Guests are housed in brick-walled dormitory rooms, share the bath facilities, and eat together in the cafeteria, where meals are served buffet style. Evenings offer volleyball and swim parties, a Monte Carlo night, a barbecue, and tennis movies. Groups are divided into foursomes by ability, and assigned to one instructor for the entire stay. Teachers are given freedom to use their own particular method. Reports here are enthusiastic; half the guests are repeat customers.

COMMENTS:

Male, 30s: *You have to work to get the most from this, but being serious about a game is an escape. Though hours of instruction seems like hard work, the atmosphere is friendly and everyone has fun. Evenings can be*

social, but are usually laid-back and quiet. There is a wide range of ages, with most people in their late 20s and 30s and others up to the 60s. There are always many singles, a good mix of men and women, and no one has to worry about finding people at compatible levels of play.
Female, 30s: *Low-key, friendly, and open, Good instruction. I felt perfectly comfortable alone.*

VAN DER MEER TENNIS CENTER, P.O. Box 5902, Hilton Head Island, SC 29938; 800-845-6138. (I—does not include meals)

Years in business: 10
Age range: 29+
Most common age: 40
Percent alone: 40
Number of participants: 7,500 annually
Male/female ratio: 1/3

Will try to arrange shares.

Dennis van der Meer, whose "tennis university" prepares tennis pros for certification for teaching, also personally supervises adult clinics at his 24-court tennis center on Hilton Head Island. The program includes stroke clinics, drill sessions, round-robins, private and group lessons. Special clinics are offered for advanced players. There are also both tennis programs and other organized activities for children, making this a good choice for single parents. Accommodations are at the oceanfront Hilton Head Inn or the Beach Arbor Villas located across from the tennis center and one block from the beach. Villa rates include membership at the Players Club Health Club, a fitness center with indoor and outdoor pools, Nautilus, Jacuzzis, and sauna. Van der Meer also offers clinics at Sweet Briar College in Virginia in the summer.

COMMENTS:
Male, 30s: *I have been to Hilton Head and to Sweetbriar alone. Both are comfortable, but most of the socializing goes on during the day, so you only meet people in your own group. At night everyone goes their own way. The people are mostly in their 30s and 40s. The adult clinic is half male, half female; the advanced group is 70 percent male. The instruction is good and the program well run, but it is for tennis, not for socializing.*

Male, 30s: *I go with a Parents Without Partners group that returns every Thanksgiving. Other than our people, there seem to be few singles there. The food and accommodations are excellent and the instructors are great, but I recommend it for single people only if they really want to improve their game.*

—

NICK BOLLETTIERI TENNIS ACADEMY, 5500 34th St. W., Bradenton, FL 34210; 813-755-1000 or 1-800-USA-NICK. (M)

Years in business: 20+
Most common age: 27–40
Year round number of participants: 5–35 weekly
Age range: 19–80
Percent alone: 40
Male/female ratio: 3/1

Will try to arrange shares.

Bollettieri runs a large junior program, as well as adult tennis weeks at his big 46-court Florida center. Five and a half hours of tennis instruction are the center of each day, including work on strokes plus the academy's "mental toughness" program, taught by a sports psychology expert. In Florida, guests are housed four per two-bedroom town house overlooking the courts, and meals are served buffet style in the recreation center. Swimming and Jacuzzi are also available and Longboat Key's beaches and Sarasota shopping are nearby. During the summer, camps also are held on four school campuses: California State University at Northridge, California; Deerfield Academy, Massachusetts; Wayland Academy, Beaver Dam, Wisconsin, and SUNY New Paltz, New York.

No references provided.

RAMEY TENNIS SCHOOLS AND FITNESS CENTER, 5931 Highway 56, Owensboro, KY 42301; 501-771-4723. (I)

Years in business: 28
Most common age: 35–45
Number of participants: 21
Age range: 19–70
Percent alone: 75
Male/female ratio: varies

Year round. Additional programs at midwestern campuses June and July. Special weeks for advanced players and for ladies only. Will try to arrange shares.

This "total immersion" program is geared to high achievers, with the day planned from 8 A.M. to 9:30 P.M. Tennis takes up 5 hours daily, or can be extended to 8 for diehards. Strategy sessions, a tennis psych program, tennis movies, and stroke presentations fill the rest of the day. Fitness testing and Nautilus training is part of this program. Four campers work with one pro, and also get to work individually with director Joan Ramey-Ford, a former collegiate champion. Campers are housed in guest cottages, a motel, or dormitory near the tennis house in Owensboro. The Tennis House is located on a working farm where an outdoor pool, fishing ponds, canoes, and horses are on the property, and a sauna and masseuse are on hand to ease tired muscles. Food is home cooked and farm fresh. At summer camps on campuses, participants live in dormitories or nearby motels, eat in cafeterias, and have use of the pool, gym, and other facilities of the school. The schools are Valparaiso University, Valparaiso, Indiana; Wittenberg University, Springfield, Ohio; Knox College, Galesburg, Illinois; and University of the South, Sewanee, Tennessee.

COMMENTS:

Male, 40s: *The ages varied from teens to 50s; people were mainly from the Midwest. You naturally get to know people, especially those in your tennis group, but we all ate meals as a group, making it even easier. Food was excellent, the accommodations fine, the program well run. It was a great experience.*

Male, 40s: *There were some singles, but mostly couples or two friends who came together. But I was alone and I didn't feel lonely. It was easy to meet people, even though I stayed at a motel in town, because we all ate together. The food was the high point of the trip. I was very impressed also by the structure of the lessons. We worked for eight hours a day, but it was spaced so that you didn't get worn out.*

JOHN GARDINER'S TENNIS RANCH, P.O. Box 228, Carmel Valley, CA 93924; 408-659-2207. (EE)

JOHN GARDINER'S TENNIS RANCH ON CAMELBACK, 5700 E. Mcdonald Dr., Scottsdale, AZ 85253; 602-948-2100. (EE)

The number of single participants is very small, but these two facilities deserve mention as the ultimate luxury in tennis camps. The California ranch has been in business for over 30 years. There are 14 courts for 28 guests. Guests are requested to wear tennis whites; for dinner, men wear jackets and ties and women dress up. Dinner is served buffet style and there are no tables for two, so guests do get to know each other. They may range from Texas ranchers to feminist lawyers, but all tend to be interesting and well-heeled people. The program includes 5½ hours of instruction and all meals. The camp operates March to November.

The Scottsdale facility, now over 18 years old, has about 100 people in the program, which runs from October to early May. Bigger and more luxurious, this ranch set in the beautiful Arizona desert upholds the high standards of the original. The program is less intense, with 3½ hours of instruction daily. The fee for the 7-day program includes two half-hour massages. Meals are served both indoors and out to take advantage of the scenery. This is the site of an annual U.S. Senators' Cup tournament that draws Washington and Hollywood biggies for charity.

No references provided.

For further listings of tennis camps, check the ads in the following publications:

TENNIS MAGAZINE, 5520 Park Ave., Box 395, Trumbull, CT 06611; 203-373-7000.

WORLD TENNIS, 3 Park Ave., New York, NY 10016; 212-340-3200.

GOLF

Golf schools based at top resorts give single vacationers a focus to the day and a way to meet people, as well as the chance to improve their game.

THE GOLF SCHOOL, Mount Snow Resort, Mount Snow, VT 05356; 802-464-3333; or Plantation Golf Resort, Crystal River, FL 32629; 800–632–6262 or 904–795–4211. (EE)

Years in business: Since 1978
Most common age: 50s
Number of participants: 50–80
Age range: 12–75
Percent alone: 25–30
Male/female ratio: Higher male

Suitable for beginners.

This popular school is based at the Mt. Snow resort from May to early October, and at Plantation Inn & Golf Resort, Crystal River, Florida, from January to April. The reason for its popularity is a low teaching ratio—four students per instructor. The schools employ the Accelerated Golf Method, a building-block approach that uses motion as the foundation for developing a strong, repeating golf swing. Videotape plus other training aids and classroom instruction are part of the 2- and 5-day programs offered.

COMMENTS:

Female, 40s: *A special effort is made to make single people feel comfortable. There is a get-together party and buffet dinner the first night, a banquet the last night, and a "captain's table" so that you can always find company for dinner. There were many more single males than females! The small teaching groups mean you get to know people well. A good learning experience, a lot of golf, and a lot of fun.*

GOLF DIGEST INSTRUCTION SCHOOLS, 5520 Park Ave., Box 395, Trumbull, CT 06611; 800-243-6121 or 203-373-7130. (EE)

Years in business: Since 1972
Most common age: Over 35
Number of participants: 20 per class
Age range: 25–65
Percent alone: High
Male/female ratio: Varies; higher male

Will try to arrange shares—easier to find for men.

Over 200 schools around the country operate under the auspices of this golfing magazine, with many top pros as teachers. Classes are held at the practice tee, the practice bunker, and the putting green, as well as on the golf course, and sports psychology is part of the curriculum. Videotapes are also used. Among the resorts and golf clubs participating are Innisbrook Resort and Golf Club, Tarpon Springs, Florida; Tucson National Resort, Arizona; North River Yacht Club, Tuscaloosa, Alabama; Mission Hills Resort, Rancho Mirage, California; Carmel Valley Golf and Country Club, California; Sea Island Golf Club, St. Simons Island, Georgia; Ocean Edge Resort, Brewster, Massachusetts; Fox Hill Golf and Country Club, Baiting Hollow, New York; Boyne Highlands Resort, Harbor Spring, Michigan; Amelia Island Plantation, Florida; Desert Mountain, Scottsdale, Arizona; Hueston Woods Golf Club, Oxford, Ohio; Chase Oaks Golf Club, Plano, Texas; Sun Valley Golf Club, Sun Valley, Idaho; Pine Meadow Golf Club, Mundelein, Illinois; Cog Hill Golf Club, Lemont, Illinois; the Golf Club at Château Elan, Brazelton, Georgia; and the Sonnenalp Country Club at Singletree, Vail, Colorado.

COMMENTS:

Female, 40s: *I've attended two schools, in Alabama and in Brewster on Cape Cod. Lodgings were different—villas in Alabama, a lodge in Massachusetts, but both were quite comfortable. Generally, there are couples and men alone; women are in the minority. You all start as strangers, quickly become friendly, and many people get together for dinner. I never ate alone. Ages were from 20s to 70s; the group of twenty is divided into two, and you get to know your own group of ten very well.*

CRAFT-ZAVICHAS GOLF SCHOOL, 600 Dittmer, Pueblo, CO 81005; 719-564-4449. (EE)

Years in business: 20
Most common age: 45
Number of participants: 24
Age range: 40+
Percent alone: 30
Male/female ratio: 60/40

Suitable for beginners. Single supplement charged; will try to arrange shares, but cannot guarantee them.

The second-oldest golf school in the country (and the only one operated by two women) holds 6-day clinics at three resort locations—

Pueblo West Inn and Golf Club, Pueblo West, Colorado; Tucson National Resort and Spa, Tucson, Arizona; and PGA West and La Quinta Hotel Golf and Tennis Resort, La Quinta, California. Groups are divided into classes of six or less, with male instructors for the men, women teaching women. In addition to the personal instruction, split-screen, slow-motion video analysis shows you what you are doing wrong.

COMMENTS:

Male, 60s: *I went alone and it was fine, though there were hardly any other singles. The people were from all over the U.S., and about evenly divided male and female. The program was well organized with good instruction and I was too tired to want to do anything at night.*

Female, 70s: *I've gone a dozen times in several locations and all are wonderful. Most people are older but they range from 30s to 70s, and while there are more couples, there are enough people who come alone. You do different workshops in the morning and afternoon, have lunch as a group and have time to play nine holes before dinner. They provide the first and last dinner. The female instructors all have been on the ladies' tour. It is not hard to meet people, but days are full and most people are too tired to go out at night.*

For additional possibilities, see the following publications:

GOLF DIGEST, 5520 Park Ave., Box 395, Trumbull, CT 06611; 203-373-7000.

GOLF MAGAZINE, 380 Madison Avenue, New York, NY 10017; 212-687-3000.

HORSEBACK RIDING, WESTERN STYLE

Why don't more single people go to ranches? It's hard to imagine a more informal, relaxing vacation. Everybody is in jeans; nobody puts on airs; "dudes" come from all over the country, and are all ages. This is a favorite family vacation, but while solo guests are few, ranches are the best example I know of why an easy ambience, family-style meals, and a common pursuit are more important for a good vacation than the presence of lots of "singles." I've not met anyone who went to a ranch alone who did not report a wonderful time.

Besides riding, many ranches offer activities such as river-rafting, short pack trips, and hiking. They are the perfect introduction to the panoramas and pleasures of the American West.

Ranches vary in ambience, but the routines at most are similar. Guests mount up the first day so that the wranglers can judge their ability. Beginners get instructions in starting, stopping, turning, and getting to know a horse. Your horse is assigned according to your ability to ride. Each day adult rides are offered morning and afternoon for both beginners and advanced riders.

Since many people arrive with little or no riding experience, lessons also are offered every day to help you sit tall in the saddle. Some wind up the week galloping across the meadows; others are content to stay with the "slow ride" each day, a trek into the wilderness that is no less beautiful when the horses move at a reassuring steady walk.

Evenings bring informal group activities from nature talks and slides to square dancing. Sometimes there is a trip to a nearby rodeo.

I've visited two very different kinds of ranches, both places that I would recommend to anyone who loves the outdoors and wants to learn to ride.

TANQUE VERDE RANCH, 14301 E. Speedway, Tucson, AZ 85748; 602-296-6275. (E)

In a sublime setting 2,800 feet high in the foothills of three mountain ranges, the ranch sits amidst millions of acres of national forest and adjoins the Saguaro National Monument, a veritable forest of giant cactus. Guests ride over silent, open desert, up rocky canyons, and into towering mountains. The food is plentiful and delicious, especially cookouts over a mesquite fire; almost every belt was out at least a notch by the end of the week. A tradition here is the early morning ride where a chuck wagon breakfast of eggs and pancakes awaits in the desert, served up against a backdrop of cactus haloed by the glow of the morning sun.

The main building of the ranch is historic, dating to the 1880s, but the 59 air-conditioned rooms in modern casitas are downright luxurious. A tennis court, indoor and outdoor pools, and a workout room are available when you are not in the saddle. Nature programs and walks are an added feature for those who are interested.

Despite the comparatively large number of guests, I met a friendly couple in the van from the airport who invited me to their table at dinner that night and I never lacked for company the rest of the week. Meals are family style, so each day was an opportunity to meet more people. The other two singles in residence were a male visitor from Japan, about age 35, and a woman in her 60s.

VISTA VERDE RANCH, P.O. Box 465, Steamboat Springs, CO 80477; 303-879-3858. (E)

This is an equally stupendous setting in the high meadows north of Steamboat Springs. At 8,500 feet, surrounded by national forest and wilderness areas and the 12,000-foot peaks of the Rockies, the air was crystal clear and the views glorious. This is a working ranch, where you can ride out with the hands to check the cattle and the fences. With only eight rustic cabins, making friends was a snap. Besides riding and eating together, guests share picnics, a white-water rafting trip, optional hiking, and hot-air balloon rides. If you don't feel at home and don't know everyone well by the time the week is over, it's your own fault. Once again, the food was fine.

At both ranches, the guests were well educated, interesting, and went out of their way to include someone who was alone.

CASTLE ROCK GUEST RANCH AND ADVENTURE RESORT, 412 County Rd., 6NS, Cody, WY 82414; 307-587-2076. (E)

Castle Rock rates a mention for its varied program, which supplements riding instruction and ranch life with a chance to try out easy adventures such as llama treks, mountain biking, kayaking and rafting, sailing and windsurfing, and rock climbing. Trips to see the sights of Cody and Yellowstone National Park are included in the rates.

COMMENTS:

Male, late 30s: *I went with my daughter. There were mostly families, just a few singles with kids and a few couples. Most adults were in their 30s* *and 40s. The days were structured, but the atmosphere was very relaxed. They had set riding times each day and many planned activities like kayaking, climbing, fishing, and llama packing. They also have a pool, so there is always something to do. They play games the first day that introduce everyone, and it is very friendly. The food was wonderful, the accommodations okay—sort of suburban rustic. The instruction was great and I had a wonderful time.*

Female, 40s: *It was a totally positive experience. Guests were mostly couples, a few families, one other single parent with his son, from all over the U.S. and from Europe. Everyone was easy to get along with and compatible. You could do as much or as little as you wanted, with the group or on your own. The food was served buffet style, and was outstanding. The staff was top-notch. I would recommend it to any single traveler, but especially those with kids.*

LAZY HILLS GUEST RANCH, Box G, Ingram, TX 78025; 512-367-5600. (I)

Years in business: 29
Age range: 1–90
Most common age: 30–50
Percent alone: 3
Number of participants: 90
Male/female ratio: 50/50
Will try to arrange shares.

This is a working ranch in beautiful country, a good choice for those who want to sample Texas-style ranching. Besides riding, the ranch offers swimming, tennis, basketball, volleyball, archery, hiking, fishing, hayrides, and cookouts. Owners say that it is a good choice for singles, even though they are few in number, because they are included when they want to be, yet are not pressured to participate in activities.

COMMENTS:

Female, 30s: *I've gone a number of times, alone and with my son. It is a working ranch with trail rides, tennis, a pool, a lovely environment. Meals are served family style, so you get to know everyone. Guests come from all over the world, and range in age from 20s to 90s. There have been a number of single people on my visits, more women than men.*

Female, 40s: *There were few other singles, but I had a wonderful time. It was easy to be alone because the owners made sure I was never by myself if I didn't want to be. The food and accommodations were excellent and there were almost too many things to do, as I came to relax. I hiked or rode in the morning, spent the afternoon sitting by a river with a family I became friendly with. The area is very beautiful and peaceful. The hayrides were absolutely wonderful. I would recommend this place to anyone.*

HOW TO CHOOSE A RANCH

There are enough ranches out West to fill a separate book, and because none attract a large number of single guests, the best bet is to get a comprehensive listing, narrow the choices by location, and write for brochures. The first determining factor will be price, since ranches can range from $450 to $1,200 a week, and from 5-star to pure rustic. When you have a few possibilities in mind, call them directly. You'll get a good idea of the flavor of the place just from the way you are received on the telephone. Here are a few things you should learn from the brochure or the owner:

- *Emphasis.* Are single adults welcome? How many came last year? Do more come at certain times of year?
- *Location.* To experience the true beauty of the West, pick a ranch with mountain views and access to rides in the wilderness. If you are traveling alone, you may prefer a ranch that will meet you or that is easy to reach from a major airport.
- *Size.* Outgoing people will do fine almost anywhere, but on the whole, it is easier to meet people at a smaller ranch.
- *Ambience.* Is this an authentic working ranch or a resort? Are accommodations modern or rustic?
- *Amenities.* If you are a new rider, chances are you will soon be a "tender-seat." You may welcome facilities such as whirlpools or the ministrations of a masseuse on the premises, services that can be found even on working ranches like Vista Verde these days.
- *Facilities.* Do you care about a pool or tennis courts in addition to riding? If so, check whether they are available.
- *Activities.* Are there options beyond the ranch itself—trips to the

rodeo, rafting expeditions, fishing, etc.? Is there an evening program?

- *Staff*. What is the ratio of staff to guests? Who gives the riding instruction? How much teaching experience do they have?
- *Horses*. Are there more horses than guests? Will you be assigned the same horse each day?
- *References*. Every ranch should be able to provide you with the names of guests who have visited recently. *Call them before you decide where to go.*

Here are sources that can supply ranch listings; some can also offer advice on selection:

ARIZONA OFFICE OF TOURISM, 1100 W. Washington, Phoenix, AZ 85007; 602-542-8687.

COLORADO DUDE AND GUEST RANCH ASSOCIATION, P.O. Box 300, Tabernash, CO 80478; 303-887-3128. Publishes annual state directory, offers guidance, sometimes offers air discounts.

TRAVEL MONTANA, 1424 Ninth Ave., Helena, MT 59620; 1-800-541-1447.

WYOMING TRAVEL COMMISSION, I-25 at College Dr., Cheyenne, WY 82002-0660; 800-225-5996; in state, 307-777-7777. Publishes state listing.

THE DUDE RANCHERS ASSOCIATION, P.O. Box 471, LaPorte, CO 80535; 303-493-7623. Publishes annual magazine-directory including Arizona, Arkansas, California, Colorado, Montana, Nevada, Oregon, South Dakota, Texas, and Wyoming.

OLD WEST DUDE RANCH VACATIONS, American Wilderness Experiences, Inc., P.O. Box 1486, Boulder, CO 80306; 800-444-DUDE, 303-444-2632. Handles 23 ranches in Montana, Wyoming, Arizona, and Colorado, and offers a central reservation service with guidance in selecting the best place for your needs.

HORSEBACK RIDING, EASTERN STYLE

For easterners who can't make the trip out West, here are a few places that teach riding in rustic, informal, and scenic surroundings:

JORDAN HOLLOW FARM, Route 2, Box 375, Stanley, VA 22851; 703-778-2285.

WEST RIVER LODGE, RR 1, Box 693, Newfane, VT 05345; 802-365-7745.

KEDRON VALLEY INN, Route 106, South Woodstock, VT 05071; 802-457-1473.

ROCKING HORSE RANCH, Highland, NY 12528; 800-43-RANCH or 914-681-2927.

ROARING BROOK RANCH & TENNIS RESORT, Lake George, NY 12845; 518-668-5767

BASEBALL

Every guy—or gal—who has ever fantasized about being a major leaguer can make the dream come true at one-week spring training camps where guests are the rookies and former greats of the game turn coach. Said one participant, "You walk into the clubhouse, grab a cup of coffee, head for your locker and your freshly laundered uniform, with your name stitched on the shirt above your number. You look around and you see stars, telling stories about the old days, and you're one of them . . . for one week, you're on the team." This participant, one of three women in the camp, not only got to play but actually got a hit in the final game, a thrill she will never forget.

Baseball camps, aptly named "Dream Weeks" by one promoter, attract as many nonathletes as aces. Nobody under 30 is allowed. Campers are coached in every phase of the game, get drafted for a team, play each other and sometimes play the pros. All talk is centered on baseball, past, present, and future. Most participants haven't played ball for years—but they have a ball. Who comes to baseball camp? One recent roster included surgeons, lawyers, a dentist, a comic-book distributor, a real estate broker, a bartender, two mailmen, a plumber, and a congressional analyst.

THE SOX EXCHANGE, P.O. Box 145, Montpelier, VT 05601; 802-223-6666. (EE)

Years in business: 5
Most common age: 43
Number of participants: 100 per year
Age range: 30 minimum
Percent alone: 20
Male/female ratio: 95/5

Will try to arrange shares.

Former Boston Red Sox greats, including the legendary Ted Williams, coach these rookies at camp in Winter Haven, Florida. After a "players' draft," seven teams are formed, each with its own manager and coach. Along with receiving coaching, the teams play games throughout the week. At night there are Sox highlight films around the bar, and the chance to listen to the pros reminisce. A third of the "rookies" are repeats. Says president Stuart Savage, "The camaraderie is so intense and the week so full that people become totally immersed in the experience and they return to real life with newfound energy and a sense that more is attainable. People have gone on to change careers, finish long-ignored manuscripts, etc."

COMMENTS:

Male, 50s: *I didn't go to socialize—I'm competitive and I went to play, but it was easy to meet people and camaraderie quickly forms. The people represented 19 states. Many had been given the trip as a gift from their wives. There was one woman. The food was "franchise food"—it could have been better. The people who run the camp do everything they can to get you involved, and you really get to know the Red Sox pros who act as your scouts, instructors, and coaches. There's lots of playing time, and free time in the afternoon and at night, when everyone went to the local bar.*

Male, 40s: *I went alone twice and I'm going again. It is very congenial. When there is free time everyone hangs out together around the pool. I've formed lasting friendships. The average age was 38 to 48; most guests were from New England, and there were five women on one of my programs. Some came just to see the Red Sox greats and didn't participate in games. A typical day starts with calisthenics in the morning, then comes a game, then lunch, then another game. Afterward, you hang around the pool, have dinner, go to the bar, then collapse into bed. It's* *better if you're into the Red Sox but anyone who likes baseball would love it.*

RANDY HUNDLEY'S BASEBALL CAMPS, INC. 244 East West Ct., Palatine, IL 60067; 312-991-9595. (EE)

Years in business: 6
Most common age: mid-40s
Number of participants: 60
Age range: 30–77; 30 minimum
Percent alone: 10–20
Male/female ratio: 95/5

Will try to arrange shares.

Randy Hundley, a former major leaguer, re-creates a big-league spring training camp in Arizona, complete with uniforms, instruction, and intrasquad games, allowing his rookies to live out fantasies of being a Chicago Cub or a St. Louis Cardinal for a week. Infield and outfield drills, batting practice, and coaching from former major leaguers like Ernie Banks, Bob Gibson, or Curt Flood are part of the activities; the grand finale is a game, campers versus the coaches.

COMMENTS:
Male, 40s: *I've attended twice. I went alone, was placed with a roommate. You can't help meeting people. Most of the men were over 40, married, but traveling on their own, and Cub fans from the Midwest. It is well run.*
Male, 30s: *I've been three times and I am going again. It is so easy to meet people—there is instant "team spirit." The men are mostly married, from 30 to 50; there were very few women. I had a great time each time and am looking forward to returning.*

Other baseball camps for adults:

DREAM WEEK, INC., P.O. Box 115, Huntingdon Valley, PA 19006; 215-938-0517. For information on weeks with the Philadelphia Phillies, call 215-938-0517; Cincinnati Reds, 513-745-7900; New York Mets, 718-706-4100; Baltimore Orioles, 301-243-9800.

LOS ANGELES DODGERS ADULT BASEBALL CAMP, Box 2887, Dodgertown, Vero Beach, FL 32961; 305-569-4900.
NEW YORK YANKEES SPORTSWORLD, 5764 Paradise Dr., Suite 7, Corte Madera, CA 94925; 415-924-8725

SAILING

Attending sailing school is a wonderful combination of learning a skill and having the exhilaration of being at sea. In a week you learn the ropes from port to starboard. You start on land, learning what to expect, then head on board with instructors. Pretty soon the crew mates are working as a team, beginning to speak the language of sailing and getting to know their boat. Friendships come easy working in such close quarters toward a common goal. By the time the week is over, the crew is usually able to chart a course and set out on its own.

STEVE COLGATE'S OFFSHORE SAILING SCHOOL, 16731-110 McGregor Blvd., Fort Myers, FL 33908; 800-221-4326 or 813-454-1700. (M)

Years in business: 25
Age range: 12–75
Most common age: 30s
Percent alone: 45
Number of participants: 60,000 graduates
Male/female ratio: 70/30

School locations: City Island, New York; Captiva Island, Florida; Cape Cod, Massachusetts; Tortola, British Virgin Islands. Will try to arrange shares—two to five per villa at Captiva Island, two per room in Tortola.

The 7-day "Learn to Sail" program for beginners is based at a resort and kicks off with a sociable get-acquainted party. Days are divided into morning classes and afternoons on the water. No more than four students are assigned with an instructor to each Olympic-class 27-foot Mooring boat, and a real bond develops among them. Once the basics are mastered, students can increase their knowledge with more advanced sailing and cruising weeks. A special live-aboard cruising course combines curriculum with a thrilling one-week sail on a 40- to

50-foot boat in some of the world's ultimate sailing destinations—Tortola in the British Virgin Islands, St. Lucia in the Grenadines, Tahiti in the South Pacific, and the Sea of Cortés, Baja California, Mexico, depending on the time of year. Graduates can become members of the Offshore Cruising Club, eligible to enjoy cruising vacations in more beautiful locales, and in the Sail Away Club, sailing regularly on club-owned boats at offshore branches.

COMMENTS:

Female, 40s: *My St. Lucia classmates, numbering just two, were also female—one slightly younger and one slightly older than me, one married and one divorced, all of us from different walks of life and enrolled for vastly different reasons. By the end of the week we enjoyed a very special breed of friendship based on a combination of shared apprehension, excitement, embarrassment, fear, joy, panic, and amazing mutual support.*

Male, 30s: *On the last day at Captiva, like kids, you stay out past the allotted time until, finally, the instructor arrives in his launch to see you home. You wish you could spend a month of sailing days like these.*

ANNAPOLIS SAILING SCHOOL, 601 Sixth St., Annapolis, MD 21403; 800-638-9192 or 301-267-7205. (M)

Years in business: 30
Most common age: 25–35
Number of participants: 3,000 annually
Age range: From 16
Percent alone: Varies
Male/female ratio: Varies

Branches in St. Petersburg, and Marathon, Florida; Charleston, South Carolina; St. Croix, U.S. Virgin Islands. Suitable for beginners; will try to arrange shares.

The nation's largest sailing school boasts 80,000 graduate sailors. Beginning students live on land, learn to sail by day aboard the 24-foot Rainbow sloop, a boat specifically designed by the school for use in teaching. Beginning courses are offered for a weekend, or for 3 or 5 days. After completing the beginner's course, you can follow with a weekend or 5-day cruise, a vacation at sea that continues your instruction. The school also offers a complete 7-day learn-to-sail vacation. Learners spend the first 2 days partly in classroom instruction, partly in short sails. The next 3 days are devoted to day-sails, and the week concludes with a weekend cruise that is both fun and a chance to practice navigation and chart reading.

Package arrangements with nearby inns are made by the school at each location. Breakfast is included, but students are on their own for lunch and dinner. St. Petersburg and St. Croix schools operate year round; Annapolis and Charleston are open from late March through October; Marathon from mid-November to Easter.

COMMENTS:

Female, 20s: *I went alone on a two-day program, liked it so much I decided to work there. The age range is about 25 to 50, but most people are in their 20s and 30s, and from the Northeast. There are a few couples and many singles, though many are groups of friends who come together.*

Male, 50s: *It was a very good experience. The instruction was excellent, and there was no problem being alone. I learned a lot and had fun, though I stayed in a hotel and there was no real socializing at night. Of 19 people, there was one couple and all the rest were single. They were quite a diverse group of people, but mostly from the Northeast.*

WINDSURFING

Want to skim the waves with the wind? Here's the place to learn.

THE SAILBOARD CENTER, 9125 U.S. 1, Sebastian, FL 32958; 407-589-2617. (M)

Years in business: 7
Age range: 18–73
Most common age: 40
Percent alone: 70
Number of participants: 10
Male/female ratio: 55/45
Will try to arrange shares.

Three certified instructors work with very small groups of students, from beginners to intermediates, starting the novices on land on a sailboard simulator, and progressing first to a small lake on the grounds and then to the Causeway, which has an average depth of 4 feet—an ideal spot for learning. A high-wind simulator helps develop new techniques or refine old ones. Mornings are typically spent on instruction, the rest of the day sailing. Guests are lodged in a turn-of-the-century home where they share meals. The 5-day program runs from October to June. The school is located on the east coast of Florida north of Vero Beach. Nearest airport is Melbourne.

COMMENTS:

Male, 30s: *When I went the group was all male, all in their 30s, and we were all soon friends. The accommodations and food are phenomenal and the teaching is excellent whether you are a beginner or advanced. The days are quite vigorous and after a few drinks at night, we were ready for bed. It's particularly good for singles because the groups are so small and the instruction is so intense and direct. You're with the same group all the time and you become very intimate.*

Female, 60s: *I've been once and I'm going again. It is a wonderful atmosphere, like an old-time ski lodge, no more than nine or ten people at a time. My group had only four, from late 30s to 60s, all interesting people. The instruction was wonderful. You spend all day surfing and it's quite vigorous. I'd recommend this to anyone, but you have to be into windsurfing, because there's nothing else to do.*

SCUBA DIVING

More Americans every year are descending to discover the eerie beauty at the bottom of the sea. Recent statistics show that around 12 million people now have their diving certification, and with it a kinship that makes it easy to find friends on any diving vacation. If you want to join their numbers, why not choose one of the great diving spots—Bonaire in the Dutch West Indies, the Cayman Islands, or the U.S. Virgin Islands—to gain your certification? The easiest way to get the most current list of courses available, as well as a selection of hotel brochures, is to contact the island tourist offices.

BONAIRE GOVERNMENT TOURIST OFFICE, 275 Seventh Ave., New York, NY 10001; 212-242-0000. Diving is what Bonaire is all about, and all major hotels have learning programs. The most luxurious accommodations are at the Divi Flamingo Beach, where Peter Hughes's Dive Bonaire is located. The most knowledgeable divers head for the no-frills Habitat, run by Cap'n Don Stewart, an island legend. Besides dive package information, ask for the color booklet *Divers' Travel Guide to Bonaire.*

CAYMAN ISLANDS DEPARTMENT OF TOURISM, 420 Lexington Ave., Suite 2312, New York, NY 10017; 212-682-5582. (Offices also in Atlanta, Chicago, Coral Gables, Dallas, Houston, Los Angeles, Tampa, and Toronto.) There is a host of places to learn to dive in the Caymans; information packets include a long list of dive packages, including the "Discover Diving" program for noncertified divers.

U.S. VIRGIN ISLANDS DIVISION OF TOURISM, 1270 Avenue of the Americas, New York, NY 10020; 212-582-4520. (Offices also in Atlanta, Chicago, Los Angeles, Miami, Washington, D.C.) Diving is only one part of the action on bustling St. Thomas, but instruction is said to be excellent at the St. Thomas Diving Club at Villa Olga, a diver-oriented resort, and instruction is available also from several diving centers.

FISHING

ORVIS FLY FISHING SCHOOLS, 10 River Rd., Manchester, VT 05254; 802-362-3622. (M)

Years in business: Since 1967	Age range: 10–92
Most common age: 20s, 50–65	Percent alone: 30–50
Number of participants: 37 per class	Male/female ratio: 3/1

This longtime sports outfitter started operations in 1967, offering the first organized fly-fishing school in the United States. The instructors at the 2½-day course are professionals who give a solid foundation that includes casting, essential knots for tying on flies, selecting the right flies for the right fish, how to read a trout stream, how to wade a stream safely, how to manipulate lines in tricky currents, and how to play, land, and release a fish. Classes are taught on the casting ponds, in an indoor classroom, and on the Battenkill, Vermont's finest trout stream. They promise that by the last morning you'll be able to catch and release rainbow and brook trout from their stocked ponds. Classes are held from early April through August. Orvis also supervises fly-fishing instruction in other locations, and runs a shooting school for hunters.

No references provided.

BUD LILLY'S TROUT SHOP, 39 Madison Ave., West Yellowstone, MT 59758; 406-646-7801. (M)

Years in business: 39	Age range: 23–63
Most common age: Late 30s	Percent alone: 50
Number of participants: 20	Male/female ratio: 50/50

Fly-fishing instruction is the specialty here, but the shop also organizes guided fishing trips, horseback riding, hiking, and touring groups in the park. Participants stay together at a nearby ranch where meals are cafeteria style and it is easy to get to know other guests. Guides look out for those who are alone and will take you out with a group or alone, as you prefer.

COMMENTS:

Male, 30s: *I go once a year. They really take care of you, pick you up at the airport, often come over to the lodge to have dinner with you. Guides are very helpful, pack great lunches, take care of everything. You can meet people hanging out in the trout shop, probably find a fishing partner, and meet people also at the lodge. It's a very relaxing vacation.*

Male, 30s: *I've been five times. It's a fantastic thing to do, and is fine alone, if you like to fish. You can socialize with the people at the ranch—it's a very warm, informal atmosphere, and you get to know everyone* *who is staying there. The guides are great; they know all the best fishing spots.*

KAYAKING, CANOEING, AND WHITE-WATER RAFTING

You can learn some of these skills on a regular rafting trip, but these programs focus on instruction.

NANTAHALA OUTDOOR CENTER, U.S. 19 West, Box 41, Bryson City, NC 28713; 704-488-2175. (I–M)

Years in business: Since 1972
Age range: 10–70
Most common age: 20–55
Percent alone: Majority
Number of participants: 3,200 yearly
Male/female ratio: Higher male

Located on a mountainside along the Nantahala River near Great Smoky Mountains National Park, this employee-owned center boasts many paddling champions and is a terrific place to learn water skills. *Esquire* magazine called the center "the Oxford of white-water canoe schools." Courses are held from April to October. They run the gamut from beginner to expert, one day to one week. Participants in the week-long courses try several rivers. Reasonable packages include instruction, room, and three meals. Lodgings range from handsome vacation cabins to motel rooms to a bunkhouse base camp. Three restaurants offer plenty of dining variety and family-style service. Courses are also offered in rock climbing, backpacking, and fly-fishing.

COMMENTS:

Female, 30s: *I've gone half a dozen times alone, and it was great every time. The program is terrific, the instructors world-class—and it's cheap! There are plenty of singles—in my last group, in fact, there was only one couple out of ten people. There are always more men, usually in their 30s and 40s. There is no social pressure; you eat as a group and it's easy to* *get to know people. Cabins are lovely, with wooded views from the balcony. The food is very good, all natural and with homemade bread. I definitely recommend it.*

Male, 40s: *I've been on lots of kayaking trips, and I think this is the best instruction in the country. I've gone several times, alone and with a friend. You feel at home as soon as you get there. Most people come alone; the majority are from the East Coast, but more seem to be coming from all over. The age range is from 20s to 50s, about 2 to 1 male. The lodges have beautiful views; the food is so good they put out their own cookbook. And the instruction is great—five students to one instructor, and very patient, understanding teachers.*

DVOŘÁK KAYAK & RAFTING EXPEDITIONS, 17921 U.S. 285 Nathrop, CO 81236; 800-824-3795 or 303-539-6851. (I)

The first licensed outfitter in Colorado, this experienced company offers instructional seminars where students begin on flat water to learn the basic strokes necessary to control a raft, canoe, or kayak, then move down the river to practice their skills in moving water. As skills sharpen, so does the challenge. Instructional trips vary from a half day to 12 days; they suggest at least 3 days for a good introduction, 5 to 7 days for a serious paddler. Seminars are held in 29 canyons on 10 rivers across the west. More Dvořák information and participants' comments are on page 114.

GREEN RIVER KAYAK SCHOOL, c/o O.A.R.S., P.O. Box 67, Angels Camp, CA 95222; 209-736-4677. (M)

Six-day trips from July through August teach how to squeeze the last drops of excitement from river-running in light, agile kayaks. Low student-to-teacher ratio means the course can be tailored to individual learning rates. See more O.A.R.S. information and participants' comments on page 113.

SKIING

Of all the many types of sports schools available, ski schools are the easiest to find. Almost every slope has midweek 5-day learn-to-ski packages at substantial savings over their weekend rates. The most comfortable way to approach this alone is to be part of a group that will remain together for the 5 days; if you simply sign up for individual lessons, you may have different classmates and instructors each day and will have little opportunity to become friendly with those in your class. Ask in advance.

The entire ski week group generally meets at a welcoming party on arrival, then is divided into smaller groups according to ability. There is the opportunity also for evening get-togethers for ski movies or entertainment. Ski lodges are friendly places, anyway, albeit crowded, and it is easy to meet people naturally during the day, at lunch, or at the bar after skiing. Singles are also paired up with other singles in the lift line, though that could as likely mean a 10-year-old as a possible dinner companion. It's all in the luck of the draw.

Lodgings can be informal meeting places as well, with guests gathering in front of the fire for drinks at the end of the day. Best bet to get to know your fellow lodgers well is to find an inn that serves dinner family style. If you are in your 20s or 30s, dorm-style accommodations are a good place to find other singles. Many ski area lodging bureaus will help steer you to the right places if you ask. Avoid condominium accommodations if you are traveling alone; they limit your sociability.

As a rule, there are more single skiers at the big, better-known resorts, more families at smaller areas. But if you are a real beginner, the giant ski meccas may not be the best choice. The crowds and the mob scene at lunch in the big lodges can be intimidating. Top ski writer Abby Rand recommends smaller areas with big mountains, such as Taos, New Mexico, and Alta, Utah. Claire Walter, author of *The Best Ski Resorts in America,* suggests Snowbird, Utah, and Jackson Hole, Wyoming, two more moderately sized areas with demanding slopes, though she adds that it is hard to beat the social scenes at Aspen and Vail.

For guaranteed company, there is the Club Med at Copper Mountain, Colorado. (M) Besides having unlimited skiing privileges on the mountain, guests here are graded for ability, then divided into groups of ten for lessons morning and afternoon, a total of 4 hours of instruction. Beginner or advanced, that much instruction is bound to improve skiing skills. Videotaping also helps demonstrate what you are doing wrong. A recent participant reports that great camaraderie grows within each group, so there is a lot of moral support and encouragement to help overcome your fears. During her week at the club, guests came from England, Australia, and France, as well as the United States. Adults' ages ranged mostly from 25 to 50, and singles were roughly one-third of the total of 450. Another third were families with children in tow. The lodge is a 5-minute walk from the lifts, so skiers can return for lunch. There is a heated room for donning and removing boots and skis, which veteran skiers will recognize as a nice little luxury. All meals are included in the price, along with ice skating, exercise classes, a sauna and Jacuzzi, and nightly entertainment and dancing. This is still Club Med—you'll enjoy (or endure) silly songs with hand motions and homemade entertainment, share a not-so-large room. But you won't lack for learning or companions. Phone 1-800-CLUB-MED for information.

Another good bet is the Vic Braden Ski College at Buttermilk Mountain, P.O. Box 1248, Aspen, CO 81612; 303-925-9229. (M—tuition only) Founded in 1987, the school aims to help skiers overcome fear and learn more about the principles of body movement that lead to success on the slopes. A test designed to pinpoint each student's best learning style helps to individualize the instruction. The approach was developed by Braden, a psychologist who made his original reputation as a tennis coach. The instructors were chosen from the Aspen Ski School.

The program gets high marks from several who have attended. Beginners, intermediate skiers who feel stuck at a certain level, and some who have given up the sport but want to come back are among those who seem to be ideal candidates. Weekly enrollment may vary from 15 to 40 people, with teaching groups limited to 6. The average age is between 35 and 50, but students have run the gamut from teenagers to those in their 70s. According to the school, the ratio is about 55 percent female, 45 percent male.

Several ski areas have discovered that females-only ski clinics are very popular with women who would rather do their slipping and sliding without a male audience. Squaw Valley, California, was the pioneer. Now you can find women's programs all over Colorado, at Aspen, Breckenridge, Vail, Copper Mountain, and Telluride.

I learned to ski at age 30, and as an adult getting a late start, I found that an accelerated GLM (graduated-length method) teaching program beginning on short skis helped me get acclimated in a hurry. I learned at Killington Mountain, Vermont, the pioneer of this approach in the East. Following are some major areas that currently offer some version of an accelerated program along with the choice of traditional teaching techniques:

ASPEN HIGHLANDS, Aspen, CO 81612; 303-925-5300.
BRECKENRIDGE SKI AREA, Breckenridge, CO 80424; 303-453-6118.
STEAMBOAT SKI AREA, Steamboat Springs, CO 80487; 303-879-6111.
ALTA, Alta, UT 84092; 901-742-3333.
PARK CITY SKI AREA, Park City, UT 84060; 801-649-8111.
SUNDANCE, Provo, UT 84604; 800-662-5901 or 801-225-4107.
MT. BACHELOR, Bend, OR 97709; 503-382-2442.
KILLINGTON, 400 Killington Rd., Killington, VT 05751; 802-773-0755.
PICO SKI RESORT, Rutland, VT 05701; 802-775-4345.
SUGARBUSH SKI RESORT, Warren, VT 05674; 802-583-2381.

Other ski areas with excellent traditional ski schools—and a lively social life:

HEAVENLY VALLEY, South Lake Tahoe, CA 95705; 916-541-1330.
VAIL, Vail, CO 81658; 303-476-5601.
MT. MANSFIELD, Stowe, VT 05672; 800-253-7311.

CROSS-COUNTRY SKIING

Cross-country enthusiasts are growing, lured by the time to enjoy the quiet and beauty of the snow-covered countryside and the lack of lift lines. Almost every major area today offers cross-country trails and instruction; a day or two of practice is all it takes to get started. Local chambers of commerce can point you to inns that have cross-country trails outside the door. But lessons won't necessarily guarantee company. If you are looking for a cross-country group, the best bet is to contact outdoor organizations such as the Appalachian Mountain Club or Colorado Mountain School (see below) or check the winter offerings of outdoor trip organizers, such as American Forest Adventures, beginning on page 89.

SENIORS ON SKIS

Once they know the basics, older skiers in search of company can find plenty of it these days. The industry estimates that 45 percent of the skiing population is over 35, and white hair is an increasingly common sight on the snowy slopes.

Ski areas are welcoming these mature skiers. Waterville Valley, a ski resort in New Hampshire, has formed a club called Silver Streakers for those 55 and over, offering member discounts and special midweek packages with many social activities. The state of Michigan has a "Silver Streak Week" when 41 ski facilities across the state provide free downhill lift tickets or cross-country trail passes to anyone 55 years of age or above. New programs are starting all the time, so if you fall into this category, by all means ask at several areas to find out what special programs may be available before you decide on your destination.

There are also national clubs for older skiers:

THE OVER THE HILL GANG (13791 East Rice Pl., Aurora, CO 87715; 303–699–6404) was founded in 1977 by three Colorado skiers seeking company in their own over-50 age group. There are now 1,500 members in 16 chapters around the country, and many more chapters are forming.

THE 70+ CLUB (104 Eastside Dr., Ballston Lake, NY 12019; 518–399–5458) is even larger; it offers special discounts as well as group trips to its 4,000 members.

Older cross-country skiers will also find many programs of interest. Here are just two possibilities:

SENIORS ON SNOW (Woodstock Ski Touring Center, The Woodstock Inn, Woodstock, VT 05091; 802-457-1100). For skiers over age 50, there are 4-day 3-night packages, including lessons and rentals, at the luxurious Woodstock Inn in one of Vermont's most picturesque settings. Program features a reception, some evening activities.

ELDERHOSTEL (80 Boylston St., Suite 400, Boston, MA 02116; 617–426–8056) includes low-cost cross-country ski trips in Vermont, Utah, and Colorado in its extensive programs for adults over age 60—and a smattering of downhill skiing, as well.

For further information on skiing, see

SKI MAGAZINE, 2 Park Ave., New York, NY 10016; 212-779-5000.
SKIING MAGAZINE, 1515 Broadway, New York, NY 10036; 212-719-6000.

OUTDOOR SKILLS

APPALACHIAN MOUNTAIN CLUB, 5 Joy St., Boston, MA 02108; 617-523-0636. (I)

Years in business: Since 1876	Age range: Up to 85
Most common age: 28–55	Percent alone: 35
Number of participants: 33,000 members	Male/female ratio: 50/50

At Pinkham Notch Camp in Gorham, New Hampshire, in the heart of the White Mountains, this active club offers year-round weekend workshops for both beginners and advanced outdoor enthusiasts. Among the many topics offered are camping, ski touring, snowshoeing, bushwhacking, map and compass reading, nature studies, mushroom hunting, ecology, music, storytelling, photography, and drawing. There are several special weekends for women. Guided hikes are also available for beginners. The lodge is sociable, with many individual hikers staying over. Meals are family style. Lectures and slides on outdoor topics are offered on Saturday evening.

Other, smaller AMC lodges with varying seasonal programs include Bascom Lodge in Adams, Massachusetts, Cold River Camp in

Center Conway, New Hampshire, Cardigan Lodge in Bristol, New Hampshire, and Fire Island Camp in Atlantique, New York (open mid-May through October).

COMMENTS:

E.B.: *I'm a longtime AMC member. The lodges are not luxurious, but they are comfortable, the people are outgoing outdoor lovers of all ages, and the club and its programs are tops.*

MOUNTAIN CLIMBING

COLORADO MOUNTAIN SCHOOL, Box 2062, Estes Park, CO 80517; 800-444-0730 or 303-586-5758. (I)

Years in business: 8
Age range: 8–60
Most common age: 25–40
Percent alone: 25–30
Number of participants: 1,500 annually
Male/female ratio: 8/2

Located in the shadow of Rocky Mountain National Park, this group offers 2- and 3-day beginner workshops teaching the proper techniques for backpacking, mountaineering, and rock climbing. Once you've learned, many guided climbs and mountain hikes are offered. Lodging is your choice of nearby motels or the no-frills very inexpensive dorm at Tlamacas North Climbers Lodge, where there is plenty of company from other climbers and hikers. Meals are not included. In winter the emphasis shifts to skiing, mountaineering, and ice climbing, and once again there are programs for beginner to advanced. The owners say: "Many people have met and become good friends through their courses and outings. In mountain travel, there is ample opportunity for a tremendous amount of honest, open discussion, and the mountain atmosphere encourages this. Our participants always exchange addresses, etc., at the end of trips and stay in contact with each other afterward."

COMMENTS:

Female, 40s: *I've been once, am going again. It was a lot of fun, there was a lot of instruction, and it was very good. All the participants were* *from Colorado, and most came alone. I signed up for a more difficult workshop, so there were few women. Ages were 25 to 50.*

Other mountaineering schools:

YOSEMITE MOUNTAINEERING SCHOOL, Yosemite National Park, CA 95389; 209-372-1335.

THE MOUNTAINEERING SCHOOL AT VAIL, INC., P.O. Box 3034, Vail, CO 81657; 303-476-4123.

JACKSON HOLE MOUNTAIN GUIDES, Box 547, Teton Village, WY 83025; 307-733-4979.

INTERNATIONAL MOUNTAIN CLIMBING SCHOOL, INC., Box 1227, North Conway, NH 03860; 603-356-5287.

WILDERNESS SKILLS

OUTWARD BOUND, 384 Field Point Rd., Greenwich, CT 06830; 800-243-8520 or 203-661-0797. (I–M)

Years in business: Since 1961
Median age: 22; one-third are over 30
Number of participants: Over 17,000 annually
Age range: All ages
Percent single: High
Male/female ratio: 60/40

Special classes offered for women over 30 and adults over 55.

Outward Bound programs are in a class by themselves. Those who participate, many of them beginners, come to be challenged mentally and emotionally as well as physically—with the wilderness as a classroom. If you want to learn about backpacking, canoeing, mountaineering, rock-climbing, white-water rafting, ski mountaineering, dogsledding, snowshoeing, or almost any other outdoor adventure, their five schools in Colorado, North Carolina, Maine, Oregon, and Minnesota are ready to teach you these skills—and much more.

The courses have five parts. Phase one is a training and physical conditioning period, giving instruction in technical skills, safety, first aid, shelter construction, wilderness cooking, environmental awareness and conservation, map and compass reading, etc. Next, these skills are applied. Groups of 8 to 12 are formed and as participants become more self-reliant, instructors turn the leadership role over to them. The third phase, the solo, is a period of solitude—1 to 3 days in the wilderness alone. Afterward, the group comes together to execute an expedition with a minimum of supervision. Then comes a final event, a last fling with your body that involves running, paddling, cycling, snowshoeing, or skiing—more miles than you may have thought possible. Finally, there is a period of reflection on your experiences, feelings, and personal discoveries during the course.

Over 140,000 alumni, from troubled youths to corporate executives to adults in a period of life transition, testify that meeting the challenges of Outward Bound has helped them to go beyond what they believed they could do and to develop new self-confidence as a result.

3

STRETCH YOUR MIND

EVER WISHED YOU TOOK BETTER VACATION PICtures . . . or could paint a picture? Would you like a better understanding of the stock market . . . or a wine list . . . or what an archaeologist actually does on a dig? What about a yen to try your hand at quilting or carving or playing the fiddle?

Whatever your interest—or your fantasy—you can indulge it on a learning vacation that stretches your mind and talents in scenic surroundings.

In a situation where everyone is learning together, there is automatically a common interest, a natural bond, and a lot of mutual support. Many programs are set up so that the group eats together, but even when meals are optional, students who have shared small classes naturally tend to get together for dinner.

The choices are enormous, as is the range of settings. You can live and paint in Italy, study wines in Germany or cooking in Provence, or learn to twang a banjo in the West Virginia hills. Here are some of the many wonderful options:

EDUCATION

Education vacations come in many forms, from formal campus settings to research in the field. Besides the programs listed here, most universities have a week of "Alumnae College" and many welcome non-alums to share the learning.

CORNELL ADULT UNIVERSITY, 626 Thurston Ave., Ithaca, NY 14850-2490; 607-255-6260. (I)

Years in business: 20+
Most common age: 30s and 40s
Number of participants: 150 per week
Age range: 30–70
Percent alone: 35
Male/female ratio: Varies

Five 1-week sessions held during July and early August in Ithaca; marine ecology workshops also held in Maine. Learning sessions take place also during spring and fall in various off-campus locations.

"A getaway for nature enthusiasts, armchair philosophers, art and music lovers, romantics and pragmatists of all persuasions," says the brochure, and indeed this largest of all summer university programs offers something for almost every interest. Classes are taught by university faculty; subject matter runs the gamut. Some recent offerings: "Behind the Silver Screen: Movies and American Culture"; "The Court of the Sun King: Louis XIV and Versailles"; "How We Know What Isn't So: The Causes and Consequences of Erroneous Beliefs"; "Culinary Workshop"; "Autobiographical Writing"; "Vegetable Gardening Workshop"; and "How to Argue Like a Lawyer Without Going to Law School."

This is a "back-to-school" week of dorm living and cafeteria dining, with all the many athletic and cultural facilities on campus open to participants. And while there is a large program for young people, which attracts many families, single adults will find plenty of company. The evaluation sheets at the end of each session are enthusiastic: Over 90 percent of the participants say they plan to return.

Cornell also sponsors interesting spring and fall programs. Some recent examples are "The Desert and the Sky," 5 days at a ranch in Tucson, Arizona, learning about the Sonoran Desert and visiting the Kitt Peak National Observatory with an astronomer; and "Cultures and Landscapes of the Chesapeake," 4 days around Chesapeake Bay, with inn and hotel lodgings.

COMMENTS:

E.B.: *The Cornell campus is magnificent, in the heart of the Finger Lakes, a region of spectacular natural gorges. I chose "Gorgeous Gorges of the Finger Lakes," a course that offered a daily walk of about three miles through the gorges, many of them remote locations tourists would ordinarily miss. It didn't feel like class—the instructor was like a knowledgeable friend who could point out a million interesting things you would never have noticed on your own, from bird calls to the marks of the last glacier. There were no assignments but readings were available if we wanted to learn more.*

Our group of a dozen ranged in age from 30 to 80, equally divided between men and women. At least half the group was on its own during class; even couples at the program tend to choose different subjects. Classmates and dorm mates provide a natural base for making friends. The cafeteria food was so-so, but the setting was another congenial place for meeting people. All you have to do is say, "May I join you?" and set down your tray. Most classes end at lunch hour, leaving time to use the campus facilities in the afternoon or just sunbathe on the lawn.

The evening schedule included a wine tasting at a nearby vineyard, a cookout, and a campus concert. If these didn't appeal, there were plenty of activities around campus as a substitute. The week ended with a banquet followed by a "graduation" party. Going to college for a week proved to be a congenial and relaxing vacation. The cost was nominal, and, as a bonus, I learned a lot.

For a directory of other summer university programs from one week to six weeks, write to Campus Vacations, 2860 Huron Way, Miramar, Florida 33025. Ask for current price of directory.

CHAUTAUQUA INSTITUTION, Chautauqua, NY 14722; 716-357-6200. (I–M)

Years in business: 115
Age range: 2–102
Most common age: 50s
Percent alone: 40–50
Number of participants: 9,000 per season
Male/female ratio: 40/60

This is where the idea of learning vacations began. Chautauqua was founded as a training camp for Sunday school teachers and evolved into a 9-week summer feast of arts and education, served up in a period Victorian village. The religious element, while still present, is optional.

The lineup of activities is staggering. Twice-a-day talks by prominent lecturers are on a new theme each week, from arts and humanities to the Americas to sports in American life. The summer school topics include the arts, languages, human relations, public speaking, nutrition, parenting, self-improvement, foreign cultures, and much, much more. Evening entertainment may feature the resident opera and theater companies, a symphony orchestra, ballet, Shakespeare performances, or guest stars from Johnny Cash to the Smothers Brothers to Chinese acrobats. And for a sporting change of pace, golf, tennis, and sailing are available.

Chautauqua lodging is outside the institution grounds in hotels, inns, guest houses, or private homes. The clientele has tended to be on the older side, but that is changing somewhat as an active children's program has begun to attract young families. For single participants, marketing director Carol Halter says, "Chautauqua is very sensitive to the single vacationer and programs many events that are perfect for people traveling alone. They're only on their own until they pass through our gates."

COMMENTS:

Female, 40s: *I've been alone and with friends; I keep going back for the intellectual stimulation. The lecturers are great and the hotels and food are very good. It's a very special place and is great for singles . . . people are friendly and it's easy to meet them.*

Female, 60s: *The program is wonderful. You buy a gate ticket and can participate in any and all activities. You can stay busy all day long. The* *group is heavily female, many widows, but also many families and a wide age range, from children to those in their 70s. There is a good number of singles and it is very suitable for them. You can stay in a hotel and have meals family style. People come from all over, but most from the Northeast. The place started as a religious institution and is still highly religious for some, but it doesn't have to be.*

SMITHSONIAN SEMINARS, c/o Smithsonian National Associates, 1100 Jefferson Dr. SW, Washington, D.C. 20560; 202-357-1350. (I–M)

Years in business: Many (no one is sure how long)
Most common age: 45–50
Number of participants: 20–40
Age range: 20s–80s
Percent alone: 60
Male/female ratio: Varies with topics; usually heavily female but more males for subjects such as aviation.

Will automatically arrange shares unless single is requested.

Three- to 5-day programs for museum associate members (membership is $20) in Washington and at top resort locations such as the Homestead in Virginia, the Broadmoor in Colorado, and Mohonk Mountain House in New Paltz, New York. A variety of topics is featured, from creative writing, music, and art to aviation and archaeology. Programs last most of the day. Washington visitors get a good discount on hotels; some of the great resorts have special-value packages.

No references provided.

HUMANITIES INSTITUTE, Box 18, Belmont, MA 02178; 800-327-1657; in MA, 617-484-3191. (M–ME)

Years in business: Since 1975
Most common age: 40–50
Number of participants: 25 maximum per program
Age range: 25–70
Percent alone: 80
Male/female ratio: 1/3

Education and culture are the focus of this varied program for those who want to learn more about the countries they visit. Some classes are based at such institutions as Cambridge and Dublin's Trinity College, where mornings are devoted to lectures and discussion, and afternoons are free for exploring the area. These 2- to 3-week in-depth seminars are equivalent to a short university course and may actually be taken for academic credit. Other noncredit trips are less rigorous, but still education-oriented, concentrating on such topics as the gardens of England, the art and architecture of Italy, or birding and wildlife in Australia. They also might include archaeological field-work in Israel or a goodwill exchange for meeting residents in China. Each program offers some sight-seeing and evening lectures. About 80 percent of the participants are teachers.

COMMENTS:

Female, 50s: *I went alone and was very comfortable. There was a diverse group, ages 30 to 65, heavily female. Mornings were spent in class; afternoons there were tours of museums or lectures. There was always something to do. The accommodations were not great, but the trip was inexpensive.*

Female, 70s: *I've been on several trips alone. It is wonderful and I always make friends. There is a nice mix of people from all over the U.S., ages 35 to 70, most in their 40s. Many are married but traveling alone. Meals are as a group and there is lots of discussion, making it easy to get to know people. There is always something to do during the week; weekends are free to do whatever you want.*

ELDERHOSTEL, 80 Boylston St., Suite 400, Boston, MA 02116; 617-426-8056. (I)

Years in business: Since 1975
Most common age: 60s, 70s
Number of participants: 160,000 annually; 50 maximum per group
Age range: Over 60
Percent single: 40
Male/female ratio: Higher female

This remarkable program for older adults who want to continue to expand their horizons offers inexpensive, short-term academic programs at educational institutions around the world. The topics? Cicero to computers . . . politics to poetry. There are over 1,000 programs in the United States and Canada alone, with 40,000 spaces available, plus international programs in Australia, Asia, Europe, North

America, Central America, South America, the Caribbean and Polynesian islands. Typical U.S. programs offer three courses that meet daily for 1–1½ hours each. Most living/dining accommodations are in dormitories, and participants have the use of the campus recreational facilities. The charge for an average 6-night program is under $300. Besides classroom courses, programs include bicycling trips, cross-country skiing, stays in country houses and private homes, in other countries, and study cruises, all at reasonable rates. Put yourself on the mailing list and three times each year you'll get a 150-page newspaper-sized catalog crammed with possibilities plus a newsletter in between with informal listings. A land-sea program in Alaska, a stay at Trinity College in Wales, a spring sojourn in the Great Smoky Mountains, a jazz course in New Orleans or a stay in New Delhi—it's enough to make younger folks want to hurry up and age!

COMMENTS:

Female, 60s: *Elderhostels have been like a life raft in an open sea. The experience opened up a whole new world to me, and I no longer will dread traveling alone or thinking about my retirement in the not-too-distant future. In fact, Elderhostel might hasten the latter.*

Male, 60s: *The history professor during our week-long session really made the French Revolution come alive. I'd never been able to sit through such a class in my high school days, but now, in a college classroom with Elderhostel, I found it riveting.*

STUDY VACATIONS ABROAD

A number of short-term study and educational tour programs are available abroad, sponsored by U.S. universities in association with colleges in other countries. Some use dorm facilities on campus, others utilize hotels. The offerings vary from year to year, so it is best to call for current information. Schools with active programs include:

UNIVERSITY OF CALIFORNIA, BERKELEY EXTENSION, Marketing Dept., 17G, 2223 Fulton St., Berkeley, CA 94720; 415-642-3112, ext. 17.

Two- and 3-week travel-study programs in Paris, the south of France, Venice, Florence, Spain, and Oxford University in England. A special program in London with the National Theatre of Great Britain gives an in-depth look at the London theater scene.

UCLA EXTENSION, Travel/Study Dept. of Marketing, P.O. Box 24901, Los Angeles, CA 90024; 213-825-9676.

Programs in cooperation with London's Royal College of Art, Sotheby's, and Cambridge University.

INTERHOSTEL. University of New Hampshire Division of Continuing Education, 6 Garrison Ave., Durham, NH 03824; 603-862-1147.

Study tours for adults over age 50 held in 15 countries, in conjunction with local sponsoring institutions abroad.

UNIVERSITY VACATIONS, 9602 N.W. 13th St., Miami, FL 33172; 800-792-0100.

Sponsors a series of 1- and 2-week cultural vacations at Oxford and Cambridge universities.

UNIVERSITY OF LONDON, Birkbeck College, Center for Extra Normal Studies, 26 Russell Square, London, England.

Offers 1-week theater study groups for adults, who read three current plays, attend the theater together to see and then discuss them. Participants live in the college dorms and come from many parts of the world.

NEW YORK UNIVERSITY SCHOOL OF CONTINUING EDUCATION, 331 Shimkin Hall, Washington Square, New York, NY 10003; 212-998-7133.

Program is based at Cambridge University.

More information on study opportunities for adults abroad can be obtained from the Institute of International Education, 809 United Nations Plaza, New York, NY 10017 (212-984-5413), and from *The Insider's Guide to Foreign Study* by Benedict A. Leerburger.

FIELD RESEARCH VOLUNTEER PROGRAMS

Assisting scientists and archaeologists in their work is a wonderful way to widen your horizons and get a new perspective on an area. As a side benefit, many of these trips are tax deductible. The cost is considered a donation to underwrite the research.

EARTHWATCH, 680 Mt. Auburn St., Box 403N, Watertown, MA 02272; 617-926-8200. (I–EE)

Years in business: Since 1971
Most common age: 35–55
Number of participants: 2,900, but divided into very small special-interest groups
Age range: 16–82
Percent alone: 50
Male/female ratio: 40/60

More than 20,000 volunteers have gone out on some 1,000 Earthwatch vacation-learning experiences in 83 countries and 36 states, helping scientists and researchers in field projects ranging from anthropology to zoology. Most participants have college degrees and are a well-traveled lot: professionals, scientists, managers, students, retirees, and teachers.

Would-be volunteers read about the projects in the Earthwatch magazine, which comes out seven times each year, then send for a more detailed briefing of the projects that interest them. The possibilities include archaeological excavations, surveys of plants, birds or animals, underwater and environmental impact studies, and research in agriculture, public health, and art history. Some recent projects: Helping a team studying the carved figures on Easter Island in the Pacific, excavating mummies in the Chilean desert, studying native costumes in Ecuador, observing kangaroos in Australia or black bears in North Carolina. Living conditions vary with the locale.

COMMENTS:

Female, 50s: *For two weeks we lived in splendid isolation studying honey eaters on Australia's Kangaroo Island. I shared a bunk room with four other women. Just outside my door were kangaroos, koalas, emus, and* *other creatures people seldom encountered outside a zoo. We did simple but necessary jobs such as hand-pollinating blooms and marking and bagging clusters of flowers for breeding studies. We also observed honey eaters and bees as they collected nectar and pollinated—or failed to pollinate—the plants. We got two days off for sight-seeing. In the evenings, we played games, sang folk songs, talked a lot. The group, ages 25 to 60, had a wide range of occupations. We were a motley and congenial crew.*

Male, 40s: *I've gone on six trips, each time alone. It was a little hard the first time, then became easy. There was about an equal mix of men and women, single and married, from varied backgrounds. How well the program runs depends on the "Principal Investigator," the person in charge. One of my trips was not so well run. I would recommend this type of vacation to other singles, but I would also say that you have to really want to do it. This is not a leisure vacation. There is work involved.*

UNIVERSITY RESEARCH EXPEDITIONS PROGRAM (UREP), University of California, Berkeley, CA 94720; 415-642-6586. (I–EE)

Years in business: Since 1976	Age range: 16–75
Most common age: 30–50	Percent alone: High
Number of participants: 5–10	Male/female ratio: Varies

Like Earthwatch, UREP programs provide the opportunity to be part of a team doing actual research in the field, this time assisting University of California scholars while gaining new knowledge, new friends, and insights into another culture. Tax-deductible contributions pay project costs and participants' expenses. Animal-related projects include studying the wildlife of Patagonia, the mule deer of the High Sierra, and the maternal behavior of Australian sea lions. Ancient rock art of Hawaii, Eskimo villages, pueblo archaeology, South American folk art, the Peking Opera, and historic preservation in California gold rush country are among other recent topics. The only requirements for participation are curiosity about the world and a willingness to invest in learning.

COMMENTS:

Female, 50s: *It was a positive and interesting experience that enabled me to see places and have experiences which I probably would not have* *had traveling with a tour group or alone. It was eye-opening, energy-expending, socially cooperating, native-appreciating, and thoroughly enjoyable, the most highly concentrated two weeks of learning and cultural immersion that I've experienced in many years of travel. The experience exceeded my expectations . . . was one of new understanding of another people and of personal growth.*

Male, 30s: *The program is well organized. I had a very good experience in Costa Rica planting trees to stop forest fires from spreading. It was especially rewarding because I was doing something for another country, a kind of mini peace corps. Our interesting group, evenly split male/female, was mostly single, ages 26 to 45. The first week was spent in a group situation; the second week we split into smaller groups to work on individual projects. Food and accommodations were satisfactory considering the location. I would definitely recommend the experience to other single people.*

FOUNDATION FOR FIELD RESEARCH, 787 South Grade Rd., Alpine, CA 92001-0380; 619-445-9264. (I–EE)

Years in business: Since 1982
Age range: 14–80
Most common age: 30s–50s
Percent alone: 40
Number of participants: 140, divided into groups of 5 to 12
Male/female ratio: 50/50

Another opportunity for volunteer research projects. This group recently has sponsored archaeology projects in California, Arizona, Canada, and the Caribbean, done botany research in Mexico, and studied folk medicine in Liberia and medieval architecture in southern France. All lodgings are shared, so singles are automatically paired. Meals are family style, and close ties automatically develop through living and working together.

COMMENTS:

Male, 20s: *The people were from all over the country, ages 16 to 70, about half male and female, a fair number married and with spouses. The program was not very structured, so you could do pretty much what you* *wanted. Meals were as a group and we all hung out together at night by the campfire. Food was very good. I enjoyed this as a single person because of the companionship of the group and the fact that there was always some activity to be involved in.*

Female, 30s: *I've been on four trips alone. It's easy because you are always busy. The people are from diverse backgrounds, ages 16 to 60s. The food is good; the program is well run, and the experiences unique.*

SMITHSONIAN ASSOCIATES RESEARCH EXPEDITIONS, The Smithsonian Institution, 1100 Jefferson Dr. SW, Washington, D.C. 20560; 202-357-1350. (M)

Years in business: Since 1988
Most common age: Mid-50s
Number of participants: 12–13 average per project
Age range: 18 to 75
Percent alone: 90
Male/female ratio: 40/60

This is a relatively new program under Smithsonian auspices, and a promising one offering some unique projects related to the museum's exhibits and collections. Among the topics are anthropology, wildlife ecology, volcanoes, history, art, military history, aviation, and space education. Locations include Washington, D.C., and Virginia, as well as Montana, Florida, Costa Rica, and London. The D.C. assistants live in a dormitory; other lodgings depend on location.

COMMENTS:

Female, 40s: *The opportunity to do archival research at the Air and Space Museum for two weeks was one of the highlights of my life; everything exceeded my expectations. We were given positions of real responsibility, treated like colleagues, and the work we did made a difference. The program was carefully structured, but it is assumed that you have a certain level of competence; for example, that once you are given directions, you can get around on the subway. There were 16 of us, ages 35 to 85, and married or single all came on their own. A welcoming dinner helped everyone get acquainted. All, naturally, were people interested in* *flying and the space program; some were retired engineers. I made good friends and exchange Christmas cards still with most of these people. We were also given a guided tour of the city, and the weekend was free to enjoy Washington.*

ARCHAEOLOGY

Ever fantasized about being an archaeologist and going on a dig? Here's your chance!

CROW CANYON ARCHAEOLOGICAL CENTER, 23390 County Rd. K, Cortez, CO 81321; 800-422-8975. (I)

Years in business: 6
Most common age: 35–55
Number of participants: 420 per year
Age range: 18–75
Percent alone: 50
Male/female ratio: 50/50

Here in the rugged terrain of the "four corners" where Arizona, New Mexico, Utah, and Colorado meet, adults join archaeologists searching for remains of the Anasazi ancient culture in the Mesa Verde region of southwestern Colorado. They learn the process of excavation, artifact identification, and interpretation by working on a dig of a 700-year-old Indian ruin, at the same time gaining firsthand understanding of the environment in which these people thrived. Participants live in round log cabins that resemble Navajo hogans, share hot meals at the lodge and sandwiches in the field. Most stay for one week.

COMMENTS:

Female, 40s: *I went alone the first time, have gone back five times and know a lot of people now. This is the best program I've ever found. The group is warm, with amazing backgrounds and levels of intelligence. The ages range from 18 to 80, about half male and female, and last time there were only three couples out of 24 people. You have classes in the morning, go to the dig site in the afternoon and early evening, have lectures after dinner. The food was family style and excellent. This program has caused several people to decide to go back to school for a master's degree.*

Male, 30s: *I've been going alone for five years. This is not Club Med, not a summer camp or play time—you are actually contributing to the archaeological work in progress. Accommodations and food are great. It's wonderful for anyone who is into archaeology or southwestern art.*

ANDOVER FOUNDATION FOR ARCHAEOLOGICAL RESEARCH (AFAR), Box 83, Andover, MA 01810; 508-470-0840. (ME–E)

Years in business: Since 1984
Age range: 15–90
Most common age: 55–75
Percent alone: 50
Number of participants: 10–20
Male/female ratio: 50/50

The archaeological expeditions sponsored by this nonprofit scientific organization study the origins of agriculture in New Mexico, dive for the fabled "Little Spanish Armada" in Belize and uncover an ancient Iroquois village near the St. Lawrence River in upstate New York. There is, as they put it, "a dig for all seasons." Volunteer "Friends of the Foundation" get basic training in archaeological techniques, typically stay 2 or 4 weeks. All work is done on weekdays, leaving Saturday and Sunday free to explore the area. Other projects are being planned in Mexico and Bolivia.

COMMENTS:

Male, 50s: *I've been on four trips alone. It is a diversified group, mostly from the Northeast but representing all the U.S., with an equal number of men and women, mostly traveling alone. None of the other men were married. The group is very congenial, always a group situation so you never feel alone; food ranges from fair to superb depending on the trip.*

Female, 60s: *The group is mostly singles or married people traveling alone. The program is well organized. I've stayed in tents, huts, and a rented house, depending on the trip. There is lots of physical labor, so everyone is pretty tired at night. The group gets along well and I recommend it for single travelers—I have been on eight of their trips.*

CENTER FOR AMERICAN ARCHAEOLOGY, Dept. B, Kampsville Archaeological Center, Kampsville, IL 62053; 618-653-4316. (I)

Years in business: 40
Age range: Teen to over 65
Most common age: 20–30
Percent alone: 80
Number of participants: 30 weekly
Male/female ratio: 50/50

On-site training in archaeological techniques through helping to excavate a series of Native American sites in the lower Illinois River valley. Meals are served cafeteria style in an open-air pavilion, an easy place to make friends. Evenings are occupied with lectures, night hikes, and informal outings in local restaurants. The programs enroll many young students; it might be wise to be sure other adults will be there when you go. Adult programs in the summer attract many teachers.

COMMENTS:

Male, 60s: *I felt a little awkward because I was the only adult—the rest were high school kids. The days were filled with long, hard work; the program was well run; the people were knowledgeable. I would go again.*

Female, 30s: *This is mostly doing, not classes. It's an intense time, working all day with planned activities at night. It's a very involving program. Accommodations are comfortable though not luxurious; the food was substantial and good.*

Publications listing other research vacation opportunities:

ARCHAEOLOGY FIELDWORK OPPORTUNITIES BULLETIN, Archaeological Institute of America, 675 Commonwealth Ave., Boston, MA 02215; 617-353-9361. $6 for nonmembers.

ANTHROPOLOGY FIELD SCHOOLS LISTING, American Anthropological Association, 1703 New Hampshire Ave. NW, Washington, D.C. 20009; 202-232-8800. $6 for nonmembers.

BACK TO NATURE

The nicest thing about nature-oriented workshops is their magnificent settings, where recreation is as appealing as the learning opportunities. Also included in this category are retreats in natural settings where the focus is on personal growth while you appreciate nature rather than study it.

AUDUBON ECOLOGY CAMPS AND WORKSHOPS, National Audubon Society, 613 Riversville Rd., Greenwich, CT 06831; 203-869-2017. (I)

Years in business: 50+
Most common age: 30s–40s
Number of participants: 55 maximum, divided into smaller field groups.
Age range: 18–80
Percent alone: High
Male/female ratio: Higher female

Adults from across the country come to the 1- and 2-week summer sessions held in the society's sanctuaries in Connecticut, off the coast of Maine, and in the Wind River Range of Wyoming. The society also sponsors a week of nature photography in national parks in Wyoming and in Maine, and international workshops, such as an on-site study of the ecology of Kenya. Other workshops are offered on topics such as beginning and advanced birding and field ecology. Winter ecology is taught amidst the beauty of Yellowstone National Park. The aim is to reintroduce you to nature, to show how all wildlife is interdependent and what you can do to protect it. Rustic lodgings are mostly dorm style; meals are buffet. Participants are all ages and backgrounds, from college students and retired seniors to teachers and firemen.

COMMENTS:

Female, 30s: *A typical day means getting up for an early breakfast, walking from about 8:30 to 11:30 with a naturalist, who is usually a teacher. The leaders are excellent and really know their stuff. There's time to rest or relax before and after lunch, then another program from 2:00 to 5:00. Depending on the weather and the topic, you might go out by boat instead of on foot. The idea is always hands-on learning. If it rains, classroom talks are held. At night there might be a guest lecturer, square dancing, a slide show, or an evening astronomy walk. The big group is divided into four small groups, and you stay with that group every day for programs, so there's plenty of chance to get to know people. Everyone has an interest in nature, and it's really nice to share that with others. There's a lot of bonding within the group.*

NATIONAL WILDLIFE FEDERATION CONSERVATION SUMMIT PROGRAM, 1400 Sixteenth Street NW, Washington, D.C. 20036-2266; 703-790-4263. (Mostly I; some M)

Years in business: 18
Most common age: 30–50
Number of participants: 400–500 annually
Age range: Infants to 70s
Percent alone: 33
Male/female ratio: Varies

Will try to arrange shares.

Conservation summits offer a week of nature education and recreation in four beautiful locations. Lodgings may be at university campuses or resort facilities; all programs serve meals in a central location, either cafeteria or family style.

The most luxurious site is Kiawah Island, South Carolina, where accommodations are in luxury villas. Participants enjoy birdwatching, early morning photography walks, beachcombing, and instruction in celestial navigation, sand dune and barrier island ecology. Plentiful recreational facilities include golf, tennis, beaching, biking, and jogging. In Burlington, Vermont, explorations along Lake Champlain shift to aquatic biology, Green Mountain geology, wetland ecology, and alpine exploration. Housing is in University of Vermont dorms or apartments. Ocean and mountain observations combine at the Pacific Northwest Summit headquartered at the University of Washington in Bellingham, Washington. On the agenda here are whale and seal-watching cruises, and educational programs on old-growth forests, tide pool ecology, mountain wildflowers, Cascade mountain geology, the salmon industry, and nature writing. The fourth summit, at Estes Park, Colorado, is reserved for teachers and scout leaders.

COMMENTS:

Female, 40s: *The age range is literally infants to senior citizens. You're up early. There are lectures and field trips, yet also plenty of free time. The hiking isn't too strenuous, so anyone can do it. In the evening there* *are slide presentations, music, or a skit and there is always one night devoted to the area you are visiting, such as a salmon cookout in Washington. Accommodations and food vary from fair to excellent depending on location, but the lodgings are always clean and adequate.*

Female, 50s: *I've been many times on my own. It is very comfortable and you get to meet people with common interests from all over the world. About half are there alone. This is as much pleasure as learning; we went on lots of hikes and field trips in beautiful areas as well as attending classes.*

THE CLEARING, P.O. Box 65, Ellison Bay, WI 54210; 414-854-4088. (I)

Years in business: 54
Most common age: 55–65
Number of participants: 28
Age range: 18–85
Percent alone: 75
Male/female ratio: 1/3

Will try to arrange shares.

Inspired by Danish folk schools for adults that stress teaching, learning, and living together in scenic surroundings, this program calls itself "a unique school of discovery in the arts, nature, and humanities." It presents dozens of courses, spring through fall, from watercolors, weaving, and design to ecology, astronomy, writing, and philosophy. Classes are taught outdoors and in the cathedrallike schoolhouse designed by Frank Lloyd Wright disciple Jens Jensen, located in a wooded setting near Green Bay. Participants live in dorms or in log and stone cabins, and enjoy family-style meals at hand-carved wood-plank tables. Inexpensive rates, no bar, hassle-free atmosphere, healthful food, time to meet interesting people, plus quiet contemplative time in unspoiled natural surroundings are part of the experience meant to be a clearing of the mind.

COMMENTS:

Female, 60s: *I have been at least 20 times. The Clearing is quiet, serene, a true retreat with time to think and exchange ideas with new people. It's inspiring. Most people are middle-aged and from the Midwest. Accommo-*

dations are simple but adequate; meals are not gourmet but good and very social, with lots of lively conversation. The scenery is just beautiful, and you really get to know everyone.

Male, 60s: *I've been with and without my wife. It is easy to be there alone. The group is mostly professionals, many single people, and many women. There is a rule that you can't sit down at the same place twice at meals, so you're almost forced to meet everyone. It is quiet and relaxed and informal, but with a purpose. I recommend it to anyone, single or not.*

STAR ISLAND CONFERENCE CENTER, P.O. Box 178, Portsmouth, NH, summer only; 110 Arlington St., Boston, MA 02116; 617-426-7988, September to June. (I)

Years in business: 73
Most common age: Varies with week's program
Number of participants: 180–240
Age range: Wide range
Percent alone: 50
Male/female ratio: Higher female

Will try to arrange shares.

Sponsored by the Unitarian Church, but open to all, the center offers arts instruction as well as birding, swimming, and boating, folk and square dancing, volleyball, and games. Each week has a different theme, such as arts, natural history, international affairs. Family-style meals and the small size of the island are conducive to meeting other people.

COMMENTS:

Female, 50s: *This is a place to get in touch with your spiritual side. There are more single people than married, more women than men. It is very comfortable to be alone. The programs are very well organized and I would recommend this to anyone. When you get there, you're not a stranger.*

Male, 40s: *I've gone for seven years, sometimes alone, sometimes with a friend. It's an easy group to get to know—meals are family style, everyone wears a name tag, about a quarter are single, but many married people come without their spouses. All activities are optional. Over half* *choose to go to morning chapel, even more to evening chapel. Workshops are in photography, painting, dance, music, drama, and writing—no experience necessary. Afternoons are free for trips to nearby islands. At night there are guest artists and folk dancing.*

A similar Unitarian-sponsored retreat in the South is the

MOUNTAIN HIGHLANDS CAMP AND CONFERENCE CENTER, 841 Highway 106, Highlands, NC 28741; 704-526-5838.

FOREIGN LANGUAGES

THE FOREIGN LANGUAGE IMMERSION PROGRAMS, The College at New Paltz, State University of New York, New Paltz, NY 12561; 914-257-2629. (I–M; Mohonk programs, E)

Years in business: Since 1981
Most common age: 45
Number of participants: Workshop groups, 12–15; foreign study groups, 20–25
Summer campus programs: 350 total, about 15 per class
Foreign trips: 20
Age range: 15–80
Percent alone: 75
Male/female ratio: 20/80

This innovative language department sponsors year-round weekend "total immersion" workshops at the New Paltz campus and in New York City, plus weekends and a 1-week session at the beautiful Mohonk Mountain House resort outside New Paltz. One- and 2-week intensive programs are held in summer at the New Paltz campus, and on language-learning vacations in Nice, France, Sorrento, Italy, and Seville, Spain.

The SUNY approach is to speak only the new language from day one, perfect for travelers who want to increase their vocabularies and learn conversation fast. Only enough grammar is taught to give a needed foundation. Two hundred to three hundred people may enroll for weekend seminars; they are divided into small groups according to ability. The summer classes meet from 8 A.M. to 1 P.M., leaving plenty of time for recreation. The Nice vacation provides lodging at a first-class hotel and instruction from 8 A.M. to 1 P.M. in conference rooms at the hotel. Native instructors double as guides and help students get the most from visiting the Riviera.

COMMENTS:

E.B.: *My weekend at SUNY was a delight. Teachers are chosen for their outgoing personalities as well as language ability and they conduct classes with flair and a sense of fun. A typical assignment: "Pick a French character and describe yourself so that the class can guess who you are." Everybody gets into the spirit, and there's lots of laughter as well as learning. The class stayed together at lunch, still speaking French. Most of us chose to have dinner together as well, though we did give ourselves an English break. The approach dredged up every word of my forgotten college French—I was really amazed. It left me in much better shape to tackle a trip to France.*

Female, 40s: *The summer program in Nice was high-quality. The age range of participants was from 21 to 70, with most people in their 30s and 40s. Most were from New York State, but there was one Texan and one New Englander. Among 19 people there was only one couple and only two men. The hotel was good, and a very nice extra was a full American breakfast included each day. There were welcoming and closing dinners, and the rest of the time the class often went to dinner together, though it was not compulsory. We also had a delightful picnic, which we shopped for together—in French! Our French-born teachers made the trip far richer. They became our friends, and we were even invited to the home of one instructor's family. You have to want to spend part of your day in France on instruction to do this, but the 5 hours seem to fly by and your first assignment each morning is to tell the class about your sight-seeing (or other activities) the previous afternoon and evening. It is a lot of fun, a very good experience, and the cost is moderate for what you get.*

For other language study opportunities abroad, contact National Registration Center for Study Abroad, 823 N. Second St., Milwaukee, WI 53201; 414-278-0631. NRCSA is a consortium of 85 universities, language institutes, and specialized schools in 12 countries of Latin America and Europe.

FOOD

The opportunity to master the authentic cuisine of France or Italy with instruction from top regional chefs and teachers gives a special dimension to a foreign location, and a view of the country most tourists miss. All of these programs include regional sight-seeing, the chance to visit local markets, and sample fine cuisine—including some that you will produce yourself. They are expensive, but participants say they are wonderful experiences worth saving for!

ROME GOURMET ADVENTURE, c/o E & M Associates, 211 E. 43rd St., New York, NY 10017; 800-223-9832 or 212-599-8280. (EE)

Years in business: 8
Age range: 25–65
Most common age: 35–55
Percent alone: 50
Number of participants: 12
Male/female ratio: 40/60

Jo Bettoja, part of a family of Italian hoteliers and author of *Italian Cooking in the Grand Tradition*, conducts her Scaldavivande Cooking School in English at a 17-century palazzo near the Trevi Fountain. Guests stay at a first-class Bettoja hotel, attend classes for 4 hours daily, then lunch on their creations. One morning is devoted to visiting the bustling Piazza Vittorio, Rome's most famous food market; another includes a guided sight-seeing tour of Rome. Other afternoons and evenings are free. The pièce de résistance comes on the last day when students travel to Caprarola for a visit to the Villa Farnese and then to Barbarano for a graduation luncheon held at the Bettojas' 18th-century villa on a 200-acre farm and hunting preserve.

COMMENTS:

Female, 50s: *I've gone alone twice. This is an extremely affluent group, a mix of married and single, and two-to-one female. The class is great, the group interesting; you feel like one of the family, and there is plenty of free time in the evening, when stores are still open. Perfect for anyone who likes to cook or eat.*

ITALIAN COUNTRY COOKING, Positano, Italy, c/o E & M Associates, 211 E. 43d St., New York, NY 10017; 800-223-9832 or 212-599-8280. (E)

Years in business: 5
Most common age: 25–45
Number of participants: 12
Age range: 20–60
Percent alone: 60
Male/female ratio: 60/40

Diana Folonari, of a noted Italian wine family, conducts this 9-day program at her home in Positano, a magnificent setting in the cliffs on the Amalfi Drive. The program begins with a reception and a talk on Italian food and wine. Five mornings are spent in class, with students preparing lunches they share. One late-afternoon session features homemade pizzas and country dishes. Special sessions on Italian wines are held as well. Participants stay in a local hotel, have one full day and most afternoons and evenings free for sight-seeing in nearby Amalfi, Ravello, Sorrento, Pompeii, and the Isle of Capri. A final, farewell dinner is held at a fine local hotel.

COMMENTS:

Male, 40s: *This is fantastic, one of the best trips I've ever made. I happened to be the only student who enrolled, and Diana and I became great friends. You stay at the best hotel in Positano, with wonderful accommodations. The area is beautiful, the wines delicious, the instruction fantastic. It's expensive, but worth it.*

THE COOKING SCHOOL OF UMBRIA, Casella Postale 127, Todi, Perugia, Italy 06059; 075/887370. (EE)

Years in business: 4
Most common age: 35–50
Number of participants: 12
Age range: 25–60
Percent alone: 50
Male/female ratio: 40/60

Will try to arrange shares.

After a 30-year career in the restaurant and hotel business in the United States, master chef Donald Soviero retired to Italy to open his own cooking school, handsomely appointed and well equipped with five professional 22-burner ranges, a separate *pasticceria* for pastry and bread making, wood-burning ovens, and plenty of work space for all. One-week sessions in English are held alternate weeks from May to early December, introducing the full range of Italian cuisine from "alta cucina" and regional specialties to breads and pizzas. Field trips to markets, bakeries, sausage makers, cheese and pasta factories, vineyards, wineries, and wine tastings, plus truffle hunts and oil pressings in season are part of the itinerary, along with visits to select restaurants that provide kitchen tours and demonstrations. Rates include lodging in a hotel in Todi, all meals, five 4-hour cooking lessons followed by lunch with appropriate wines, excursions, visits to a minimum of four restaurants, and a festive final banquet prepared by Chef Soviero.

COMMENTS:

Female, 40s: *The instruction was much more meaningful because it was preceded by historical descriptions and explanations of regions and cuisines. I didn't really know what to expect of this week; it exceeded my greatest expectations. I hope I have an opportunity to return. I loved the school and the area and the warmth extended by Donald and his able assistants.*

Male, 50s: *An excellent program and I was pleasantly surprised by the supplemental wine program, which was excellent in itself. I especially enjoyed the presentation of the history and produce of each region, critiques of the restaurant food as it was served to us, and the personality of the chef—sufficient humor alternating with seriousness to keep everyone's attention.*

MARCELLA AND VICTOR HAZAN'S MASTER CLASS AT HOME IN VENICE, c/o Susan Cox, P.O. Box 285, Circleville, NY 10919; 914-692-7104. (EE)

Years in business: Since 1985 | Age range: 30–50
Most common age: 35 | Percent alone: 33
Number of participants: 6 | Male/female ratio: 50/50

A few times each year, these noted culinary authorities open their 16th-century palazzo to a select group of students interested in Italian cooking and wine. Classes are loosely structured and intimate, with a chance to experience at close range the Hazans' approach to cooking.

The week opens with an overview of the course over espresso, an escorted tour of the historic produce and fish market at Rialto, and a midday banquet at one of the hosts' favorite Venice restaurants. Classes begin the morning of day 2 and continue for the next 5 days, running for 5 hours. Afterward, students share the dishes they've made at a leisurely luncheon. During each meal, Victor Hazan presents and discusses rare wines from his private cellar. Despite the high cost, the demand for this course is great—reservations are accepted 2 years in advance.

LA VARENNE IN BURGUNDY, c/o Ecole de Cuisine La Varenne, P.O. Box 25574, Washington, D.C. 20007; 202-337-0073. (EE)

Years in business: 13
Age range: 35–60
Most common age: 35–60
Percent alone: 50
Number of participants: 10
Male/female ratio: Varies

One-week programs in summer and fall designed by Anne Willan, noted founder of Ecole de Cuisine La Varenne in Paris, combine cooking instruction in Burgundian and seasonal cuisine with fine living at the 17th-century Château du Fey in northern Burgundy. Each program is conducted by a different food personality, sometimes Willan herself. Meals are prepared by a La Varenne chef and include tastings of wines, cheese, and other regional specialties. The week includes 4 half-day participation classes and one demonstration, plus excursions to the market at Joigny, a visit to historic Sens, wine tasting in Chablis, and meals at two 3-star restaurants—the Côte Saint-Jacques in Joigny and l'Esperance in Vézelay. The château has a pool, tennis courts, woodland and garden paths.

COMMENTS:

Male, 40s: *This was the most relaxing vacation I've ever had. I left my wife at home, went to enhance my cooking skills. In my group of ten, there was only one couple—everyone else came alone. The instruction was excellent. We had classes in the morning, preparing a lunch. Then we went to local cheese makers or vineyards, or had free time to sightsee or relax. Dinner was either prepared by our chef or we dined out in a 3-star restaurant. We all had a wonderful time.*

Male, 30s: *The people were interesting; most were alone and from diverse backgrounds. The trip was special because there was nothing touristy about it . . . cooking was the main focus, and because there were few in the group, you really got to know people. I would highly recommend this to anyone who likes to cook . . . or to eat!*

COOKING SCHOOL AT L'ABBAYE DE SAINTE CROIX, Route Val-de Cuech, 13300 Salon-de-Provence, France; c/o David Mitchell & Company, Inc., 200 Madison Ave., New York, NY 10016; 212-696-1323. (EE)

Years in business: Since 1987
Most common age: 30–60
Number of participants: 6–12
Age range: 20–82
Percent alone: 15
Male/female ratio: Varies

This small week-long winter cooking course in the heart of Provence gives students the opportunity to prepare elegant four-course dinners with professional instruction, then enjoy the results together with their chef, Yves Sauret. Though the chef speaks French, translators are on hand to make sure you get every detail right. The setting is a restored 12th-century monastery, which is now a luxurious 4-star Relais et Château hotel, set high above the plain with an unobstructed view of the Mediterranean. The weather in winter is usually in the 60s. Besides cooking instruction, the week includes excursions with the chef to the local market and to shop for kitchen equipment, and visits to Avignon and Les Baux with meals at noted local restaurants.

No references provided.

For a list of cooking schools around the world, order "The Guide to Cooking Schools" from Shaw Associates, 625 Biltmore Way, Coral Gables, FL 33134; 305-446-8888. Ask for current prices.

WINE

These "universities" attract wine lovers from around the world. Some students are in the wine business and need this knowledge professionally; others are strictly amateur enthusiasts who want to learn in depth about the wines of the country, and have an enjoyable vacation at the same time.

GERMAN WINE ACADEMY, P.O. Box 1705, 6500 Mainz, West Germany, or German Wine Information Bureau, 79 Madison Ave., New York, NY 10016; 212-213-7036. (M)

Years in business: 16
Age range: 21–70
Most common age: 35–50
Percent alone: No records
Number of participants: 20–40
Male/female ratio: 60/40

No shares arranged; single supplement is small.

Six days of learning about German wines include lectures in English by local experts, travel to grape-growing regions for visits to vineyards and cellars and a wide spectrum of tastings. Seminars are based at the academy headquarters, a 12th-century monastery called Kloster Eberbach. Students are lodged for 5 nights at the charming Hotel Schwan in Oestrich/Rheingau, and spend one day on a Rhine cruise with an overnight at the Alte Thorschenke at Cochem, one of Germany's oldest hotels.

Areas usually visited include the Mosel, Rheingau, Rheinpfalz, Baden, and Rheinhessen regions. An 11-day "Super Seminar" adds cultural visits to castles, museums, and other places of historic interest to the wine lectures, and leaves some free time for shopping and sight-seeing. There is also an advanced course for those with a basic knowledge of German wine.

COMMENTS:

Female, 30s: *Some come for business, some for personal interest, but everyone shares the basic interest in wines; several people came alone. Because groups are small and you travel and eat together every day, it's very congenial and you get to know everyone.*

Male, 40s: *I came first with a companion, came back to the advanced session alone, returned a third time with my 21-year-old daughter, and always had a ball. About half are couples, the rest come alone, and there was plenty of company even for those in their 20s or 30s. I think this is one of the great bargains of the world—the food is great and you taste more than 250 wines. As the wine flows so does the fun. Even on the bus we sang songs and told jokes. It was a constant party.*

ITALIAN WINE ACADEMY, 10 Garnock Ave., Toronto, Canada M4K 1M2; 416-465-8305. (ME)

Years in business: 3	Age range: 20–60
Most common age: 30s and 40s	Percent alone: 50
Number of participants: 20	Male/female ratio: 60/40

Toronto wine writer and instructor Robert Black organizes 6-day programs in English on the wines of Italy, offered in spring and fall, and headquartered on a wine estate in Sienna. The Tuscan week begins with an overview and a tasting session of the wines of Tuscany, held at the National Wine Library, a showcase for Italian wines housed in a 16th-century fortress. Each day following, the group visits a different winery for a talk, a tasting, and lunch. Students learn about the basics of wine making, viticulture, and wine etiquette. Time is allotted also for sight-seeing in the ancient towns and lush countryside of the area. Rates include lodging, lectures, tastings, continental breakfasts, and a total of eight lunches and dinners. Similar programs for other regions may be planned for the future.

COMMENTS:

Male, 40s: *We saw parts of Italy we would never have seen on our own, and learned a great deal about the Italian style of wine making, from sparkling vermouth to grappa. It was educational and a very good experience. The group is limited to 20. Much of the time is occupied with learning about wine, and we ate our meals together, so there is no problem being alone. My group was mostly male, and mostly Canadian, though there were participants from Connecticut and Mississippi. There was only one woman in my group.*

OTHER FOOD AND WINE VACATIONS

THE WINE SOCIETY OF AMERICA'S WINE DISCOVERY TRIPS, Hale House, 1 Bennett Common, Millbrook, NY 12545; 800-367-2675. (EE)

Changing annual wine-study trips have included Portugal, and Burgundy and Bordeaux in France. One special trip is a barge cruise through Burgundy with Steven Spurrier of l'Académie du Vin in Paris and Becky Wasserman of le Servet in Beaune. Check for current year's offerings.

LIMITED EDITIONS, 373 Commonwealth Ave., #601, Boston, MA 02115-1815; 617-266-8450. (EE)

Offers a number of upscale cooking and wine-tasting courses in Europe. Director Patricia McNally estimates that half of the participants come alone. She arranges shares. Some of their programs:

The Château Country Cooking Course (EE). Taught by Michelin-starred chef Alain Corvi at Le Domaine de la Tortiniere, a historic château in the Loire. Morning cooking classes are complemented by afternoon excursions to regional wine cellars and visits to the renowned châteaus. Limited to 15.

French Cooking at Château de Montreil (EE). A 5-day program taught by Michelin-starred chef Christian Germain at a Relais et Château property in northern France. Three-hour morning classes are followed by afternoon excursions to regional wine and cheese cellars. Limited to 8.

Tuscan Cuisine with Lorenza de' Medici (EE). Lorenza de' Medici is hostess and instructor for a 1-week course at Badia a Coltibuono, a wine estate in the Chianti countryside not far from Florence. Three- to 4-hour hands-on classes are followed by a sampling lunch, sightseeing in the area, and evening dining at the region's best restaurants.

Wines of Bordeaux (E). Based in the Château La Grange de Luppe, 6 days are spent exploring the region. Each day's itinerary includes daily excursions to area châteaus with lunch en route, vineyard and cellar visits, wine tastings, and dinner. Included are the great châteaus of Latour, Margaux, and Saint-Emilion.

PHOTOGRAPHY

Sharpening your ability with a camera not only makes for a rewarding vacation, but gives you skills that will enhance your travel pleasure forever after, guaranteeing wonderful personal souvenirs from any trip.

MAINE PHOTOGRAPHIC WORKSHOP, 2 Central St., Rockport, ME 04856; 207-236-8581. (M)

Years in business: 17
Most common age: 30–40
Number of participants: About 150 per week
Age range: 18–75
Percent alone: Varies
Male/female ratio: Varies

With the picture-perfect Maine coast village of Rockport as subject matter and inspiration, one of the nation's leading educational centers for photography offers 1-week workshops from June to September. Classes range from Photography I and beginning darkroom techniques to master classes in many aspects of the craft from portraits to landscapes, in black-and-white and color, taught by some of the top people in the field. There is also a special 2-week workshop for beginning amateurs. This is a chance to deepen your appreciation of the photograph as well as to understand more about the process of taking better pictures, with exhibits in the gallery and slide shows by the masters to illustrate what is possible.

Classrooms, labs, accommodations, and dining rooms are interspersed in buildings throughout the village, all within walking distance of each other. Meals are served buffet style and are shared by all at communal tables. In the planning stages, possibly ready for 1990, is an 11-acre complex of studios, classrooms, a theater, and lodgings.

No references provided. Letters from past students say: "There was such an excitement in the air that I jumped out of bed each morning looking forward to being surrounded by such creative, loving, and interesting photographers."

"A high-energy, intensely inspirational experience. I have never worked such long hours and had so much fun. Not to mention the fact that I learned in quantum leaps."

TRAVEL PHOTOGRAPHY WORKSHOPS IN SANTA FE, P.O. Box 2847, Santa Fe, NM 87501-2847; 505-982-4979. (M–no meals included)

Years in business: 8
Most common age: 55–65
Number of participants: 20
Age range: 30–80
Percent alone: 60
Male/female ratio: 50/50
Will try to arrange shares. Not suitable for beginners.

Serious amateur photographers learn from noted travel photographer Lisl Dennis, with the inspiring Santa Fe landscape as subject matter. Many are world travelers who want to learn to convey a better sense of place on film. Two days are spent on photo-trips with on-location demonstrations, traveling one day to ghost towns and a Spanish colonial museum, another to Taos through the Rio Grande Valley, photographing Anasazi petroglyphs, chili stands, the famous Ranchos de Taos church, and the 800-year-old Taos Indian pueblo. Students stay in the Hotel La Posada in Santa Fe. Dennis also leads photography tours.

No references provided.

NATURE PHOTOGRAPHY WORKSHOPS, 5210 Hurbert Rd., Spruce, MI 48762, 517-727-3260. (I)

Years in business: 3
Age range: 30–60
Most common age: 45
Percent alone: 40
Number of participants: 20
Male/female ratio: 50/50

Roommates are assigned, though the single supplement is small. Suitable for beginners.

Week-long workshops are held by two professional nature photographers at Tahquamenon Falls on Michigan's upper peninsula, with lodging at a nearby Comfort Inn, and at Sleeping Bear Dunes National Lakeshore, based at the Leelanau Center for Education. More programs are planned in Ohio, California, West Virginia, Missouri, and Arizona, as well as a session in Kenya. About 20 percent of the time is spent viewing instructional slide programs, the rest in the field, where the two directors are on hand to supervise and advise. For this specialized type of photography, students are taught to use a long lens, tripods, how to shoot by moonlight, and how to stalk animal subjects.

COMMENTS:

Female, 30s: *I've gone alone twice—it's the best vacation I've ever had. The instruction was excellent, with lectures and trips available every day, early morning photography sessions before breakfast if you choose to get up. All of the meals and trips are with a group, making it easy to be part* *of things. About half the participants each time have been single, evenly divided between male and female, ages from 20s to 60s; most from Michigan or the Northeast. I've recommended this vacation to my own single friends.*

Male, 30s: *I went alone as a helper/instructor. It doesn't matter whether you are married or single, the activities are as a group. There's a nice mix of hobbyists and serious photographers. My group had more males, a fairly even number of married and single. If you go to all the lectures and group shoots, the program is fairly structured, but you can do what you want, and you are free to just hang around and take your own shots if you choose.*

For other U.S. and foreign workshops, see the monthly listing in *Peterson's Photographic Magazine*, 8490 Sunset Blvd., Los Angeles, CA 90069; 213-854-2200. There are many workshop advertisements in other photography publications such as *Modern Photography*, 825 Seventh Ave., New York, NY 10019; 212-265-8360; or *Popular Photography*, 1515 Broadway, New York, NY 10036; 212-719-6000.

ART

An art-oriented vacation is more than a chance to develop a lifelong hobby; it means looking at a new locale from a different point of view—with the painter's eye—truly absorbing the details of the landscape and the architecture. The following are among hundreds of art workshops held around this country and abroad each year. For a comprehensive listing, look for the annual directory of art schools and workshops usually published in March in *American Artist Magazine*, 1515 Broadway, New York, NY 10036; 212-764-7300.

ART WORKSHOP, 463 West St., Apt. 1028H, New York, NY 10014; 212-691-1159. (M)

Years in business: 14
Age range: 17–80
Most common age: 40–60
Percent alone: 50
Number of participants: 10–20
Male/female ratio: Majority female

All are assigned roommates unless they specify singles. Suitable for beginners.

Inspiring settings from Mexico to Italy are the specialty of this workshop run by two experienced art instructors. Groups for the 3-week program in Assisi, Italy, are housed in clean and simple rooms in an English-speaking convent, unless they prefer hotel accommodations in town. They meet on the covered terrace of the garden for classes in painting, drawing, collage, and design. Work and play at your own pace is the motto, so there is time to enjoy the convent pool and to explore the countryside. Two days are left completely free for excursions. Breakfast and lunch are included in the tuition.

Groups for the 10-day program in Mexico stay either at Rancho Rio Caliente, a hot-water spa in the mountains outside Guadalajara, or at the Aristos hotel on the grounds of the Instituto Allende art school in San Miguel de Allende. Class days are interspersed with free days for trips or time for sight-seeing. If they wish, students may paint away from the class and return for critiques at the end of the day.

COMMENTS:

Female, 40s: *This is an excellent program with no pressure. It was very easy to get to know everyone. My group was all women, ages 16 to 72, half of whom were single, and with all levels of art training. The food and the atmosphere were wonderful. We had painting instruction in the morning, afternoons free, and ate all meals together. A few times each week there were lectures and slide presentations. We went to local concerts or went swimming on our own.*

Female, 50s: *A group of very interesting people from all over the U.S. and Europe, mostly women and mostly single. We stayed in a guest house run by nuns with strict rules—you had to dress appropriately for the dining room. But the food was wonderful and the teachers creative. The views were beautiful. Teachers provided a painting theme each day, but you could paint whatever you wanted if you preferred. There was a certain amount of time for peer criticism. We tended to stay together in the afternoon, and the whole group often went out for dinner. It was excellent. I would recommend this to any single person.*

INTERNATIONAL ART PROGRAMS, LTD., 41 Union Sq., Room 314, New York, NY 10003; 212-980-7053. (E)

Years in business: 5
Most common age: 50s, 60s
Number of participants: 25–30
Age range: 35–80
Percent alone: High
Male/female ratio: 60/40

Will arrange shares. Suitable for beginners.

Cadenabbia, a town on the shores of Italy's Lake Como, is home base for 3-week workshops in oils, pastels, and sculpture. Work includes portraits, landscapes, and still lifes. Studios are in the first-class hotel where students are housed, but much of the work is done outdoors with glorious scenery for inspiration. Classes last 5 hours, with the rest of the day free for sight-seeing. There is great bonding, says instructor Diana Willis; after a week, the students are taking care of one another.

COMMENTS:

Male, 70s: *I was the oldest—the rest of the group ranged in age from the 30s and up, with most probably around 50. Of 20 people, there were three couples, and one other single male. We all got along well. The instruction was excellent in every media, the sculpture as well as the painting. Good for any age if you want to improve your art skills; I hope to go back this year.*

LA ROMITA SCHOOL OF ART, 1712 Old Town NW, Albuquerque, NM 87104; 505-243-1924. (I)

Years in business: 22
Most common age: 40–50
Number of participants: 19–20
Age range: 30–70
Percent alone: 50
Male/female ratio: 1/8

Shares usually compulsory. Suitable for beginners.

Two 4-week summer programs held in the glorious Italian Umbrian hill country between Rome and Florence give participants a chance to tour as well as paint. Studio days are interspersed with visits to such towns as Spoleto, Assisi, Florence, Siena, and Perugia. The school is housed in a 16th-century monastery with modern facilities.

COMMENTS:

Female, 40s: *Well organized, every detail taken care of, so we were free to concentrate on lessons. We spent three days in the monastery near Rome, three days in Florence. Participants were mostly well-educated women. Accommodations were dorm style with two to a room and bathrooms shared. Good food, good value, and very easy for a single.*

Female, 20s: *Good organization and excellent food. As a photographer, I found the holiday geared more to artists, but we saw non-touristy Italy and were able to mix with local people. It was like combining my hobby with foreign travel. The group was mostly women over 40; there was only one couple on the trip.*

PAT NORTON WORKSHOP, Norton's Landing, Barbeau, MI 49710; 906-647-3416. (I)

Years in business: 20
Most common age: Varies
Number of participants: 10-20
Age range: 20–60
Percent alone: 50
Male/female ratio: 1/3

Suitable for beginners.

Two 1-week summer sessions held in a scenic northern Michigan area not far from Mackinac Island. Lodging is in cottages and rates include meals. Ms. Norton also leads workshops in Greece.

COMMENTS:

Female, 40s: *We were treated like family and very well looked after. I did not take the art classes, but did some painting on my own and took trips in the area. The group was mostly female; I felt very comfortable as a single and would go again.*

CAROLINE BUCHANAN, 36976 Soap Creek Rd., Corvallis, OR 97330; 503-745-5253. (I–M)

Years in business: 12
Most common age: 50s
Number of participants 20–24
Age range: 30–65
Percent alone: 70
Male/female ratio: 1/4

Suitable for beginners.

Learning workshops on the magnificent Oregon coast, with participants lodged in motels or inns, and also on the San Juan Islands, where most of the group stays in one hotel. Buchanan also offers a 2-day workshop, called "The Uncertain Artist," at her Soap Creek studio. For non-artists only, this is the perfect place to try painting with other novices. She also leads sketching tours to Greece and the South Sea Islands.

COMMENTS:

Male, 50s: *I was very at ease alone. The age range was 30s to 60s, most in the group married but without their spouses. Only 2 men out of 18 people. There were a few people from the East but most from Oregon and Washington. It's relaxed, good for beginners or dabblers. The organization was excellent. You get out of the instruction what you put into it.*

Female, 40s: *It was wonderful, and easy to meet people. Everything was a group situation, yet there was no social pressure. You could be by yourself if you liked but you never felt left out or lonely. Age range was 20s to 60s, no couples, almost all women. Great instruction in the morning, then afternoons free to swim or walk or whatever. In the evening we evaluated the paintings or went out in groups.*

BEN KONIS ART WORKSHOPS, 712 W. 17th, Amarillo, TX 79102; 806-373-8458. (M–E)

Years in business: 20
Most common age: 40–55
Number of participants: 20
Age range: 23–65
Percent alone: 50
Male/female ratio: 2/3

Suitable for beginners.

Konis, a southwestern artist who presents workshops at summer art schools around the country, also leads art-oriented trips to Hawaii and Mexico with instruction in capturing the local scenery.

COMMENTS:

Female, 40s: *The course was very well organized, the setting beautiful. There was no pressure to take part in activities. The group was mostly middle-aged, mostly female. It was a very enjoyable holiday, single or not.*

THE ARTNERSHIP, INC., P.O. Box 1418, Sarasota, FL 34230; 800-237-6286. In Florida, 800-222-6286. (I–M)

Years in business: 25+
Age range: 25–75
Most common age: 55–65
Percent alone: 30–40
Number of participants: Average is 30
Male/female ratio: 25/75

Guests are matched with roommates unless singles are requested; there is a single supplement. Suitable for beginners.

One- and 2-week workshops at a variety of scenic sites with instruction by two experienced artist-directors to help you translate the beauty into watercolors. Locations include Key West (motel lodgings); Harbor Inn on Monhegan Island, Maine; Purity Spring Resort in New Hampshire; Ghost Ranch, 55 miles from Santa Fe in New Mexico; Bell Rock Inn in Sedona, Arizona; and Harbor Lite Lodge on the Mendocino coast of northern California. One foreign trip is planned annually. Each morning starts with a lecture-demonstration forming the core of the day's teaching points. Instructors stay on hand to assist, and do constructive critiques at the end of the day. Slide/cassette programs are available in the evenings.

COMMENTS:
Female, 60s: *These are the best-run workshops I have been to. It is a wonderful trip because you can combine art with companionship; art breaks all barriers, and young and old mix easily. This is a particularly good choice for older women.*
Female, 60s: *The teachers are very good and the program is geared toward work. The group I was in included lots of retired couples and married people, and a few singles, with females outnumbering the males two to one. It was easy to meet people because you had to carpool to all the destinations—all you have to do is to extend yourself a little.*

ART TREK, P.O. Box 807, Bolinas, CA 94924; 415-868-1836. (E)

Years in business: 8
Most common age: 30–45
Number of participants: 12–16
Age range: 23–69
Percent alone: 60–70
Male/female ratio: 50/50

Suitable for beginners.

Watercolor painting instruction in exotic locales—France, Tahiti, the American Southwest, Indonesia—combined with sight-seeing and activities in each area. Some trips are in conjunction with the University of California extension in Santa Cruz.

COMMENTS:

Male, 30s: *I went to Tahiti, and it was just great. We visited several islands by boat and small plane, including some really isolated spots that we would never have seen on our own. I was one of only two males in our group of 16, ranging in age from 28 to 70, but age or sex did not matter. We all shared an interest in painting, the area was brand-new to all of us, and I think everyone had a good time. The opportunity to paint in such surroundings was exceptional, and really motivated me to continue on my own.*

ARTS, CRAFTS, MUSIC, AND MORE

These multifaceted programs have something for almost everyone.

CREATIVE WORKSHOPS AT DILLMAN'S SAND LAKE LODGE,

Box 98, Lac du Flambeau, WI 54538; 715-588-3143. (I)

Years in business: 54
Most common age: 50
Number of participants: 120
Age range: 25–80
Percent alone: 30
Male/female ratio: Higher female

Suitable for beginners.

For the past 10 years, this family-run resort has offered a weekly roster of painting and photography workshops from late May to early October to supplement the many sports facilities of the lodge. A long list of art choices is available along with the chance to learn silk screen, calligraphy, or duplicate bridge, survey Native American culture, or try your hand at journal writing. Guests are housed in the lodge; reasonable tuition includes room, breakfast, and dinner.

No references provided.

ARROWMONT SCHOOL OF ARTS AND CRAFTS, P.O. Box 567, Gatlinburg, TN 37738; 615-436-5860. (I)

Years in business: Since 1945
Most common age: 40–65
Number of participants: 40–100 per week
Age range: 18–80
Percent alone: 20
Male/female ratio: 1/3

Will try to arrange shares. Suitable for beginners.

A visual arts complex on 70 wooded acres adjacent to the Great Smoky Mountain National Park. One- and 2-week summer workshops draw men and women of all ages and levels of ability who wish to learn both traditional and contemporary crafts. Classes in basketry, quilting, weaving, and enameling as well as painting and drawing and work in clay and fibers are conducted by more than 100 visiting faculty members. Students are housed in simply furnished dormitory rooms in cottage-type buildings. Home-cooked meals are served in a congenial dining room. Having everyone together makes for a warm atmosphere.

COMMENTS:

Male, 40s: *This is an intense learning experience, the best school of its type. It is fine to be here by yourself, as about half the students come alone. Most are women. People come from all over the world.*

Female, 30s: *I had a very pleasant experience. My group was mostly women, and many of the men who did come were with their wives, but it was a great mix of people. People here leave their lives behind. It's like summer camp—easy to become close quickly. The instructors are very well qualified. It's a good place to go alone.*

HAYSTACK MOUNTAIN SCHOOL OF CRAFTS. Deer Isle, ME 04627; 207-348-2306. (I)

Years in business: 38
Most common age: Mid-30s
Number of participants: 80
Age range: 18–80
Percent alone: 30
Male/female ratio: Varies

Located in a handsome complex in a spectacular setting on the coast of Maine, Haystack attracts many accomplished artisans, but also offers a 2-week program, called "Square One: A Session for Beginnings," for artists who want to explore a new medium or individuals who want to begin seriously studying a particular art. Courses in clay, fibers, metals, wood, and glassblowing were offered in a recent session.

COMMENTS:

Female, 40s: *This is a working vacation . . . there's always something to do and you can go from area to area and learn several types of crafts. How structured or loose the course is depends on each instructor. The atmosphere is very warm and people come away extended creatively. Most students are female—some professional women, some retired.*

Female, 30s: *There's a cluster of serious art students, and most of the older people are there for vacation. About half are single or came alone. There's a nice balance of public and private time. People come here to have an experience with others who are interested in crafts, and it's not just surface—they form lasting friendships. The food is terrific, very healthy and appetizing. There's something to do all day, and at night there is usually a slide show or a dance or some sort of program.*

AUGUSTA HERITAGE CENTER, Davis & Elkins College, Elkins, WV 26241-3996; 304-636-1903. (I)

Years in business: 16
Most common age: 25–45
Number of participants: 1,400
Age range: 10–75
Percent alone: 30–40
Male/female ratio: Varies but about 50/50

Singles matched in dorm rooms.

Appalachian arts, from fiddling, blacksmithing, and basketry to whittling and folk painting, are the focus of this excellent 5-week summer program. Dance, storytelling, songwriting, performance, and music from bluegrass to Cajun are also included in the list of 90 workshops, most of which run for 5 days. Room and board includes housing in twin-bed college dorms and three daily meals on campus. The program ends with a 3-day folk festival with home cooking galore and music and dancing that leaves toes tapping for weeks after.

COMMENTS:

Female, 30s: *It is very easy to meet people, and 75 percent are alone. It's fairly even male and female. I went for the dancing; the days were strenuous, the instruction very good. The dorm rooms and food are not good, but that's not why you go. It is creative time.*

Female, 40s: *There's no way you would feel alone here. A wide variety of people come from all over the U.S., all ages but mostly in their 20s and 30s. Some of the classes are very structured, running from 8* A.M. *to 5* P.M.*, then resuming at night. There are dances at least twice a week and people who come for the music classes hold jam sessions in the evening. Most of the people here lead some type of alternative life-style; they are happy to meet each other, and many lasting friendships are formed.*

MUSIC AND ART INTERNATIONAL WORKSHOPS, 11309 N. Glenbrook Lane, Mequon, WI 53092; 414-242-9039. (I)

Years in business: 17
Age range: 16–85
Most common age: 45–60
Percent alone: 20
Number of participants: 250–300
Male/female ratio: 1/10

Music study is not suitable for beginners; beginners okay for art or photography.

Musicians, artists, and photographers come together for this multifaceted workshop held in Eisenstadt, Austria, a few minutes south of Vienna. Housing is in clean, simple double rooms in two student hotels. Music instruction is not for beginners, though there are topics such as Recreational Chamber Music for less-serious students. Courses in Japanese *sumi-e* painting and photography are appropriate for all.

No references provided.

INTERNATIONAL MUSIC CAMP SUMMER SCHOOL OF FINE ARTS, P.O. Box 27, Bottineau, ND 58318-0027; 701-228-2277, ext. 246. (I)

Years in business: 33
Most common age: Teens, but there are adult programs also
Number of participants: 2,200 over 7 weeks during summer
Age range: 10–75
Percent alone: 99
Male/female ratio: 1/3

Many classes suitable for beginners; piano, band, or orchestra classes require prior study.

As the name suggests, this is primarily a study camp for musicians and it attracts many teenagers and music instructors, but a variety of adult classes in the arts are offered, including guitar, ballet, modern dance, creative writing, and painting. Classes are divided according to students' abilities, from beginning to advanced. Adults are also able to enjoy concerts and recitals, ranging from classical to jazz, by faculty and artists-in-residence.

The camp is located in the picturesque International Peace Garden, a 2,200-acre oasis of formal gardens, lawns, lakes, and wilderness areas straddling the border between North Dakota and Manitoba, Canada. The garden is run jointly by a nonprofit U.S. and Canadian organization that is a symbol of friendship between the two countries. Men and women are housed in separate dormitories. Meals are served cafeteria style in a new, modern dining hall.

COMMENTS:

Female, 50s: *About equally divided between Americans and Canadians, plus a few Europeans. Most are married but come alone. I never felt out of place being alone. The program is very well run, highly recommended for anyone who plays an instrument and wants to learn more. There is a very creative atmosphere.*

Female, 60s: *The teachers are marvelous. The music study is intensive. The food is not good but overall it was a wonderful experience and ideal for anyone who plays an instrument. They have a children's camp also, so there are lots of kids around.*

4

TRY ADVENTURE TRAVEL

"ADVENTURE TRAVEL" IS A CATCHALL TERM FOR a score of ways to get back to nature, to see unspoiled countryside or untouched wilderness areas, to be actively involved with the environment and with your fellow travelers. It is an escape from the pressures of urban living, as well as a welcome change from passive travel that shows you the world through the windows of a tour bus. Since groups are small and camaraderie between participants is strong, the percentage of single vacationers who choose this kind of vacation is predictably high.

For years, this type of travel was considered exotic, limited to hardy backpackers or thrill-seekers who delighted in climbing Mt. Everest or careening over dangerous rapids in a rubber raft. But owing to their explosion in popularity over the last 20 years, adventure trips have become accessible and safe for almost everyone.

Some statistics from a tour operator's recent catalog chronicle this boom. By 1949, eighty years after John Wesley Powell completed his first descent of the Colorado River, only 100 people had ever rafted through the Grand Canyon. By 1972, the National Park Service was forced to limit traffic on the river to 17,000 people a year! According to a recent estimate, well over 2 million Americans have now participated in an adventure travel trip.

With so many people signing on, the number of operators offering adventure outings has zoomed to well over 2,000, and the variety of trips has grown to match. Just a few of the choices include rafting, backpacking, back-country skiing, horseback trekking, and mountain climbing, and gentler pursuits such as biking and walking trips, sailing, and safaris in four-wheel-drive vans. Tour operators commonly grade their offerings to suit a wide range of abilities, making it easy for travelers to make a wise choice.

These trips are offered on the seven continents and almost every place on earth from the sub-Arctic ice floes to the jungles of the equator to the placid countrysides of Europe or the United States. You can take your choice of camping out or staying in quarters that are positively plush, particularly on the many inn-to-inn walking and biking tours available.

Two of the world's truly great travel destinations, Nepal and East Africa, come under the "adventure" category.

The following pages offer a small sampling of the great selection available. The listing represents some of the longer-established operators or the more unusual adventure choices, and runs the gamut from rustic to deluxe. Use the additional references given in each category to find more operators in whatever area interests you most.

The majority of these outdoor trips are priced per person, with no single supplement. When necessary, operators try to arrange shares. Where single supplements do exist, they tend to be low. Luxury trips with a substantial supplement are so indicated.

A warning: More than any other type of trip, adventure travel depends for its success and safety on the experience and skill of the operator, so check references carefully before you make your choice.

OPERATORS WITH TRIPS IN MULTIPLE CATEGORIES

WORLD ADVENTURE/AMERICAN YOUTH HOSTELS, INC., P.O. Box 37613, Washington, D.C. 20013-7613; 202-783-6161. (I)

Years in business: 50+
Age range: 18–75
Most common age: Under 35
Percent alone: 90
Number of participants: 9–10 per trip
Male/female ratio: 50/50

World Adventure offers budget-priced bicycle and hiking trips, less strenuous trips by van, and other varied travel adventures such as canoeing, cycling, snorkeling, and sailing expeditions, open to everyone from teens to seniors. Trips are graded beginner, intermediate, and advanced. Adult trips are for all ages over 18; some trips are especially for adults over 50. Among the 60-plus offerings are trips in the United States, Canada, Central and South America, and Iceland, plus 9 European itineraries. Participants stay in hostels, with separate dormitory-style lodgings for males and females, and kitchens where all pitch in to prepare meals. A few hostels have cafeterias. All have common rooms for socializing. Beds come with mattresses, pillows, and blankets; each traveler needs to bring sheets or, instead, bring or rent a sleeping sack.

COMMENTS:

Female, 20s: *I had an absolutely magical trip. Thanks for the awakened eyes to see the English greens, the chance to smell the lush meadows, and hear the birds while I whistle my own songs and fill my heart with great people.*

Male, 30s: *An excellent trip and one of the greatest experiences of my life. I was pleased with the hostels, the bike group, and the organization of the trip. Without AYH I would not have been able to make such an adventurous trip and I would not have such beautiful memories of biking in England.*

Male, 60s: *Great trip, excellent group of people I traveled with.*

AMERICAN FOREST ADVENTURES, P.O. Box 2000, Washington, D.C. 20013-2000; 800-323-1560 or 202-462-3088. (I)

Years in business: Over 50
Most common age: 40s (but very evenly spread over all ages)
Number of participants: Up to 18
Age range: 20–65
Percent alone: 50
Male/female ratio: Varies

Programs sponsored by the American Forestry Association are designed to provide safe wilderness experiences with a good guide, good food, and good friends, says the director. The association contracts with reliable outfitters for each trip. Many are camping trips at moderate cost. Among the offerings are horseback riding, hiking, canoeing, kayaking, rafting, fishing, llama trekking, cross-country skiing, natural history safaris, and international tours. There is an occasional trip for singles only.

No references provided.

NANTAHALA OUTDOOR CENTER, U.S. 19 West, Box 41, Bryson City, NC 28713; 704-488-2175. (I–E for some foreign excursions)

Years in business: 17
Most common age: 20–55
Number of participants: 3,200 yearly
Age range: 10–70
Percent alone: High
Male/female ratio: Varies

This outdoor teaching center has a long roster of adventure trips for all abilities. Among the choices: White-water rafting in the southern Appalachians; kayaking and rafting through the Grand Canyon; canoeing in Alaska; cycling tours in North Carolina, Tennessee, Mississippi, Wyoming, Colorado, and the San Juan Islands of Washington; hiking with lodge accommodations and short backpacking trips from the Center. Foreign excursions include biking in England, kayaking in Baja California or eastern Mexico, canoeing on the Rio Grande, white-water rafting in Costa Rica, Nepal, France, Chile, Scotland, and New Zealand.

See page 34 for comments on the program.

APPALACHIAN MOUNTAIN CLUB, 5 Joy St., Boston, MA 02108; 617-523-0636. (I–E for some foreign excursions)

Years in business: Since 1876
Most common age: 28–55
Number of participants: 33,000 members
Age range: 5–85
Percent alone: 35
Male/female ratio: 50/50

Hiking, climbing, cross-country skiing, canoeing, snowshoeing, and rafting are among the pursuits of this venerable, conservation-minded club, the oldest in the nation, with local chapters throughout the Northeast. The club maintains a lodge at Pinkham Notch in the White Mountains of New Hampshire, where workshops on outdoor skills (see page 40) are held year round. Eight huts spaced along the Appalachian Trail in the mountains provide sleeping accommodations for hut-to-hut hikers and cross-country skiers. Guided overnight hikes are held from Pinkham Notch. Other permanent lodges with varying programs include Bascom Lodge in Adams, Massachusetts; Cold River Camp in Center Conway, New Hampshire; Cardigan Lodge in Bristol, New Hampshire; and Fire Island Camp in Atlantique, New York (open mid-May through October).

AMC also sponsors dozens of major excursions throughout North America and abroad, organized and supervised by members. They range from trekking the Andes to hiking in Norway, traversing Scotland's highlands "by ridge and rail" to sailing Maine waters in a windjammer.

COMMENTS:
Not relevant, since each trip has a different organizer.

SIERRA CLUB NATIONAL OUTING PROGRAM, 730 Polk St., San Francisco, CA 94109; 415-776-2211. (I)

Years in business: 80+
Most common age: Not given
Number of participants: 4,000 total, 10 to 25 per outing
Age range: 10–80
Percent alone: 50–75
Male/female ratio: Not given

Another longtime leader in conserving and appreciating the wilderness, the Sierra Club annually offers about 250 outings to every region of the United States and 40 or so to foreign countries. Trips ranging from 4 days to over 3 weeks in length include backpacking, hiking trips using a single base camp, biking, rafting, canoeing, and sailing. All are cooperative ventures with volunteer leaders, and everyone pitching in with cooking and chores. The trips require varying degrees of stamina and experience, but the catalog clearly characterizes each outing, with advisories such as "Prior backpacking experience and leader approval are required," or "Enjoy spectacular mountain scenery on this moderate trip." Base camp trips tend to be easy to moderate, and are a good idea for beginners, since they allow for taking the day off if you are weary. A supplement is printed for each trip spelling it out in detail.

COMMENTS:
Not relevant, because trips vary with the leader.

ADIRONDAK LOJ/ADIRONDACK MOUNTAIN CLUB, P.O. Box 867, Lake Placid, NY 12946; 518-523-3441. (I)

Years in business: Since 1870s
Most common age: 30–50
Number of participants: 46
Age range: 20–80
Percent alone: 30
Male/female ratio: 50/50

Educational workshops, field trips to see wildflowers or birds, hikes, and cross-country skiing are among the programs of this venerable club for outdoorsmen and nature lovers. The lodge provides simple accommodations and family-style meals at modest rates.

COMMENTS:
Male, 40s: *There's lots of diversity because accommodations vary from a dorm for 46 to bunk rooms for 4 to 6 to private rooms. People come from all over; about half are single, and men outnumber women. There are classes in kayaking and winter sports. A family atmosphere makes it easy to strike up conversations, and everyone is friendly. The staff is wonder-*

ful. This attracts outgoing well-educated people and is great for singles who are into the outdoors.

AMERICAN WILDERNESS ADVENTURES, 7600 E. Arapahoe Rd., Suite 114, Englewood, CO 80112; 303-771-0380. (I–M)

Years in business: 10
Age range: Wide
Most common age: 25–42
Percent alone: 40
Number of participants: Varies
Male/female ratio: 4/5

The American Wilderness Alliance, conservationists who want to share the wilderness they love, sponsors over 80 "soft" adventure trips, many requiring no previous outdoor experience. They range from 1 to 21 days and are as challenging or relaxing as you choose. River rafting in Alaska or the West, kayaking, canoeing, or sailing in Hawaii or Alaska are some of the possibilities. Backpack or horseback treks are also offered. All participants learn camping techniques, and a bit of human and natural history and geography; some study trips emphasize archaeology or ecology. Special programs offer seminars on self-discovery, personal and career growth, and a few choices for women only. Grand Canyon river trips and other longer-length raft trips are the favorite choices for singles. Trip participants get a free six-month membership in the Alliance.

COMMENTS:

Female, 30s: *This is a group situation with very outgoing people from teens to 50s. I was the only single person, but it was fine and I found good company with the guides. The instruction was very good and so was the food. I'm going again.*

Male, 40s: *I've taken many trips alone—you never know who you will meet, as the groups are quite different each time. Most often there are five or six per group, mostly males in their 20s or 30s. There are group activities and time to explore by yourself. You hike to campsites, some two to five hours, depending on the terrain, work together on projects. The food is quite good and the organizers run a good program.*

AMERICAN WILDERNESS EXPERIENCE, P.O. Box 1486, Boulder, CO 80306; 800-444-0099. (I–M)

Years in business: 17
Most common age: 30–40
Number of participants: 2,000 annually
Age range: 25–60
Percent alone: 35
Male/female ratio: 45/55

Horseback treks, fishing trips, llama trekking, backpacking, ranch vacations, Hawaiian sailing and whale-watching adventures, Alaskan wildlife safaris, and international trips to Peru, Mexico, and China are among this group's many offerings. Combo trips are made up of riding and rafting. AWE also has a roster of 23 dude ranches, and promises to help vacationers select the right one. Requirements for trips: good physical condition—"old enough to get on a horse and young enough to stay on." But they advertise "The Civilized Way to Rough It" and promise comfort and good food. A growing number of people in their 60s are signing on, they say, so there is now a discount to lure more. A third of the participants are repeats.

COMMENTS:

Male, 30s: *I've taken four trips by myself, found the groups about half singles and even numbers of males and females. Most were in their 20s and 30s, from all walks of life, from all over the country. The program is very well managed. I've recommended it to other single friends.*

Female, 30s: *There were mostly families on my ranch stay, with 6 singles out of 19 people. Average age was 30s and 40s, but guests ranged from children to one set of grandparents. The accommodations were fine and each day there was a choice of activities—riding lessons, trail rides, fishing. At night we sat by the fire in the lodge and talked or sang songs. It was a pleasant experience and one I would recommend to singles, especially those with kids.*

OVERSEAS ADVENTURE TRAVEL, 6 Bigelow St., Cambridge, MA 02139; 800-221-0814 or 617-876-0533. (M)

Years in business: 10
Most common age: 30–50
Number of participants: 15 per trip, 2,000 per year
Age range: 20–70
Percent alone: 60
Male/female ratio: 46/54

Among the wide-ranging activities of this large outfitter are camping trips on the plains of Africa and in Australia's outback, trekking through the Himalayas and the Andes, rafting on the Amazon and cruising to the Galápagos Islands of Ecuador, hiking and camping in Hawaii, trekking Mt. Fuji and visiting the country inns of Japan, and touring Costa Rica and Java.

COMMENTS:

Female, 60s: *On my OAT safari, half the people were traveling alone; singles shared tents. Ages were from 28 to 62. The food was delicious, the level of cleanliness was incredible, and we were always together for meals so you were almost forced to get to know everyone. We all got along well and had a wonderful time.*

Male, 40s: *I've gone on two trips with this operator, once alone. Almost half the people were traveling alone, generally a few more women than men. The ages were 20s to 70s and they came from all over the U.S. Things are well run, the food is very good, and you need never feel lonely.*

HIMALAYAN TRAVEL, INC., P.O. Box 481, Greenwich, CT 06830; 800-225-2380 or 203-622-6777. (I–M)

Years in business: Since 1972
Most common age: 40
Number of participants: 600 annually
Age range: 25–70
Percent alone: 50
Male/female ratio: 50/50

As the name suggests, Nepal is the prime focus of this group, but they also offer trekking, wildlife safaris, river rafting, Galápagos cruises, and overland expeditions in South America, India, Turkey, Morocco, Greece, the Alps and Pyrénées, and many other exciting locales. Many of the Nepal trips can be combined with extensions to countries such as India, Burma, and Bhutan.

All trips, including Nepal treks, are graded A to E for difficulty. "A" trips are generally sight-seeing with no sustained walking, and utilizing hotel or lodge accommodations. "B" trips, which involve 4 to 6 hours of trekking, are said to be within the ability of any "weekend athlete."

COMMENTS:

Female, 30s: *The program is excellent, the equipment they provide is great—a down jacket, sleeping bag, water bottle, pack—everything. The food was delicious. We were up at dawn and trekked all day. You could go at your own pace and didn't have to keep up with anyone. If we were in a town, we stayed in guest houses, if not, we camped. It's very cold at night in Nepal! After dinner we sat around and really talked.*

The group got along very well. The age range was 28 to 66, the majority in their 30s and 40s. Two of us were from the U.S., the rest were from England. Two guys came together, all others were by themselves; 50/50 male/female. I'd recommend this for anyone who is a little adventurous. If you need to take a shower every day, it's not for you.

Male, 40s: *I've gone to Nepal twice, alone and with a friend. Neither trip had many Americans. Most were Australian and British, ranging in age from 30s to 50s. On the first trip there was one couple, all the rest had come alone. On the second, there were four couples out of 14 people. The food was terrific on one trip, terrible on the other. In both groups there were interesting, mature people who became close before the trips were over. The only way to see these views is to walk, so people are willing to put up with a certain degree of discomfort to do it. If you like to hike and rough it a bit, and like mountain scenery, it's for you.*

SOBEK EXPEDITIONS, INC., P.O. Box 1089, Angels Camp, CA 95222; 209-736-4524. (M–E)

Years in business: Since 1973
Most common age: 35–45
Number of participants: 3,000 annually, small individual groups
Age range: 30–50
Percent alone: 60
Male/female ratio: 60/40

The whole world is the territory for these adventure specialists. Trekking, hiking, rafting, biking, climbing, skiing—they cover all the adventure categories, plus cultural tours to exotic locales for the less athletic. In 1982, Sobek joined with 40 other adventure travel operators to form Sobek's International Explorers Society, a cooperative offering of 200 worldwide adventure opportunities, described in one big color catalog. Trips are listed in five categories from easy to strenuous, and range from climbing Mt. Everest to canoeing in New Guinea to taking African safaris by van.

COMMENTS:

Female, 30s: *I went on a rafting trip alone but I never felt alone. The people were ages 20 to 60, half single, twice as many men, and a very interesting group. The food was great, and the leaders even brought hot coffee to each tent in the morning. We all got along and had a great time. The scenery was spectacular, and the instruction was also great. You could do as much or as little paddling as you wanted.*

ALASKA WILDLAND ADVENTURES, P.O. Box 259, Trout Lake, WA 98650; 800-334-8730 or 509-395-2611. (E–EE)

Years in business: 12
Age range: 8–80
Most common age: 40ish
Percent alone: 40
Number of participants: 18 per trip
Male/female ratio: 35/65

This group offers hiking, rafting, camping, boat trips, natural history safaris, cruises, and a sportfishing camp, all in the national parks and refuges of the great Alaskan wilderness. Part of the thrill is close-up views of wildlife such as bald eagles, moose, brown bears, caribou, puffins, and seals. Some trips use rustic cabins, others are camping expeditions, and some offer a taste of both. For those who don't want to rough it, there is an "Executive Safari" with indoor dining, and a "Senior Safari," a less strenuous trip for older travelers that still ventures way off the beaten path.

COMMENTS:

Female, 60s: *Fantastic, I've never been on a better trip. The guides and food were wonderful; there was something new and different to do every day. Most people were in their 40s and 50s, but the range was to 75. There were more women than men, more single than married, brought together by their spirit of adventure. Days were well organized, but there was no regimentation.*

WOMANTREK, 1411 E. Olive Way, P.O. Box 20643, Seattle, WA 98102; 206-325-4772. (I–E)

Years in business: 5
Most common age: 35–65
Number of participants: 300 total
Age range: 22–80
Percent alone: 75
Male/female ratio: All female

Off-the-beaten-path adventure for small groups of women only (with female guides) run the gamut from biking, rafting, sea kayaking, trekking, skiing, llama pack trips, and leadership courses to deluxe tours. Destinations include Peru, India, Nepal, Greece, China, Nova Scotia, Africa, Mexico, Thailand, Galápagos Islands, Tibet. Ski trips are in Washington and New Mexico. Camaraderie and the opportunity of a lifetime for women who are looking for experiences of personal importance and who wish to see the world, says the brochure. Some white-water trips include workshops on management, leadership, and personal renewal.

COMMENTS:

Female, 40s: *I've gone on three trips, alone and with a friend. The groups were made up of very intelligent people, and I formed lasting friendships with women from age 20 to 60. The guides are knowledgeable and the programs first-rate.*

Female, 60s: *I went on a safari alone and it was fine. The groups were small, only seven on my tour. The women's ages ranged from the 30s to 60s, but most were in their 40s and single, and mainly from the West Coast. Everyone got along well. It was a wonderful experience.*

RAINBOW ADVENTURES, 1308 Sherman Ave., Evanston, IL 60201; 312-864-4570. (M–E)

Years in business: 7
Most common age: Late 40s, early 50s
Number of participants: 10–20
Age range: 30–79
Percent alone: Owner says the majority are married but traveling alone; some are widowed or divorced, a minority never married.
Male/female ratio: All female

Worldwide adventure travel for women over 30, from "Play hooky weekends" to 3-week world journeys. Trips are rated easy, moderate, or challenging. Many trips are designed for beginners who want to enjoy adventure travel within a supportive and noncompetitive environment. Activities include cross-country skiing, river-rafting, horseback treks, hiking, horsepacking, and llama treks in the United States and Canada, plus a walking holiday in England, canal boating in Wales, and a China adventure by foot, plane, train, boat, and bicycle.

COMMENTS:

Female, 40s: *I've gone hiking in the UK, staying in small family hotels and sharing rooms. I've also gone cross-country skiing in Wisconsin and camping on a glacier in Alaska. The women have diverse backgrounds, but share a love for adventure. They come from all over the U.S., but predominantly from Illinois and Wisconsin. Good organization; will go again.*

Female, 70s: *I've taken four trips, including hiking and canal boating in England. The trips are well organized and I've always made good friends with women of all ages.*

Older travelers who want a taste of outdoor adventure at a relaxed pace may want to look into the six-day program for people over 50 offered by Mount Robson Adventure Holidays, Box 146, Valemount, British Columbia, VOE 2Z0, Canada; 604-566-4351. It includes hiking, canoeing, and sight-seeing in the heart of the Canadian Rockies. The operators, who have offered the program for five years, say that there are many single participants. Ages range from 50 to 80, average age is 62.

HIKING/WALKING IN EUROPE

Walking trips with comfortable lodgings awaiting each night are a lovely way to linger through some of Europe's beautiful areas, far from tourist crowds. There are trips for every ability, from rugged mountain hiking to a relaxed pace in the gentle countryside. A van carries all the gear; walkers need only a light day pack for an extra sweater, a slicker, or snacks.

FRED JACOBSON ALPINE TRAILS, LTD., c/o Chappaqua Travel, Inc., 1 South Greeley Ave., Chappaqua, NY 10514; 800-666-5161 or 914-238-5151. (M)

Years in business: 15
Most common age: 40–60
Number of participants: 15–25
Age range: 30–70
Percent alone: 30–50
Male/female ratio: 40/60

Fred Jacobson, the pioneer of organized hiking for Americans in the Swiss Alps, leads scenic 2-week hiking trips with accommodations in charming and comfortable 3- and 4-star village inns along the way. Everyone shares meals at tables for four or eight. Each trip offers a daily choice of moderate or strenuous hikes. The trips have been singled out by "Hideaway Reports" as superior; more than half of the participants are repeaters and their friends. In 1989, easier 1-week trips were added as well as a winter African excursion offering a combination photo game safari to Tanzania and a climb up Mt. Kilimanjaro.

In winter, Jacobson also offers downhill skiing in Zermatt, and cross-country skiing in Pontresina, the Maloja, Kandersteg, and Saignelégier. These are highly personalized trips that are led daily by professionals. Registration is limited.

COMMENTS:

Male, 40s: *The program is not overly structured—you can be with the group or do your own thing. The people are congenial, outdoorsy, mostly good hikers, ages 45 to 60, and reasonably affluent, with a few more females than males. The majority are married but there are enough singles to make you feel comfortable in the group. The program is tops, the food and accommodations are outstanding, and there's always something to do. Everyone had a good time.*

Female, 40s: *This is not a typical tour. You hike most of the day, have a chance to do your own thing. The ages range from 20 to 60. The people were terrific. Food and accommodations were wonderful.*

BAUMELER TOURS, 10 Grand Ave., Rockville Centre, NY 11570; 800-6ABROAD or 516-766-6160. (M)

Years in business: 27
Most common age: 40s–50s
Number of participants: 20–35
Age range: 35–60
Percent alone: 33
Male/female ratio: 40/60

This well-established company has an office in Lucerne as well as in the United States, so there is an international mix of people on many of their walking tours in the Tuscany region of Italy, Provence in southern France, and England's Stratford-upon-Avon country. Trips vary in difficulty, with the most challenging hiking in the Swiss Alps. Lodgings typically are in one or two good middle-class inns, with coaches used to transport the group between home bases and the start of scenic walking areas. (Also see biking tours on page 102.)

COMMENTS:

Male, 20s: *I was the youngest in the group but I had a great time. We walked through Tuscany and Umbria, stopping in small villages you would ordinarily miss. An average day meant walking about 2½ hours in the morning, then either picnicking or meeting the bus to be transported to some nice place for lunch. After lunch we walked another 2 to 3 hours. There were few hills and the pace was easy. We walked 11 out of 14 days. There were breaks for time on your own and for sight-seeing in cities like Florence and Siena. I enjoyed it so much I went back a second time. It's a great way to meet people. Walking and sharing meals every day, you become very friendly. On the whole, this was a sophisticated group, more so than what you'd find on an average bus tour. Everyone is very congenial and wants to mingle.*

BUTTERFIELD & ROBINSON, 70 Bond St., Toronto, Ontario, Canada M5B 1X3; 416-864-1354; in U.S., 800-387-1147. (EE)–includes airfare to Europe)

Years in business: 23
Most common age: 45–55
Number of participants: 18–24
Age range: 30–70
Percent alone: 30
Male/female ratio: 40/60

Single supplement; will try to arrange shares.

This is a top-of-the-line organization, with luxury accommodations and food. The easiest trips average 8 to 12 miles or 3 to 5 hours of walking each day on gentle terrain. More strenuous itineraries may cover 10 to 12 miles, involving some climbing. Each person goes at his own pace, and a van is posted at several points so that walks can be shortened if necessary. Areas covered are the Alsace region in Germany, Bordeaux and the Dordogne Valley in France, the Lake District and Tuscany in Italy, the Cotswolds in England, and the Swiss Alps. (Also see under biking tours on page 102.)

GREENSCAPE, c/o Tours of Britain, 5757 Wilshire Blvd., Suite 124, Los Angeles, CA 90036; 800-423-3740 or 213-937-0494. (E)

Years in business: 7
Most common age: 35–55
Number of participants: 14
Age range: 20–70
Percent alone: 50
Male/female ratio: Higher female

Single supplement; will try to arrange shares.

This British company offers inn-to-inn country walks through the Cotswolds, Dorset, and Devon, with gentle itineraries covering 7 to 8 miles per day. More demanding itineraries include the southern Highlands of Scotland, where the program sets out on daily walks from a single home base in Aberfolye, and an inn-to-inn tour across the moors of Exmoor, with participants carrying their own gear. The operators have representatives in Canada and Australia as well as in the United States, making for an interesting mix of English-speaking companions.

No references provided.

COUNTRY CYCLING TOURS, 140 W. 83d St., New York, NY 10024; 212-874-5151. (M) (See data under Bicycle Tours below.)

While primarily a cycling tour operator, CCT has recently added walking trips, and the list of destinations keeps expanding. Possibilities include short walking trips in the Massachusetts Berkshires, the Connecticut countryside, and on the coast of Maine, as well as moderately priced week-long tours of the Yorkshire Dales of England, the French and Italian Alps, Israel, and China. All use inn accommodations. The domestic tours are a good way to try out the walking experience. (Also see under biking tours, below.)

BICYCLE TOURS

Bicycle touring offers an in-depth look at beautiful parts of the United States and the rest of the world with congenial company and plenty of time to explore off the beaten path. Tours are available for beginners as well as for experienced riders and all tour operators offer rental bikes, helmets, and other necessary equipment. The tour company maps out a choice of detailed bike routes of varying difficulty. Some bicycle tours camp overnight, but most are "inn-to-inn," with a different comfortable lodging destination each night. Depending on the pace and the choice of routes, you can vary your daily mileage. Everyone is together for breakfast and dinner. Many tours also offer the option of a lunch pool with everyone chipping in and sharing picnics assembled en route by the hosts. Or you may choose to try restaurants along the route. A van accompanies the tour, carrying all the luggage, equipment for repairs, and extra bikes for emergencies. Known as the "sag wagon," the van is also readily available if your legs are weary and you want a ride to the inn.

BACKROADS BICYCLE TOURING, P.O. Box 1626, San Leandro, CA 94577; 415-895-1783. (M)

Years in business: 9
Most common age: 30–50
Number of participants: 26 maximum per tour
Age range: 25–65
Percent alone: 40
Male/female ratio: 50/50

Backroads tours cover every western state from the Canadian Rockies to California wine country, and Yellowstone, Bryce, Zion, the Grand Canyon, and Mesa Verde national parks; other destinations include the Baja peninsula; Hawaii; the Shenandoah Valley of Virginia; Australia; New Zealand; Bali; and the Loire Valley in France. Some are camping trips, some are cycling excursions from inn to inn, and some offer a choice of either. Tours vary greatly in their demands and are clearly labeled in the catalog for beginner, intermediate, and advanced riders. The usual daily ride can be cycled comfortably in 3 to 5 hours, but bikers frequently take all day, enjoying the scenery and attractions and picnicking along the way. Trips range from 5 to 17 days.

For those who want to test their legs before setting out on a longer route, weekend inn-to-inn tours are available in northern California and the Monterey peninsula.

COMMENTS:

Female, 30s: *I've done a number of their programs, sometimes alone, sometimes with friends. It is very easy to be alone as there are more singles than couples. The people are from all over the world, with equal numbers of men and women from early 20s to 70. I've made many friends that I keep in touch with. The people are highly educated, health conscious. The best thing about the program is the people who run it. They take care of everything, and you get pampered. The food is amazing and the hotels are luxury. It's ideal for women alone because it is nonthreatening.*

Male, 30s: *I've taken eight tours. The average group is half singles. It is easy to meet people, and you quickly become like a family. About half the group is from California, the rest from all over the U.S. and the rest of the world. It is an upscale crowd. There are several routes to choose from each day, and you can bike as little or as much as you want. The food is very good, the accommodations are fine, though not elegant.*

COUNTRY CYCLING TOURS, LTD., 140 W. 83d St., New York, NY 10024; 212-874-5151. (M)

Years in business: 12
Age range: Over 30
Most common age: Late 30s, 40
Percent alone: 75
Number of participants: 22
Male/female ratio: 40/60

Trips in New England and Virginia, Cape Cod inn-to-inn tours, and winter rambles in Florida, St. Croix, and Guadeloupe are on this interesting biking agenda, as well as cycling in France, England, Ireland, Holland, and China. Comfortable inns are home base and days are planned with enough leisure time built in so that everyone can pedal at his or her own pace and stop and sightsee along the way. Newest additions to the agenda are walking tours in Wales and England and windjammer cruises off the Maine coast.

COMMENTS:

Male, 40s: *This is a first-class organization. I've taken three international trips, including a cycling tour of China, as well as domestic trips. There is a fairly equal split between couples and singles, male and female. The people are special and I've made good friends. I would definitely recommend these trips.*

Female, 30s: *I've taken many trips with this company and highly recommend it. The accommodations in China were not luxurious, but the trip was very exciting. The group is mostly ages 30 to 45 and is geared to singles who are expected to share rooms, although this is not compulsory. I've also done trips with Butterfield and Robinson of Toronto—more expensive and more couples.*

VERMONT BICYCLE TOURING, Box 711, Bristol, VT, 05443; 802-453-4811. (M)

Years in business: 17
Most common age: 35–55
Number of participants: 5,000 total
Age range: 22–70
Percent alone: 50
Male/female ratio: 45/55

This outfit is the originator of the inn-to-inn idea in Vermont, but they don't limit tours to their home state. Sail-biking excursions off Cape Cod and the Maine Coast, and biking in England, Hawaii, and New Zealand are also on the schedule. Bike trips are divided by ability. Five-day wanderer tours for beginners and intermediates give a choice of 20 to 35 miles or 35 to 45 miles daily; Vagabond tours for intermediate and advanced cyclists cover 35 to 45 or 45 to 70 miles. Itineraries vary, some including 2 nights per inn rather than a new stop every night.

COMMENTS:

Female, 30s: *This is a wonderful way for singles to travel and I've taken four trips with this group. The kind of people who are attracted to biking* *are friendly and outgoing. The 18 days we spent in New England was the best trip of my life. The accommodations are nice, the food is almost too good. The group has breakfast together, cycles, meets for a picnic lunch, then goes on to the next inn to swim or soak in the hot tub together. Everyone meets for dinner. These trips are very well run and I definitely recommend them.*

Female, 20s: *I was very comfortable on a trip to New Zealand alone. There were only two or three married couples. The group ranged in age from 27 to late 50s and came from all over the U.S. We stayed in hotels, always had dinner together. You could do what you wanted each day, pick your routes and go at your own pace. It was a great trip.*

BIKE VERMONT, INC., P.O. Box 207, Woodstock, VT 05091; 802-457-3553. (M)

Years in business: 12
Age range: 18–65
Most common age: 30–50
Percent alone: 25–35
Number of participants: 15–20
Male/female ratio: 1/2

Inn-to-inn bicycle tours in the beautiful Vermont countryside with a new destination every night. Vermont is hilly, but this company's weekend trips and shorter midweek tours are within the reach of beginning cyclists, and the support van is available when you need a rest. Average runs are 20–25 miles a day. This is "a nonthreatening, relaxing vacation," say the organizers. "We don't bike as a group, so everyone is biking at his or her own pace. It is easy to make new friends."

COMMENTS:

Male, 40s: *I've taken several tours. There is good mix of singles and couples, plus children from about age 12. Backgrounds vary, but generally the adults are highly educated professionals. It is easy to make friends.*

Female, 20s: *I've done this for six years. When you share a sport, there's automatic camaraderie and all ages mix. You have breakfast together, then set out at your own pace, alone or with others. You meet people along the way, stop together for hot chocolate or a cold drink, and you* *make friends. I always come home with names and addresses, and often you plan to come back with these people.*

EUROPEDS, 883 Sinex Ave., Pacific Grove, CA 93950; 408-372-1173. (E)

Years in business: Since 1981
Most common age: 30–50
Number of participants: 17 maximum
Age range: 18–72
Percent alone: 50
Male/female ratio: 45/55

This firm is best known for backroads itineraries in France. At last count there were eight, including the Dordogne, the Pyrénées foothills, Champagne/Burgundy, Provence, and the south Brittany coast. In 1987 Europeds became the first American tour operator to offer a mountain-bike tour in Europe. Called "Pedal & Pole," it includes off-road cycling and glacier skiing. Biking routes are chosen for cultural richness and beauty. Three- and 4-star hotels at reasonable rates are promised, as well as three representatives on each tour—a mechanic, along with the leader and driver.

COMMENTS:

Female, 40s: *It was easy to be alone, even though most in the group were married couples. There were 22 of us, from 16 to 65, a few more women than men, but fairly even, and with a range of cycling abilities. The food and accommodations were wonderful and it was a great experience.*

Male, 30s: *I went on two trips alone. There was a mix of people from mid-20s to 70, mostly in their 30s and 40s and more females. Most were single—we had only two couples out of 21 people. I'm from the East; most seemed to be from the West Coast. We came from diverse backgrounds yet everyone got along well. Many days you would cycle for a while, then stop to sightsee. We covered about 30 miles a day at our own pace. Food and accommodations were good. I recommend it highly.*

BUTTERFIELD & ROBINSON, 70 Bond St., Toronto, Ontario, Canada M5B 1X3; 416-864-1354; in U.S., 800-387-1147. (EE; includes air from U.S.)

Years in business: 23
Age range: 30–70
Most common age: 45–55
Percent alone: 30
Number of participants: 18–24; 5,000 annually
Male/female ratio: 40/60

Single supplement; will try to arrange shares.

This long-established company has a full roster of luxury biking tours through France, Italy, England, Ireland, Germany, Denmark, Austria/Hungary, Spain, and Portugal. All feature elegant country accommodations (usually 2 nights at each stop) and top restaurants, including some Michelin all-stars. There are stops for tastings at regional wineries, as well. Routes are rated for difficulty, but participants should be able to ride at least 3 to 4 hours a day.

COMMENTS:

Female, 40s: *This is expensive, but it's the best vacation I ever had and I am going again. About half the group was unattached, equal numbers of men and women, and everyone quickly formed a close-knit group. The couples usually split up at meals and ate with different people. Ages were 25 to 63, interesting folks from the U.S. and Canada. Days were flexible, at your own pace. They take very good care of you, and there are a lot of repeat customers.*

Female, 30s: *I've been several times. There were a lot of people from the East Coast, more couples than singles, usually more women than men. Sometimes we met for activities like wine tastings; sometimes you cycled at your own pace all day. The lodging and food are tops and most meals are eaten as a group. I'd recommend it to all singles as long as they don't go expecting to meet somebody special.*

BAUMELER TOURS, 10 Grand Ave., Rockville Centre, NY 11570; 800-6ABROAD or 516-766-6160. (M)

Years in business: 27
Age range: 35–60
Most common age: 40s–50s
Percent alone: 33
Number of participants: 20 to 35; 12,000 annually
Male/female ratio: 40/60

Small single supplement; will try to arrange shares.

Because they are headquartered in Switzerland, Baumeler gets an international mix of people on many of their biking tours in Holland, France, Germany, Austria, Italy, England, and Switzerland. Tour managers are multilingual. Trips range from an easy 20 to 45 miles per day to a rugged 25 to 60, and from moderate to luxury rates.

No references given for biking; see Walking Tours, page 100.

CHINA PASSAGE TRAVEL SERVICE, 168 State St., Teaneck, NJ 07666; 800-247-6475 or 201-837-1400. (EE)

Years in business: 10
Age range: 25–65
Most common age: 33–50
Percent alone: 70
Number of participants: 25–65
Male/female ratio: 50/50

Guests are automatically given roommates; if none are available, there is no extra supplement.

These specialists in Asia travel offer cycling itineraries in China and Thailand, ideal ways to get a leisurely, close-up view of these fascinating cultures. Where available, accommodations are in air-conditioned hotels with private baths, but they may be in dorms or guest houses in some locales.

COMMENTS:

Male, 20s: *I had a wonderful time. We had both a national and local guide who were very helpful, and we got to see things most tourists never do—a hospital, a school in session where the children had never seen Westerners before, factories, etc. Most of the people were in their 20s and 30s; two were in their 50s and 60s. There was one couple and one mother and daughter, but the rest were single, about half of them male. Only one week was given to cycling—the rest of the time the route was too hilly so we used tour buses. My only complaint was that I wish we had stayed longer in each city, maybe seen one city less. Find out who's gong to be on your trip—I heard that the group that followed mine had more families and people didn't get along as well.*

Female, 30s: *These were serious travelers rather than serious cyclers; we* *biked as a group, got along really well, ate together, had free time at our destinations in the afternoon. The group was from the U.S., Canada, and England, about half single, a few more women than men. I would definitely recommend this.*

There are many other bicycle trips in special locales from the Pacific Northwest to the Caribbean. *Bicycle USA Tour Finder* (6707 Whitestone Rd., Baltimore, MD 21207; 301-944-3399) is a comprehensive directory of over 150 bicycle tour operators in the United States and abroad, published by the League of American Wheelmen. Check for current price.

SAILING

Take to the sea for a windswept adventure like no other, with lazy days of snorkeling and swimming in solitary coves, convivial shipboard fun at night, and stops in picturesque ports where the big ships can't follow.

WINDJAMMER BAREFOOT CRUISES, 1759 Bay Rd., Miami Beach, FL 33139; 800-327-2601 or 800-432-3364 in Florida. (M)

Years in business: 40
Most common age: 30–40
Number of participants: 66–122
Age range: 25–55
Percent alone: 60
Male/female ratio: Varies; about equal

Will try to arrange shares.

"The thought of a tall ship to a remote island turns people on," says the captain and founder of this Caribbean fleet which offers sailing vacations on five classic sailing ships. The fleet is based in St. Thomas, Tortola, St. Martin, Antigua, Grenada, and Freeport on its various itineraries and each month visits more than 50 islands on 6- and 13-day outings. This is not a luxury cruise but a chance to experience the exhilaration of sailing and to get to small, isolated islands. The cabins are small, but they are air-conditioned and have private toilets and showers. Meals are buffet style on ship or picnics ashore and complimentary drinks are served throughout the day. Dress is always informal and entertainment can be wacky—toga parties on the beach, steel-drum bands on board.

COMMENTS:

Female, 30s: *I took this trip with my 12-year-old son—it is great for both singles and single parents. About half the adults were single, ranging in age from 20s to 50s and 60s, a few more women than men. We were from many parts of the country with very different backgrounds, but everyone had a wonderful time. The food was fantastic, the cabins comfortable and air-conditioned. We sailed mostly at night, spent days on the islands. The crew is great and tells you the ins and outs of each new port. At night there was always an activity. I made a lot of friends—and I can't wait to go on another trip. It's the best vacation I've ever had.*

MAINE WINDJAMMER ASSOCIATION, Box 317P, Rockport, ME 04856; 800-MAINE-80. (I)

Years in business: 50
Age range: 16–80
Most common age: 20–40
Percent alone: 25–30
Number of participants: 20–37
Male/female ratio: Varies, fairly equal

This fleet of 11 nostalgic 19th-century two-masted "tall ships" sets sail each summer from June to September from Camden, Rockland, or Rockport for Penobscot Bay to explore the evergreen coast and the islands of Maine, and sleep in quiet anchorages of unblemished beauty. Ships range from 64 to 112 feet; there are single cabins, or singles may share; rates are a real bargain. Passengers can help with the halyards and lines, keep a lookout for seals and ospreys, watch the lobstermen setting out traps, or just lie back and soak up the sun. Family-style meals featuring New England chowder, "Down East" lobster bakes, and Main blueberry pie are not the least of the attractions!

COMMENTS:

Male, 30s: *I've been twice, and it was great. I was looking for something I could do without pressure to find a partner, and this was it. There were*

a few other singles, but it hardly mattered because with such a small group sharing meals and bath facilities, it was informal and comfortable for everyone. The sailing was terrific, and the food was fantastic.
Female, 40s: *I really enjoyed it and am thinking of going again. There were people from age 30 to one man in his 70s, and 9 out of 23 of us were single. Everyone got along and enjoyed each other's company.*

Tall ships also sail out of Mystic, Connecticut, around Long Island Sound and from Annapolis, Maryland, in Chesapeake Bay. For information, contact Mystic Whaler and Mystic Clipper, 7 Holmes St., Mystic, CT 06355; 800-243-0416 or 203-536-4218.

RIVER-RUNNING SPECIALISTS

What's so great about running a river? Those who love it call it "River Magic." One longtime operator says he has found that the cooperation required to meet the challenge of the river facilitates relationships, opens lines of communication, enhances personal growth, and helps participants develop lasting friendships more than any other form of outdoor recreation he has ever experienced—which explains why so many river trips are available and why so many people sign up for them.

SHERI GRIFFITH EXPEDITIONS, P.O. Box 1324, 2231 S. Hwy. 191, Moab, UT 84532; 800-332-3200 or 801-259-8229. (I–M)

Years in business: 16
Age range: 23–50
Most common age: 25–40
Percent alone: 50
Number of participants: 25
Male/female ratio: 60/40

This operator boasts of "Outdoor Adventures with a Touch of Class," priding herself on top food on 5- to 7-day river-running adventures and canoe trips on the Greene, Colorado, and Dolores rivers. There are runs for beginners to experts, plus some interesting specialty trips, such as "Expeditions in Luxury," a luxurious outing in Canyonlands National Park; "Professional Development Seminars" that combine river running with strategies for personal growth; a "Holistic River Experience," and a 14-day "Club Colorado" river run that takes in several national parks. Some river trips are combined with other outdoor activities such as horseback expeditions, hiking treks, jeep excursions, houseboating, mountain biking, and hot-air ballooning. A white-water run in Costa Rica is also offered.

COMMENTS:

Male, 30s: *To a man, every person on the trip would have jumped at the chance to go again . . . tomorrow, if not sooner.*

Female, 30s: *A well-organized, smooth-running operation with a courteous, knowledgeable, and fun staff. Their ability in the kitchen was unmatched. The trip was a bargain.*

ECHO: THE WILDERNESS CO., INC., 6529 Telegraph Ave., Oakland, CA 94609; 415-652-1600. (M)

Years in business: 17
Age range: 7–70
Most common age: 30s–40s
Percent alone: Varies
Number of participants: 3,000 per year
Male/female ratio: 50/50

River-rafting trips—the usual, plus specials that include entertainment such as wine tastings, storytelling, and music, and self-esteem workshops for women. Other special trips combine rafting with biking or fly-fishing; one offering is a hiking, snorkeling, and birding adventure in the Virgin Islands, with home base aboard a sailing or motor yacht and every day spent on a different island. U.S. rafting trips are held on the Salmon River in Idaho, the Rogue River in Oregon, the American, Tuolumne, and Salmon rivers in California, and on the Colorado River in the Grand Canyon in Arizona.

COMMENTS:

Female, 20s: *I've gone alone twice and been very comfortable. Everything is done as a group. The trips are well run; there is a comfortable mix of men and women (a few more women), an age range of 15 to 65. The groups are diverse and interesting and there are plenty of single people.*

Female, 40s: *I've been on many trips and I think this is one of the top* *companies due to the excellence of the equipment and the guides, who are bright and very good with people. No one is pushed beyond his or her comfort level. The food is wonderful and healthy. The people range from single parents to couples and single women in their 20s. It is very easy to meet and get along with everyone and I've made lasting friends.*

OUTDOOR ADVENTURE RIVER SPECIALISTS (O.A.R.S.) INC., P.O. Box 67, Angels Camp, CA 95222; 209-736-4677. (M)

Years in business: 18
Most common age: 25–45
Number of participants: 16–25
Age range: 18–54+
Percent alone: 25
Male/female ratio: 50/50

Will try to arrange shares.

With this outfitter you can camp under the stars if sleeping bags are your bag or have the thrill of rafting and the comfort of bed-and-breakfast inn lodgings at night. Choose the challenge of Class V rapids or trips with an "oar" option, meaning the guide does all the paddling, while guests sit back and enjoy the ride. O.A.R.S. offers 5- to 13-day outings on the Colorado River in the Grand Canyon, and a wide variety of 2- to 12-day trips on the American, Salmon, Kern, Klamath, and Tuolumne rivers in California; the Rogue River in Oregon; the Salmon and Snake rivers in Idaho; the Dolores, Green, San Juan, and Yampa rivers in Utah; and the Snake River in Wyoming. There are "floats" for the less adventurous in the Grand Tetons and on the Snake River. The catalog ranks each trip for solitude and remoteness, scenery, side hikes, and wildlife, as well as the difficulty of the rapids.

COMMENTS:

Female, 30s: *I've gone on two trips alone. You can have time to yourself if you want it, but you never have to be alone. My groups ranged from age 20 to mid-60s; about half were singles and two-thirds were male, and they were from all over the country. The people were great, very congenial. You switch boats each day so you get to meet everyone. The food was terrific and we slept under the stars. If you have a spirit of adventure, this is a great experience.*

Male, 30s: *I've gone on five trips, alone and with my wife. Many of the people are married but come alone. We were up at sunrise, did everything from running rapids to hiking. You get to know everyone, as you switch boats. You can do as much or as little work as you want. There is good food and lots of it. It's a good introduction to rafting—easy, relaxed, and anyone can do it.*

DVOŘÁK'S KAYAK & RAFTING EXPEDITIONS, 17921-B U.S. 285, Nathrop, CO 81236; 800-824-3795 or 303-539-6851. (I)

Years in business: Since 1969
Most common age: 25–35
Number of participants: Over 2,000 total; 12 to 25 per trip
Age range: 25–35
Percent alone: 60
Male/female ratio: 50/50

Dvořák's was the first licensed operator on the Colorado River. It has grown to offer trips through 29 canyons on 10 U.S. rivers and on rivers in Mexico, Australia, and New Zealand. Among the states covered are Arkansas, Colorado, Utah, New Mexico, Wyoming, and Texas, where rivers used include the Salt, Rio Grande, Salmon, North Platte, Gunnison, Rio Chama, Green, Dolores, Colorado, and Arkansas. Some trips combine with a day or more of fishing, hiking, horseback riding, or mountain biking.

COMMENTS:
Female, 30s: *A wonderful experience, the finest thing I've ever done. There were seven of us, all single, age 30s to 50s, about equal numbers of men and women. We stayed in tents, had wonderful, healthful food. The instruction was great—but even less-physical people can enjoy this trip, as you don't have to paddle if you don't want to.*
Female, 30s: *This was a great thing to do. I went with my 10-year-old son, and though he was the only child, it was no problem—the guides took care of him, and were wonderful helping him fish when we hit calm water. We slept in tents, had great food. There was just one couple—from New Zealand—the rest were future guides on their first trip.*

For more outfitters, *Western River Guides Association Outfitters Directory* (7600 E. Arapahoe Rd., Suite 114, Englewood, CO 80112;

303-771-0389) offers a comprehensive listing of river-raft expeditions in the western United States.

HORSEBACK TREKKING

If you want to see spectacular remote wilderness areas that are hard to traverse on foot, a horseback trek offers an unforgettable experience. Judging from those who have done it, the food and camping accommodations en route are amazingly fine. You don't have to be an experienced rider to sign on—just willing to pay for your pleasure with a bit of saddle-soreness. Enthusiasts swear it's worth it.

ADVENTURE TRAILS OF THE WEST, INC., P.O. Box 1494, Wickenburg, AZ; 602-684-3106. (M–E)

Years in business: 5	Age range: 20–80
Most common age: 30–50	Percent alone: 30
Number of participants: 500 total	Male/female ratio: 40/60

Horseback vacations scheduled annually across some of the most beautiful landscapes in Arizona—the Grand Canyon, Monument Valley, Canyon de Chelly, and high pine country—as well as in the wilderness of Australia. Some of the 25 two- to five-day rides are restricted to good riders; others welcome beginners who are taught safety and comfort while the more experienced riders go off on alternate trails. The operators provide comfortable sleeping tents, portable toilets, and an experienced cook who can do wonders over a campfire. They've even figured out a way to provide hot showers.

COMMENTS:

Female, 30s: *It is very easy to come alone because the owners of the program make you feel like part of the family from the moment you get there. You're always part of a group. About half the people are single. My groups have had a few more women, but were fairly equal male/female. The program is absolutely wonderful and you get to see things most tourists don't, to meet Navajo Indians, and see incredible scenery you can reach only on horseback. The guides were great, as were the horses. It's very relaxed and easy to get to know people. There's music* *and lots of talking around the campfire at night. I've made many treasured friendships.*

Male, 30s: *I like this so much I've been back more than a dozen times. It is very easy to be alone. The people are ages 25 to 85, and mostly professionals with diverse backgrounds. On the harder rides, there were mostly men; otherwise it is about half and half singles and couples, men and women. Days average 6 hours of sight-seeing on horseback, camping in a different place each night, and excellent catered meals. You form a real camaraderie. But I don't think this is for an inexperienced rider.*

RALPH MILLER'S WILDERNESS PACK TRIPS, P.O. Box 1083, Cookie City, MT 59020; 406-222-7809. (EE)

Years in business: 17	Age range: 25–50
Most common age: 30–40	Percent alone: 20
Number of participants: 4–8	Male/female ratio: 50/50

On horseback across the open country of Yellowstone National Park, you are in the pristine wilderness that tourist crowds never see, spying elk and bison and moose and bunnies, and reveling in unspoiled nature. One-week, 10-day, or 2-week horseback trips are offered from June to mid-September by this much acclaimed outfitter. After 13 years on the trails, Miller is a true pro; his specialty is the remote area in the northeastern section of the park around Yellowstone Lake and the Shoshone National Forest. Miller owns his own horses, knows them well, and matches the right horse to the right rider. The pace is set at a walk and no previous riding experience is necessary, though you can expect to have a case of saddle-soreness along the way. Miller's wife, Candy, is said to create miracle meals over the campfire.

COMMENTS:

Male, 40s: *Our group included one couple and five singles (two of them women), ages late 20s to 50s, mostly from the Midwest. This is a rough-it trip, not luxurious, but very well organized and with great food cooked over the campfire. We did lots of sight-seeing on horseback, some hiking, and some fly-fishing. I would definitely recommend this to anyone.*

Female, 30s: *I had an unusual trip, just one other woman and the leaders. We spent three nights in one place, two in another, days hiking or riding. The food was fabulous, the experience wonderful, and I would love to do it again.*

TRAIL RIDERS OF THE WILDERNESS, c/o American Forest Adventures (see page 89).

For more than 55 years, this program has introduced people of all ages to the beauty of the back country on 5- to 8-day trail rides. Some 18 trips are available annually, including to North Carolina's Great Smoky Mountains, most of the southwestern and western states and Banff National Park in Canada. Trail Riders is now part of American Forest Adventures and is included in their catalog.

For a list of all horse-packing trip outfitters licensed by the National Park Service in Yellowstone, contact Visitor Service Office, Yellowstone National Park, WY 82190; 307-344-7381.

TWO SUPREME ADVENTURES: NEPAL AND EAST AFRICA

NEPAL

There are many mighty mountains in the world, but the trip to the Himalayas is unique. Since it remains on my dream list, I asked Ben Wallace, who helps organize trips for Himalayan Travel (see page 93), and who has visited 60 countries and lived in Nepal for 3 years, to explain why this experience is so remarkable.

The lure of Nepal is the people as much as the mountains, he says. What makes this different from other mountain treks or climbs is that the trails you follow are the only roads in this remote region, the lifeline of the villagers who live here. Every day you pass through two to six villages, seeing intimately a fascinating and totally different way of life. You can linger, visit homes, and observe how people live, cook, farm, and work. Staying in local homes is an option. Most people come to Nepal thinking the thrill is going to be the big mountains and the views, but find instead it is the local life that is the indelible memory, the cultural rather than the physical experience that is the highlight.

Ben says that most people once were drawn to Nepal for the physical challenge, but that a higher percentage today are looking for something else, a total change from their life-style and environment. The least strenuous treks usually mean 4 to 8 days on the trail, walking 4 to 6 hours a day, with the maximum ascent of about 1,500 feet—within the ability of anyone who does any exercising at home.

Trekking can be mindless, he says, in that all you need do is put one foot in front of the other. Everything is taken care of for you. Someone else puts up and takes down the camps, carries all gear, does all the cooking and cleaning up. You are free to simply soak in the experience. Many people today sign up for the shorter 1-week treks, then spend another week sight-seeing or rafting. Ben believes, however, that the longer trips deeper into the mountains are the most rewarding. Those who take the shorter trips enjoy the country but seldom come back. People who spend the time to really immerse themselves in the culture are hooked—they almost always return.

How much stamina does the trip take? Ben explains that the degree of difficulty has three components: the duration of time on the trail, how much altitude is gained or lost, and the living conditions. "Someone who is very fit but not used to living in a tent, a jogger for example, may be able to stand up to the physical challenge but not be happy about spending three weeks in a tent.

"Altitude affects people differently—and the same people differently on different days. Above ten or eleven thousand feet, almost everyone feels some discomfort, perhaps headaches. A good operator knows this and allows plenty of time for acclimatization. A serious problem is extremely rare. And there is plenty of leisure time. How fast you walk is up to you. The idea definitely is not to get there in the fastest time, but to appreciate both the culture and the scenery around you. Even the faster walkers seldom hurry on to camp. They take side trips or just take more time to enjoy their surroundings."

The food on a trek is a pleasant surprise. A sample menu might include onion soup topped with melted yak cheese, sweet and sour chicken over vegetable fried rice, and cake, baked over the campfire. As in any third world country, there may be an occasional stomach bug to contend with. All treks include a medical kit and someone who knows how to use it.

When to come? The trekking season is from late September to mid-May.

SAFARI!

Joining a KLR safari to see the big game in East Africa was a longtime travel dream come true for me—but the reality outdid even my fondest fantasies.

Nothing you've read or seen in picture books can prepare you for the deep emotion that wells up on viewing these beautiful creatures at close range, living free in their own environment. It is a jolt of joy and wonder that fills the senses and goes straight to the heart.

Strangers soon become close friends on safari because of this shared emotion and the excitement of the trip. It makes no difference whether you are on your own or with a companion. You are all fellow hunters, intent on prowling the national parks and game preserves of Kenya and Tanzania, ready to aim your binoculars and shoot on sight with your camera.

The targets are ever-changing. Lightning-swift cheetahs stalking graceful gazelles. A pride of lions sleeping in the sun. Hordes of dizzily striped zebras, big and small. Giraffes batting their eyelashes and nibbling daintily at the treetops. Thousands of wildebeests standing around like a congregation of bearded old men. Herds of elephants trumpeting and splashing in a water hole. A family of rhinos staring out like giant near-sighted Mr. Magoos. Every day, every park holds a new discovery.

The trip is easy for a single traveler because every detail is handled for you. From the moment you are met by a tour representative in Nairobi, you are part of a carefully attended group. There seemed no common denominator for the people who chose this trip. The high price meant that the majority of those I met at the lodges were over age 50, but there were younger people as well, and even an occasional family who had brought young children to share the adventure.

While no physical exertion or danger is involved, safaris come under the adventure category because the travel required is difficult. The distances between parks are great. Rutted roads are often unpaved, sending up dust or mud, depending on the weather. We were out by 6:30 A.M. many mornings, since the animals are most active just after daybreak, and we often drove for hours searching for the bigger game. No one could stay awake much past 10:00 P.M. The thrill is worth it all.

In Kenya, the best known of the parks is the Masai Mara Game Preserve at the northern tip of the Serengeti Plains, where literally millions of animals graze and hunt. In two days in this park, we spotted over 30 species of animals, and untold numbers of exotic birds.

Other parks have their own specialties. Lake Nakuru is known for huge flocks of pink flamingoes, Amboseli for its large herds of elephants. Samburu Game Reserve, in northern Kenya, has its own species of zebras and giraffes with markings different from those to the south. At Treetops, you stay up late to watch animals congregating outside at a softly lit water hole. At the Mt. Kenya Safari Club, the place made famous by the late actor William Holden, there is a break, a day spent relaxing in luxury, dining sumptuously, and coming back to find that the logs in the fireplace in your room have been magically lit for you.

After a fabulous week in Kenya, we were unsure as to what more could be waiting for us in Tanzania. The answer was simply the most spectacular animal watching in the world.

Ngorongoro Crater, an inverted volcano, is one of the wonders of the world, a veritable Noah's ark. In Kenya, we had driven long stretches searching for the elusive big animals. Here, the naturalist guide who drove us down by jeep had only to say, "Now we'll look for the lions," and there they were. Then, "Here's where the rhinos stay"—and there they were.

Serengeti National Park, with its huge numbers of animals, is overwhelming in its beauty and richness. A recent census counted a quarter of a million gazelles, an equal number of zebras, another quarter million of other species including cheetahs, lions, and other predators, and well over a million wildebeests.

Even the smallest of the national parks, Lake Manyara, was rewarding, with an amazing variety of animals owing to the topography, which ranges from lush jungle to flat plains. One sight here fills you with amazement—lions that climb the trees in order to nap undisturbed by the park's large herds of elephants.

We were worried about lodging when we crossed the border into

Tanzania. Kenya is relatively prosperous, and with over a million visitors a year has learned how to provide safari guests with creature comforts. Accommodations were not so different from rustic park lodges in the United States. But Tanzania is poor and undeveloped, and we had been warned to expect difficult living conditions.

"Difficult" meant that we lacked hot water at times and the electricity might be turned off from midnight to 6 A.M. Still, the beds were comfortable and every room had a private bath. I've had worse accommodations in Yosemite Park. The striking architecture and scenic locations of the lodges were a wonderful surprise. True, the food left much to be desired, but when the main course did not please, there were plenty of fresh vegetables and rolls to fill in.

For me, the extraordinary animals made a few inconveniences more than worthwhile. In fact, if I could return to only one country, Tanzania is where I would choose to go.

Safaris are expensive, but they are a once-in-a-lifetime experience. Start saving.

CHOOSING A SAFARI

There are many operators offering safaris that vary in price, from budget trips via open trucks with nights spent in sleeping bags to trips that include comfortable vans and accommodations and the services of skilled guides. Deluxe tours such as those sponsored by the Smithsonian Institution add the services of a naturalist. The most luxurious trips of all are the tented safaris, where the cooks pride themselves on turning out remarkable fare over the campfire. Governors Camp in Kenya is a local legend.

Wildlife is abundant and weather is mild year-round in East Africa, but the "long rains" period from late March through May is not a good time for animal viewing. The big herds of the Serengeti are in Tanzania in the winter months, in Kenya from mid-July to September.

To compare trip costs, look at the actual days spent on safari. Tours that spend extra days in Nairobi may sound like more time for your money, but bed-and-breakfast accommodations in a city are not the point of an African trip.

The most important thing to check is that you will be *guaranteed* a window seat in your van. According to Ralph Hammelbacher of

KLR, a company that won the American Society of Travel Agents Award for African travel, other important questions to ask before you choose an operator are these:

- How long has the company been in business?
- Is Africa their main destination or just one of many?
- Are departure dates guaranteed regardless of how many people sign up?
- How large is the total group? (Over 25 is unwieldy.)
- How many seats per touring vehicle?
- Will you have a naturalist along in addition to the driver-guide?
- What airline will you fly and where will you stop en route? All airlines make a stop in Europe. Changing plans in Amsterdam is an advantage, because Schiphol Airport is particularly easy to navigate and it is a quick and inexpensive train ride into town if you have several hours to spend.
- Will you have day rooms during the stopover between Europe and Africa, or simply wait around at the airport?
- Where will you stay when you land in Nairobi? (The Norfolk is the great old hotel.)
- Is the operator a member of the U.S. Tour Operators Association?
- Most important—can they furnish first-hand references from travel agents or recent former passengers?

Among the better-known operators specializing in safaries are:

ABERCROMBIE & KENT, INTL., 1420 Kensington Rd., Suite III, Oak Brook, IL 60521-2106; 800-323-7308 or 312-954-2944. Years in business: 27. A & K maintains its own offices and staff in Kenya and Tanzania. (EE)

KLR INTERNATIONAL, 1560 Broadway, New York, NY 10036; 800-221-4876 or 212-869-2850. Years in business: 17. KLR contracts for services through the best local tour operators and guides in Kenya and Tanzania. (EE)

UNITED TOURING INTERNATIONAL, INC., 1315 Walnut St., Suite 800, Philadelphia, PA 19107; 800-223-6486 or 215-545-1355. Years in business: Since 1947. This Nairobi-based company is one of the biggest in the safari business and has a wide variety of tours. (E–EE)

OVERSEAS ADVENTURE TRAVEL, 6 Bigelow St., Cambridge, MA 02139; 800-221-0814 or 617-876-0533. Years in business: 10. Budget safaris. (E)

TRACKS, c/o Himalayan Travel Inc., Box 481, Greenwich, CT 06836; 800-225-2380 or 203-622-6777. Years in business: 10. British-run budget safaris; mostly young people. (E)

For more adventuring ideas:

SPECIALTY TRAVEL INDEX (305 San Anselmo Ave., Suite 217, San Anselmo, CA 94960; 415-459-4900) publishes a quarterly listing of ads from over 400 operators of adventure and specialty trips of all kinds. It is the source used by many travel agents. Sample index listings: Elephant Ride, Environmental Education, Equestrian Tours, Festival Tours, Film History, Fishing, Foliage Tours, Windjamming, Windsurfing, Winery Tours, Women's Tours. An annual subscription is $8.

FORCE 10 EXPEDITIONS LTD. (P.O. Box 8548, Waukegan, IL 60079-8548; 800-922-1491 or 312-336-2070) is a booking organization that publishes an adventure guide of over 300 trips of all kinds. It has an Adventure Club with a yearly membership fee that includes a newsletter and discounts on reservations.

ADVENTURE GUIDES, INC. publishes Pat Dickerman's *Adventure Travel* (36 East 57th St., New York, NY 10022; 212-355-6334), a comprehensive sourcebook for backpacking, hiking, horse pack trips, biking, boating, and other adventures such as dogsledding, ski touring, ballooning, and nature expeditions in the United States and abroad. Write or phone for mail-order price of current edition.

5

GET INTO SHAPE

IMAGINE A VACATION THAT SENDS YOU HOME slimmer, trimmer, free of stress, and full of energy. That's what you can expect from a visit to one of the new superspas, a healthy vacation experience that is gaining a growing group of advocates from both sexes. Because spas are a "you" centered vacation, dedicated to making you look and feel better, they are perfect for solo travelers, and a large number of guests choose to come alone.

Forget about the old "fat farms." Today's spas might better be called "health resorts," geared as much to the overstressed as to the overweight. Exercise means hiking or tennis as well as calisthenics, and, until you've tried it, you won't believe that a low-calorie diet can be so satisfying.

A week at a spa is designed to show how quickly the results of regular exercise and healthy eating can be seen in your measurements and morale. And to make up for the ache of unaccustomed exertion you get wonderful pampering massages and other rewards to ease away the pain.

Spa vacationers pay premium prices for their daily regimen of about 1,000 calories and enough exercise to burn them off. Yet advocates declare it is a worthwhile investment. For along with a week or two of healthy living, a good spa aims to give a lifetime bonus—education and inspiration for a healthier life-style when you return home. Many spas also teach stress-control techniques to keep you calm, collected, and better able to stick with your good intentions.

At a good spa, guests can learn, often for the first time, exactly how their bodies function—how they react to stress, inactivity, different types of exercise, and different types of food. One of the most important benefits is finding out how to eat well without gaining weight. For those who have talked about exercising without doing anything about it, a spa can be a motivation center, reinforcing good intentions and generating lasting new attitudes and behaviors.

Good-natured sharing of the agonies of sore muscles and longings for forbidden treats creates a common bond among guests that quickly cements friendships. Many guests who meet at spas plan future visits together.

For men who fear that spas are still mainly for overweight women, a pleasant awakening may be in store, since the opposite is often true today. People who come to spas tend to be those who are fit or want to be. They are usually people who take care of their bodies.

THE SPA ROUTINE

A typical spa day begins with a brisk walk before breakfast. There is a choice of exercise classes, which are spaced throughout the day. The exercises include a balanced mix of aerobics, workouts for body conditioning, and stretching and yoga for both strength and relaxation. Aquatic workouts are part of the routine, turning exercise into fun and games in the pool. Many spas have weight machines and special muscle-building and stretching sessions just for men so they can accommodate the increasing number of male guests.

Between the workouts come the rewards: soothing massages, relaxing whirlpools, saunas, and steam baths that erase tension and aches. A variety of treatments is offered, such as facials, hydrotherapy massage (done in a tub using soothing streams of water), and herbal wraps, mummylike wrappings of scented moist sheets that draw out body impurities, soften the skin, and relax muscles. Attendants report that many men whose macho upbringing made them reluctant to try these treatments discover they have been missing out on some of life's pleasanter luxuries and immediately sign up for repeats.

There is also plenty of time for a leisurely lunch—and a dip in the pool or an hour in the sun with a good book.

At day's end, though strong alcohol and fattening hors d'oeuvres are definitely not part of the spa regimen, some places do allow a glass of wine at dinner, and many have pleasant predinner "mocktail parties" that offer sparkling water and conversation along with carrot sticks and surprisingly tasty low-calorie dip. All the food, in fact, is a pleasant surprise. The menus are sophisticated, and cleverly served so that every meal has an appetizer, salad, main course, and dessert. While portions are small, wily spa nutritionists know that after four courses, most people do not feel deprived.

Evenings include speakers, how-to hints for establishing good health habits at home, or talks and movies just for entertainment. A number of spas now offer workshops in biofeedback and other behavior-modification techniques.

A week's stay is recommended to get the full benefit of a spa. Some warn you when you arrive that day three typically is a day of muscle soreness and doubts for those unaccustomed to exercise. Each day following, however, finds you feeling better—and better about yourself.

CHOOSING A SPA

Although the basic programs at spas are similar, the ambience can vary as much as the price range, which runs the gamut from a few-frills $800 to over $3,500 a week. At the top of the scale, and the ultimate spa experience, according to many people, is the Golden Door in Escondido, California, with serene Oriental decor and a staff that outnumbers the guests by 3 to 1. Reflecting current trends, the former all-female spa now offers special weeks for men.

Most opulent of the spas is the $30 million Doral Saturnia International Spa Resort in Miami, combining European treatments, Tuscan cuisine, and American exercise. Every lavish guest suite has a Jacuzzi and a garden.

At the other end of the spa spectrum is the coed Ashram, also in California, described by one recent guest as "a boot camp without food." The raw-food diet and rigorous regimen designed to test guests to the limit of their physical endurance may not be everyone's cup of herbal tea, but those who survive declare it almost an existential experience, and many do return.

Some spas are permissive, leaving it to guests to decide how much or how little activity they want to participate in. Others expect you to maintain a schedule, figuring that if you wanted to loll on the beach, you would have chosen a different vacation.

And locations vary. Some are in the middle of a city, others in the middle of nowhere; some are part of a larger resort, others are independent operations. And there are still traditional spas that are for women only.

Spa guest references weren't too helpful, since all were raves. After visits to a number of spas, however, I do have recommendations for best bets for single guests. At the top of the list are two coed "fitness resorts," Rancho la Puerta and Canyon Ranch. Each attracts an active, generally fit, and interesting mix of guests. My favorite place for pampering and a solid educational program is The Spa at Palm-Aire, one of the long-established spas in Florida. Here is what each has to offer:

RANCHO LA PUERTA, Tecate, Baja California, Mexico (about an hour south of San Diego; guests are met at no charge at San Diego airport); reservations 800-443-7565; in California, 800-422-7565; 150 guests, 30 percent male. (E–EE)

This rates my first-place vote for tranquillity, beauty, and value. The 150-acre complex, filled with flowers and fountains and ringed with boulder-strewn mountains, was born in 1940, long before the fitness boom. It remains a find for any world-weary traveler who wants a rejuvenating getaway in lovely surroundings. Guests stay in Mexican casitas decorated with hand-painted tiles and folk art. Accommodations have no phones or TV; most do have fireplaces, freshly stacked with wood and ready to be lit each night.

You do as much or as little as you please here and eat as much as you want—not as hedonistic as it sounds, since the diet is vegetarian and you can hardly avoid losing weight. Eighty percent of the vegetables are grown in the ranch's own organic gardens, and you've never tasted fresher or better. Fish is served twice a week; otherwise, main dishes are pastas, lasagnas, Mexican tortillas and beans, and other dishes that belie their calorie count.

The guests are professionals from all over the United States and Canada. The age range is 25 to 65, but because the Mexican location makes this spa a better buy than many of its American competitors, the average age tends to be younger than at most of the more costly spas, and many trim 20s and 30s are around. Everyone arrives on Saturday, many alone, and by the time you have hiked, exercised, and dined together for a couple of days, you all feel like old friends. The relaxed, friendly, and low-key atmosphere extends to the health and beauty services. You come here for renewal, not expert pampering.

There are lots of tennis courts, lit for night play, and five separate pools, some very private. Most of the lodgings also offer private decks for sun-bathing or star-gazing. This is the one spa I could imagine coming to for sheer enjoyment, even if you never went near an exercise class.

CANYON RANCH, 8600 E. Rockcliff Rd., Tucson, AZ 85715; 800-742-9000 or 602-749-9000. Coed; 250 guests; 35 percent male. (EE)

An East Coast spa opened in 1989 in the Berkshire Mountains of Massachusetts, but this was too late for press date.

The ambience at this first-class facility is charged with energy, even though higher rates are reflected in a slightly older (and often celebrity-studded) clientele. The gyms and the health center are state of the art; the staff is crackerjack; the menu is varied and delicious; and the beauty treatments are first rate. Single guests have the daily option of joining a group table or dining alone. People who come here love it, but while they may recharge, they don't really escape from the real world. Dress can be a competitive fashion parade of designer leotards and sweat suits, TV and telephones are very much part of the decor of the hotel-ish guest rooms, and there is a fax machine in the office that gets a lot of use from guests keeping up with business.

Canyon Ranch is blessed with wonderful desert and mountain surroundings, but unlike Rancho la Puerta, where the trails adjoin the spa, you must board a van to reach the starting points of the hikes. Some people prefer this because it allows for more variety and is more challenging. Hiking is a big part of the program, and special weeks are devoted to it for those who want a more rigorous schedule.

A Life Enhancement Center is a self-contained part of the spa that focuses on helping participants overcome such habits as smoking or overeating. The Behavioral Health Department of the Center uses all the latest techniques, including private counseling, biofeedback, and hypnotherapy.

THE SPA AT PALM-AIRE, 2501 Palm-Aire Dr. N, Pompano Beach, FL 33069; 800-327-4960 or 305-975-6028. Coed. (EE)

Separate facilities and programs for men and women accommodating about 80 women and 30 men.

Founded in 1971, Palm-Aire predates many of today's trendy spas. It has never lost its loyal following, being one of the most solid programs around—a rare combination of warmth, pampering, competence, and well-informed advice. Each guest is given a daily suggested schedule, with the difficulty of classes based on an initial interview and evaluation of the participant's ability. The beauty treatments are sublime; the exercise instructors hit just the right note of enthusiasm without overdoing. Assigning classes ensures against overcrowding, which sometimes occurs at other spas. Many of the nutrition talks are offered at a group lunch table, so you can fit them in and enjoy a bit of sociability at the same time. Regardless of the high price and well-heeled clientele, I've not found another spa that teaches so much in such a down-to-earth, commonsense, easy-to-follow way. My own diet was permanently changed because of their influence.

Like most spas that are part of a larger resort, Palm-Aire accommodations are handsome and plush, and the sports facilities of the complex are lavish. Spa-goers have a separate dining area, so they are not tempted by the regular menu—a point to watch out for at a resort. Florida seems to attract guests that are more sedentary than those found at fitness resorts in the West. There is a lot of emphasis here on weight loss. Many movie stars have been to Palm-Aire; Elizabeth Taylor has visited so many times, they named a suite for her.

GOOD-VALUE SPAS

Finding spas is easy. They are mushrooming all over the country, so much so that several books are devoted to sizing them up. What is not easy is finding one that is reasonable in price. Here are a few suggestions:

THE OAKS AT OJAI, 122 E. Ojai Ave., Ojai, CA 93023; 805-646-5573. Coed; 80 guests. (M)

Fitness and exercise is the forte of director Sheila Cuff, whose moderately priced spas in Ojai and Palm Springs represent good value. With plenty of her vigorous exercise classes and a careful diet, guests are sure to lose weight. This spa opened in 1977 in the center of a quaint arts-oriented town about 90 minutes north of Los Angeles. It attracts many young career women including starlets from the Los Angeles area. About 20 percent of the guests are male. The staff says that 85 percent of the guests come alone.

THE PALMS AT PALM SPRINGS, 572 N. Indian Ave., Palm Springs, CA 92262; 619–325–1111. Coed; 90 guests. (M)

This sister to the Oaks has a similar program and a similar clientele. It is equally well priced.

COOLFONT, Berkeley Springs, WV 25411; 304-258-4500. Coed; 20 guests. (I)

A 5-day "Health Retreat" is the special offering of this rustic health-minded resort in the mountains not far from Washington, D.C. Included in the program are exercise classes, hikes, yoga, massage, health education classes, self-improvement seminars, hot tubs, and nourishing low-calorie foods. The retreat can be extended by combining it with a "Fitness Weekend," a 2- or 3-day regimen. The wooded setting is beautiful and serene; there are no phones or TV in the simple chalet-style rooms to break the spell. Evenings offer a range of cultural offerings—musicians, poets, and other artists. A very special place.

NEW LIFE SPA, Liftline Lodge, P. O. Box 144, Stratton Mountain, VT 05155; 802-297-2534. Coed; 30 guests. Runs late March to mid-September. (M)

Set in an attractive alpine lodge near the mountain, this active program includes exercise classes, mountain walks, weight training, an indoor pool, and a healthful low-fat, high-fiber, high-carbohydrate diet. The small size of the group makes for a highly personal program monitored to each guest's needs. The facilities, leadership, and setting are first-rate. Stratton's golf and tennis facilities are also open to participants.

MEXICAN SPAS

Though nowhere near the class of Rancho la Puerta, two additional Mexican spa resorts deserve mention because their rates are so much lower than American spas.

RANCHO RIO CALIENTE, Guadalajara, Mexico; c/o Barbara Dane Associates, 480 California Terr., Pasadena, CA 91105; 818-796-5577. Coed; 80 guests; no shares arranged. (I)

Located in a secluded pine forest 18 miles from Guadalajara, this small, casual, very rustic hot-springs resort is an incredible bargain. The program stresses hiking, hot mineral-water baths; also offers horseback riding, relaxing yoga, and massage. Beauty treatments are available, but they are not stressed here. Meals are vegetarian; many of the foods are grown in their own garden. In keeping with the away-from-it-all feeling, there are no TV sets or telephones on the premises.

IXTAPAN HOTEL AND SPA, Ixtapan de la Sal, Mexico, c/o E & M Associates, 211 E. 43d St., New York, NY 10017; 800-223-9832 or 212-599-8280. Coed; 50 spa guests; no shares arranged. (I–M)

Part of a 600-acre resort complex based around therapeutic warm springs, the spa facilities occupy the fifth floor of a 250-room hotel. The weekly package includes daily massages, three facials, three nail and scalp treatments, and two Roman bath treatments as well as a daily aerobic and aquatic exercise class. Guests can use the spa dining room, where meals equal 800 calories a day, or the regular resort dining room. Everyone dresses up at night. Other diversions are tennis, horseback riding, and evening concerts, movies, and nightclub entertainment. Cars meet guests in Mexico City for the 2-hour drive to the hotel.

The above listing is just a sampling of the many spas to consider, and there are promising new locations such as Canyon Ranch in Massachusetts and Topnotch in Stowe, Vermont, that were not ready for review at press time.

RESEARCHING THE POSSIBILITIES

A good way to begin researching spa possibilities is to read up on the available choices. Check magazines for the latest roundups, or a bookstore or library for more comprehensive coverage. Some good book choices are:

THE SPA BOOK: A GUIDE TO THE TOP 101 HEALTH RESORTS IN AMERICA, by Judith Brode Hirsch (1988, Perigree Books, Putnam Publishing Company, 200 Madison Avenue, New York, NY 10016). A thorough survey with good factual data on each spa.

THE BEST SPAS by Theodore B. Van Italie and Leila Hadley (1988, Harper & Row, 10 East 53d Street, New York, NY 10022). A big, comprehensive volume.

THE SPA BOOK: A GUIDED PERSONAL TOUR OF HEALTH RESORTS AND BEAUTY SPAS FOR MEN AND WOMEN, by Judy Babcock and Judy Kennedy (1983, Crown Publishers, 201 East 50th Street, New York, NY 10022). Though missing some of the newer spas, this is still a good choice for capturing the real flavor of the spas listed.

THE SPA FINDER 1987–88 (Spa-Finders Travel Arrangements, Ltd., 734 Broadway, New York, NY 10003-4856). A paperbound catalog of fitness spas with short descriptions of over 200 spas. Published by a travel company that specializes in spa vacations.

Pick several spas whose approach, location, and rates seem to meet your needs and write for brochures. A brochure will tell you a lot about the philosophy of the spa, its facilities and schedules, and it should show a typical guest room. It will tell you whether massages and other services are included in the fee or are extra. It should also describe the menu, the number of calories served, whether larger portions are available if you want them, and whether the emphasis is on a balanced diet or a vegetarian menu.

If you still have questions after reading the brochure, don't hesitate to phone the spa's fitness director. Ask about the number of single guests or male guests if it is a concern. Find out whether there is someone who seats you at meals to be sure you have company when you want it. Spa vacations are expensive, and since there are many options, you should be sure you are making the right choice for your own needs.

SPA TRAVELING SPECIALISTS

The popularity of spas has spawned a couple of specialty travel agencies who promise to keep up with the field and suggest the right places for varying tastes and budgets. They are:

SPA-FINDERS TRAVEL ARRANGEMENTS, LTD., 784 Broadway, New York, NY 10003-4856; 800–ALL–SPAS. (Specializes in European spas)

SPA TREK INTERNATIONAL, INC., 470 Park Avenue S., Suite 1404, New York, NY 10016; 212–779–3480.

6

JOIN A TOUR

IF YOU'RE DREAMING OF SEEING THE WORLD, you'll find that tour companies are in the dream-fulfillment business. They print up shiny brochures showing the world's wonders, which they wrap up for you in neat, easy packages.

These packages offer many advantages. On a prepaid tour, you can sit back and let somebody else take care of all the details of travel. A tour relieves you of the chores of getting around on your own in unfamiliar cities, choosing hotels, deciding where to eat, making restaurant reservations, and planning every day's sight-seeing. You'll never have to worry about transporting luggage or finding your way to a hotel. And if your luggage does not arrive, it's the tour manager, not you, whose job it is to follow through.

Tour buses generally offer comfortable seats and big windows that give you the best views as you travel. Not the least of the appeal of a tour is the cost. Because of the economies of group buying, tours almost always save you money over trying to duplicate the same trip on your own. In peak season, the clout of a tour company often ensures room reservations that an individual cannot wangle.

Some tours also offer roommate-matching services to avoid the single supplement, allowing a big saving for solo travelers. Single sojourners also enjoy the advantage of companionship, especially important at mealtime. Most often, a block of tables is reserved for tour members and a single person would naturally join other members of the group.

Tours are a natural for a first trip to Europe, or for travel in the Orient or the South Pacific where getting along and getting around may seem more complicated than in the Western world. Tours with a special focus such as art or cuisine may appeal to those who have traveled more widely.

THE DOWN SIDE

Despite the many pros of group travel you should not sign on for a tour without understanding the realities as well. In exchange for the advantages, you give up the right to set your own schedule. There's a set time for bags to be left outside your hotel room door each morning, for breakfast, and for departure—and those times are likely to be early! The average tour is also geared to covering as much ground as possible, so you have little opportunity for browsing or lingering. On a typical "Continental Introduction" grand tour, for example, the highlights in one 3-day area might include a canal cruise and the Rembrandts at the Rijksmuseum in Amsterdam, Cologne cathedral, a Rhine cruise, Heidelberg, Nymphenburg Palace in Munich, the Bavarian Alps, and a walking tour of Innsbruck—a lot to take in over a short period of time. You get a sampling, not an in-depth view. And sometimes you get more than you can absorb. You know the old joke—"If this is Tuesday, this must be Belgium. . . ." It's easy for everything to become a blur on a whirlwind tour.

And while motor coach travel may sound restful, most tours take a lot of stamina. Besides those early departures, there is a lot of walking. Buses are often prohibited from parking in the center of town and are restricted to coach parks. You will get a good bit of exercise just getting to attractions, climbing hills to castles, and following the guides.

Of course, just because you've paid for the full tour doesn't mean that you must climb every hill or see every church on the itinerary. It's perfectly okay to decline and meet the group afterward. But when the bus is ready to roll, you'd better be on board.

The size of the group also limits your choice of lodgings and restaurants. Intimate inns and cafés cannot accommodate a busload of tourists. So you'll be staying in the larger commercial hotels chosen for their ability to handle a group well, and often offered fixed menus in large restaurants, unless you want to pay extra to venture out on your own. Nor is gourmet fare the rule, except on deluxe tours. Some hotels and restaurants may be better than you expect; others will be quite ordinary. Many tours do not include lunch in order to allow you the chance to visit some small local places on your own.

You should also be aware that most motor coach tours tend to attract older travelers. According to the National Tour Association in Lexington, Kentucky, approximately 70 percent of U.S. motor coach tourers are 50 and older. And the number of travelers by themselves is small, seldom more than four or five per busload. That doesn't mean that couples are not good company, simply that it is not realistic to expect a lot of fellow singles. Budget tours tend to attract more singles as well as a larger number of younger passengers; companies that guarantee shares are also more likely to attract people on their own.

Despite these warnings, the makeup of any one tour is unpredictable, and sometimes you may luck out. One single woman I know reported, "I took a Globus Gateway 2-week tour of the Orient by myself and to my delight had about eight single people between 30 and 55 for companionship, including several bachelors and widowers—which the brochure definitely did not guarantee."

What about those tours designed exclusively for singles (Chapter 8)? By all means consider them—thousands of people do. But sign on with the advance knowledge that the greater proportion of the travelers is likely to be female. Single women in any case outnumber single men and they seem more hesitant about striking out on their own. Choose a singles tour as you would any other—because the destination or itinerary intrigues you. And don't be surprised or dismayed at the scarcity of male company.

The one element that makes or breaks a tour is the tour director or escort. It is up to the tour director to see that everyone shows up on time, to appease the inevitable grumblers, and to set a tone of goodwill and fun for the group. Ideally, this person should be all things to all people—friendly, outgoing, humane, intelligent, articulate, witty, well informed, and ever tactful. Directors are usually college educated and those conducting European tours may speak two to four languages. The better established the tour company, the better the chances that you will have an expert tour director.

CHOOSING A TOUR

Knowing both the good and not-so-good about group tours, if you are ready to sign on, a little homework in choosing your tour will ensure a more successful trip.

The first consideration is strictly a monetary one. Tours come in three classifications: budget, first class, and deluxe, based on the type of hotels used. Decide on your price range and compare the offerings within it.

You'll also need to choose between general sight-seeing or special-interest tours. There are many varieties of specialized tours concentrating on everything from castles to cuisine. These tours most often are deluxe, but if the itinerary is really exciting to you, it may be worth the splurge. A shared interest helps ensure you will find compatible company.

Most group tours are all-inclusive, meaning that they take care of both air and land arrangements, most meals, and an escort who is with the group for the entire trip. Local guides may be used in each destination, since it is difficult for a tour escort to be an expert on everything. However, the better operators do have one person who stays with the group throughout even if someone else gives the specialized talks. On trips for special-interest groups, particularly those sponsored by museums and universities, the escort is usually also a well-qualified specialist whose knowledge can add a lot to your trip.

Many escorted tours are available also as land packages only, in case you want to combine them with independent travel. Sometimes you can use the group air arrangements from an independent city package and fit in a land tour to make up your own itinerary.

To evaluate what makes one general tour more desirable than another, gather a number of brochures covering the areas you want to visit, and do a bit of comparison shopping. A good travel agent can supply you with plenty of material to get you started, and can tell you which companies have pleased their clients in the past.

Compare brochures in the following areas—and if some of your questions are not answered, talk to your travel agent or call the tour operator directly.

- *Cost.* Figure out the cost of each trip on a daily basis by dividing the total price by the number of nights offered. Days are not a safe guide, because many tours start at noon or dinnertime and end with breakfast. Generally, you get what you pay for—better hotel, restaurants, etc. But it's well to compare.
- *Food.* Meals are an important element in any tour. How many meals are offered? Do you have a choice of selections or are you limited to a preselected fixed menu? Are there any dine-around options?
- *Accommodations.* The hotels used by the tour should be noted in the brochure. Look them up in a guidebook to find out how they are rated. If the brochure makes up a name for categories, such as "tourist class," find out what that means. Do all rooms have private baths? Also check whether hotels are centrally located. It's nice to be able to take a walk in the morning or spend time in shops on your own, not so nice to be stuck miles outside the city.
- *Airline.* Will you travel on a regularly scheduled plane or a special charter flight? If a charter, who runs it? Is departure guaranteed or will your flight be canceled if a sufficient number do not sign up?

- *Pace.* How hectic is the program? Do you have time to rest up from jet lag when you arrive at your destination? Look for tours that spend more than one night in a location. Time to catch your breath during the day and free time for shopping or a bit of sight-seeing on your own will be welcome.
- *Group size.* Will there be one, two, or three buses? How many passengers per bus? When tour groups are too large, there are delays getting into hotels and jams at tourist attractions.
- *Reputation.* There are scores of tour operators—a number of whom cancel unfilled trips—or, worse yet, go bankrupt with your money in the till. You should know how long the company has been in business and whether it belongs to the United States Tour Operators Association. That membership means the company has operated for at least 3 years and has solid references. The association also sets stringent requirements on insurance, liability, and financial responsibility. For a list of members, contact the USTOA, 211 E. 51st St., New York, NY 10022.
- *Guaranteed rates.* This can be a big advantage in case of extreme fluctuations in the value of the dollar.
- *Guaranteed departures.* This is the operator's pledge to run the tour as promised regardless of how many sign up.
- *Fine print.* Read carefully both tour descriptions and the page at the back of the brochure—the one *without* the pretty pictures—to find out exactly what is and is not included. There are many kinds of limitations. The brochure should be explicit as to exactly what your tour price covers. Membership fees needed to qualify for the trip, refund regulations, trip cancellation and trip interruption insurance, departure taxes, travel accident insurance, and medical payments are among the items that may or may not be covered.

There are dozens of tour operators, and since each tour may vary in the number of participants and the expertise of the guides, travel agents who use the companies frequently are your best references. Listed below, as a starting point, are a few long-established tour operators. They include Maupintours for trips outside the United States, Westours for Alaska and western Canada, and Tauck Tours for

U.S. itineraries, all the top choices in *Travel-Holiday Magazine*'s annual reader poll.

GENERAL TOURS

COSMOS TOURS, 95-25 Queens Blvd., Rego Park, NY 11374; 800-221-0090; or 150 S. Los Robles Ave., Pasadena, CA 91101; 800-556-5454. Budget tours to Europe, in the United States, and to Canada.

Years in business: Since 1961
Most common age: 45, though about one-third are under 30
Number of participants: Averages 39
Age range: 20–85
Percent alone: Over 33
Male/female ratio: Higher female

Guaranteed room shares for single guests.

GLOBUS-GATEWAY, 95–25 Queens Blvd., Rego Park, NY 11374; 800-221-0090; or 150 S. Los Robles Ave., Pasadena, CA 91101; 800-556-5454. First-class tours to Europe, United States/Canada, Orient, South Pacific.

Years in business: 50+
Most common age: 55
Number of participants: Averages 36
Age range: 20s–80s
Percent alone: 30
Male/female ratio: Higher female

No shares arranged.

MAUPINTOURS, 1515 St. Andrews Dr., Lawrence, KS 66045; 913-843-1211. Luxury tours to Europe, Asia, Africa, South Pacific, United States/Canada.

Years in business: 38
Most common age: 50+
Number of participants: Averages 25
Age range: Varies
Percent alone: 25–30
Male/female ratio: 50/50

Will try to arrange room shares.

WESTOURS, 300 Elliott Ave. W, Seattle, WA 98119; 206-286-3535. Luxury tours to Alaska and the Canadian Rockies; the company is affiliated with Holland American Cruise Lines.

Years in business: 42
Most common age: No reply
Number of participants: 36 per motor coach
Age range: No reply
Percent alone: No reply
Male/female ratio: 2/3

Will try to arrange room shares.

TAUCK TOURS, Box 5027, Westport, CT 06881; 203-226-6911. A family-owned business, now in its third generation, offering luxury tours in the United States and Canada.

Years in business: 65
Most common age: 55–70
Number of participants: 40
Age range: 55–70
Percent alone: 15–20
Male/female ratio: Entire group, 40/60; single passengers, 10/90

Will try to match single roommates.

Some well-regarded luxury tour operators are:

ABERCROMBIE & KENT, 1420 Kensington Rd., Oak Brook, IL 60521; 800-323-7308 (in Illinois, 312-954-2944).

HEMPHILL HARRIS, 16000 Ventura Blvd., Encino, CA 91436; 800-421-0454 or 213-906-8086.

LINDBLAD TRAVEL, 8 Wright St., P.O. Box 912, Westport, CT 06881; 203-421-0454.

TOURS FOR OLDER TRAVELERS

SAGA INTERNATIONAL HOLIDAYS, 120 Boylston St., Boston, MA 02116-9804; 1-800-343-0273. (I–M, including airfare)

Years in business: 38
Most common age: 60s–70s
Number of participants: 35–40
Age range: Over 60
Percent alone: 15
Male/female ratio: Varies, but higher female

Will try to arrange shares.

This pioneer in tours for mature travelers offers an extensive catalog of trips across the United States, Canada, and Europe, plus cruises and easy "adventures" to Australia, New Zealand, the Far East, South America, and Kenya.

SPECIAL-INTEREST TOURS

There is truly a tour for every interest, whether your love is food and wine, sports, cave art, doll houses, bird-watching, or rockhounding. Because the itineraries are unique, you can't compare these in the same way you would general tours. References from past participants are the best way to judge whether you want to sign on. Assume that most special-interest tours will fall into the "very expensive" category, unless otherwise indicated. Here are some of the possibilities:

ARCHAEOLOGICAL TOURS, 30 E. 42d St., Suite 1202, New York, NY 10017; 212-986-3054. (EE)

Years in business: 20
Most common age: 50+
Number of participants: 24–30
Age range: 30–75
Percent alone: 30 average
Male/female ratio: 40/60

Will try to arrange shares.

Luxury tour groups are accompanied by expert scholars who stress the anthropological, archaeological, and historical aspects of destinations that include Italy, Greece, Turkey, Israel, Egypt, Morocco, France, Spain, Yugoslavia, Guatemala, China, Indonesia, Thailand, and India.

COMMENTS:

Female, 30s: *I've been on trips to Turkey, Sicily and Italy, Cypress, and Crete. There were many people traveling alone on all. Most were in their* *late 40s and 50s and there were more women than men. The program is excellent and very structured, with most of the time spent at dig sites. The accommodations and food were the best available considering where we were.*

Male, 50s: *I've been to Sicily, China, and Yugoslavia alone; all were very good experiences. Though the trips are expensive, the group is not just rich people. Many are the people who save up and take a trip every other year. Most were interesting professionals. The destinations are interesting, the itineraries are meticulously planned, the days are active. I highly recommend it.*

QUESTERS TOURS AND TRAVEL, INC., 257 Park Ave. S, New York, NY 10010-7369; 212-673-3120. (EE)

Years in business: 15
Age range: 25–80
Most common age: 55–70
Percent alone: 45
Number of participants: Varies
Male/female ratio: 20/80

Will try to arrange shares; if cannot, will absorb the single supplement.

A host of tours accompanied by naturalists whose knowledge of the areas greatly adds to the experience. Culture is also part of the focus, as at Machu Picchu, where the architecture and the history of the Inca city are studied as well as the birds and wildflowers of the area. Other destinations include Hawaii, Alaska, the western United States, Mexico, Panama, Costa Rica, Guatemala, South America, the Caribbean, Norway, Scotland, the Greek Isles, Australia, New Zealand, the Himalayas, and much of Asia.

COMMENTS:

Female, 40s: *I've gone on seven trips alone. About half the participants come by themselves, are ages 20 to 80, and there are more women than men. They are from all over the world. Most come to get away from it all, to get back to nature. On some trips there has been a lot of free time, on others everything is group oriented, but you are always free to do what you want to and pursue whatever aspect of the area interests you.*

There is a lot of driving through wonderful scenery, but this is definitely not the usual sight-seeing tour.

Female, 70s: *I've taken many tours, but these are the best. I've returned ten times and find many people who go again and again. There is a good mix of singles and couples; most of the singles are women. The group is always highly intelligent—this kind of trip does not attract duds—and it is easy to make friends. The tour leaders are excellent and informative.*

ANNEMARIE VICTORY'S DELUXE GOURMET TOURS, 136 E. 64th St., New York, NY 10021; 212-486-0353. (EE)

Years in business: 10
Age range: 45–70
Most common age: 55–60
Percent alone: 50
Number of participants: 10
Male/female ratio: 40/60

Will try to arrange shares.

Food lovers will find that even reading this catalog is a delicious experience. These ultraluxury tours, limited to 10 people, include Italy, Austria, Switzerland, Belgium, Luxembourg, France, Portugal, Spain, Morocco, China, Hong Kong, and Bangkok. All focus on the finest dining in each destination, but there is also generous time for sight-seeing.

COMMENTS:

Female, 50s: *The best of everything—fine small hotels, flowers in your room, the best guides, plenty of free time, never rushed or hectic, wonderful food. On three trips, the average age was 40 to 55; the biggest number of participants was eight. I was often the only person alone, but you eat together and quickly get to know everyone. I can't say enough good things about these trips.*

Male, 40s: *We had just four people, ages 46 to 72. Everything was deluxe, the days were varied, the food was superb. It was a wonderful experience that I would gladly repeat.*

MOZART'S EUROPE, c/o New Voyager Tours, Inc., Deer Lane, Pawlet, VT 05671; 802-325-3656. (EE)

Years in business: 5
Most common age: 40–60
Number of participants: 26 maximum
Age range: 32–80
Percent alone: 50
Male/female ratio: 35/65

Will try to arrange shares.

Mozart lovers, here are your dream trips. There are three variations of this deluxe 2-week grand tour of Mozart's Europe, all including Salzburg, Mozart's birthplace. One itinerary visits the state operas in Vienna, Prague, and Budapest; another includes the Vienna/Baden Summer Festival, the Switzerland Summer Festival in Engadine, and the Bregenz, Austria, festival. The third combines the Vienna and Budapest state operas with the Würzburg Mozart Festival and the Hohenems, Austria, Schubertiade. Many private concerts and demonstrations are performed on the instruments used by Mozart.

COMMENTS:

Female, 50s: *This trip exceeded anything I've ever done. My group was older than most—from over 60 to 80—with more women than men and only five or six single people. Still, I made lasting friends, and the tour operators are wonderful people who are always available for companionship. The trip goes to all the pertinent Mozart places, to the opera in Vienna and Salzburg. It is a perfect trip for anyone who loves Mozart.*

Female, 30s: *The trip was a mental adventure, a musical dream come true. Though most of the group was older and married, it was still easy to be there alone. The people were interesting, and I never felt left out. I was sent the name and telephone number of my roommate before the trip, so we had a chance to get to know each other a little bit even before we left. The leader/owners are especially warm and were like parents to me. The hotels and food were tops and there was plenty of time to do what you wanted. This is for anyone who likes Europe and music.*

INTERNATIONAL TRAVEL PROGRAM, 92nd Street Y, 1395 Lexington Ave., New York, NY 10128; 212-427-6000, ext. 599. (E–EE)

Years in business: 8
Most common age: 50s
Number of participants: 25–30
Age range: 20s–60s
Percent alone: 80
Male/female ratio: 25/75

Will try to arrange shares.

This venerable New York cultural institution recently expanded a long-established program of weekend bus tours by including an international program of special-interest tours. Some examples: Spain: Art and Architecture; Portugal: History, Wine, and Crafts; Italy: Palazzos and Paintings; and France: the Cannes Film Festival. These tours have some unique features. Applicants are personally interviewed before being assigned roommates, making for a better chance of congeniality. A meeting is held in New York before the trip to talk about the destination and give everyone a chance to meet. There is a minimum of two nights in each destination. Dinner is not included in the group itinerary to allow participants to try smaller restaurants in each locale. At the end of the day, the group leader suggests possibilities in a variety of price ranges and sets up small groups for each, so that you need never worry about dining alone.

COMMENTS:

Female, 30s: *Most participants were female and from the New York area, well educated but not necessarily well traveled. The art-oriented program in France was wonderful, the guides in Europe superb, and you were free to leave the group if you wanted. In Paris, for example, I went off on my own. I've always traveled mostly on my own, but I found it so relaxing not to have to worry about details, I will probably do it again—with this group. I learned far more about art than I would ever have done alone.*

AMERICAN JEWISH CONGRESS INTERNATIONAL TRAVEL PROGRAM, 15 E. 84th St., New York, NY 10028; 800-221-4694 or 212-879-4500. (E–EE)

Years in business: 31
Most common age: 50+
Number of participants: 25 average
Age range: Wide
Percent alone: 20
Male/female ratio: 1/4

Will try to arrange shares.

AJC tours go to Israel and 41 other countries on six continents. African safaris, Nile cruises, and Far Eastern odysseys, Russia, and Costa Rica are among the long list of choices. Tour members have a heritage and an interest in Jewish affairs in common. They often meet Jewish residents in other countries and see sights of special cultural or religious interest.

COMMENTS:

Female, late 20s: *I've been on two trips alone, to Morocco and on safari in Africa, and to Egypt and Israel. I chose singles trips, so most people were in their 20s and 30s, though all ages were represented. Women outnumbered men, but everyone seemed to be from similar backgrounds, and were fairly successful professionals. Everything was great in Egypt and Israel—guides, food, accommodations. In Africa, the guide left something to be desired and the trip was less structured, meaning you had to do a lot more on your own. I highly recommend the Israel trip with this group, but have reservations about Africa.*

Male, 30s: *I've been on three trips: singles tours to Israel and to Spain and an "adventure tour" with mostly couples. The singles trips average 130 people, so you can't get to know everybody, but you are divided into tour buses, and you do become very friendly with the people on your bus. Two-thirds of each group was from New York, and women always outnumbered men. I enjoyed the adventure trip because it was less structured than a guided bus tour. These trips aren't like the "love boat"—people are there to travel with others their own ages and with similar interests, not to look for a partner. The group leaders are very good, and I would recommend the tours to anyone.*

ROCKY ROADS, INC., 169 N. Quaker Lane, West Hartford, CT 06119; 203-523-0637. (I)

Years in business: 4
Age range: 8–76
Most common age: 20–40
Percent alone: 50
Number of participants: 12–20
Male/female ratio: 50/50
Will try to arrange shares.

Weekend guided gem- and mineral-collecting tours in Maine, a 6-day tour to Mexico, and plans for other areas where gems are plentiful. Most participants are from the New York–New England area.

COMMENTS:
Female, 30s: *The leaders were very knowledgeable and accommodating, going out of their way to make sure you feel welcome, and the other people were very easy to talk to. We'd go to a quarry in the morning, have afternoons free to be alone or stay with the group. Ages were 10 to 70, some families, some singles. We stayed in a lodge with so-so food. You should bring your own collecting equipment because what is furnished is not great, but it is a good experience for anyone interested in gems and minerals.*
Female, 70s: *The percentage of singles was small, and there were many couples with children, but it was a delightful weekend and lots of fun. You could do your own thing in the mines but the leaders were there to help or to tell you what you had found. The accommodations were clean, the food plain; both were adequate.*

Following is a sampling of other special-interest tours (all in the EE category unless noted):

COUNTRY HOMES & CASTLES, 118 Cromwell Rd., London, England SW2 4ET; 01-370 4445. American reps: Sue Duncan, Atlanta, 404-231-5832, or Sandy Harris, New York, 212-472-9441.

Upscale tours focusing on needlework, gardens, theater; also arranges for individual stays in country homes.

BRITAIN'S COUNTRY HOUSES, FRENCH CHÂTEAUX-HOTELS AND COUNTRY INNS, Abercrombie & Kent (see address under general tours, page 141).

Upscale country tours throughout Britain and France, with accommodations in grand and historic lodgings.

IN THE ENGLISH MANNER, c/o Rolfes Travel, 301-244-0077; Hayes Travel, 800-234-8877; or Travel Etcetera, 818-441-3134.

Fourteen-day tours focusing on northern England and its literary giants of the past, such as the Brontë and Wordsworth, as well as celebrated castles, mansions, and gardens.

THE BRITISH CONNECTION, 2490 Black Rock Turnpike, Suite 240, Fairfield, CT 06430; 800-727-2771 or 203-227-0700.

A U.S. link to more than 200 special-interest vacations in Great Britain operated by small British companies. Trips focus on a wide range of subjects from art, music, and antiques to gardens and King Arthur country in Wessex. One economy "travelbug" tour uses camping and hosteling accommodations to hold down the cost of touring Britain and Scotland.

TOURS OF BRITAIN, INC., 5757 Wilshire Blvd., Suite 124, Los Angeles, CA 90036; 213-937-0494.

A variety of tours including the Villages of Great Britain, Golf in Ireland, Castles of Scotland, plus theater and antiquing weekends.

RUFFINO'S TUSCAN EXPERIENCE, c/o Annemarie Victory, 136 E. 64th St., New York, NY 10021; 212-486-0353.

Giovanna Folonari Ruffino, of a noted Italian wine family, serves as hostess during 9 days of exploring the culinary and cultural heritage of Tuscany. Participants stay at the deluxe Excelsior Hotel in Florence, and travel daily to a different Tuscan town for sight-seeing, cooking demonstrations, and a special Ruffino wine tasting.

SCANDINAVIAN COOKING TOUR, Tunlare Travel Organization, 101 Hillside Ave., Williston Park, NY 11596; 516-877-1720.

Groups go behind the scenes at gourmet restaurants, cooking schools, bakeries, and chocolate factories. Participants dine at top Oslo restaurants.

SCANDINAVIAN KING PACKAGE, c/o Crownline Tours, 3300 S. Gessner, Houston, TX 77063; 800-255-9509 or 713-977-6916.

This specialized itinerary features deluxe dining in restaurants recognized by the Michelin Guide in Stockholm, Copenhagen, and Oslo.

GARDEN TOURS, c/o Serendipity Tours, 3 Channing Circle, Cambridge, MA 02138; 617-354-1879.

Garden tours in the United States and abroad are this operator's specialty. Trips are accompanied by landscape designers and other professionals.

PHOTOGRAPHY TOURS

Tours oriented to photography provide plenty of time and opportunity for bringing home great pictures.

Inexperienced photographers setting out on a tour that promises instruction and critiques should be sure that other novices are along. It is also well to know the ratio of participants to tour leaders to be sure you will receive personal attention. You should also get references from people who have traveled with your leader. Great photographers may or may not be great travel guides.

CLOSE-UP EXPEDITIONS, 1031 Ardmore Avenue, Oakland, CA 94610; 415-465-8955. (EE)

Years in business: 13
Age range: 35–75
Most common age: 55–75
Percent alone: 65
Number of participants: 8–12
Male/female ratio: 50/50

Will try to arrange shares. Suitable for semibeginners.

This is an intensive program for those interested in travel and nature photography. Groups are small, and the pace is geared to picture taking, with transportation in vehicles that can go almost anywhere and stop quickly. Driver-guides are skilled photographers who share their knowledge. Itineraries are planned around light and weather conditions and the slower pace needed for careful photography. Good early morning and afternoon light conditions occasionally require altered meal times. Recent destinations have included Baja California, the Southwest desert, the California coast, New England in autumn, Nova Scotia, Alaska, Yugoslavia, New Zealand, Costa Rica, Scandinavia, the south of France, Wales, and the English countryside. Trips range from 10 to 25 days.

COMMENTS:

Male, 30s: *I found the prices a little high and did not consider the leader a good naturalist. However, this was a relaxed holiday, not rushed like other photographic tours I have taken, and the trip was well organized. The group was about equally male and female, with most traveling by themselves.*

Male, 30s: *I made a trip to Costa Rica with my mother. The age range of my group was from 35 to late 60s and 70s, and about half were single. The program is well run and good for a beginner wanting to learn something new on vacation. The food and accommodations were fine. You have the freedom to do what you want, though it is generally a group situation because of the locale—you can't go off by yourself at night in the Costa Rican rain forest!*

PHOTO ADVENTURE TOURS, 2035 Park St., Atlantic Beach, NY 11509; 516-371-0067. (EE)

Years in business: 4 | Age range: 10–80
Most common age: 25–70 | Percent alone: 50
Number of participants: About 20 | Male/female ratio: Varies

Will try to arrange shares. Suitable for beginners.

Billed as a comfortable way to discover the wonders of the world, these tours cover Iceland, Russia, Israel, the Caribbean, India, and "Navajo Land" in New Mexico, Arizona, and Utah. Guides discuss the history, geology, geography, and culture of their countries. A qualified local photographer is also on hand to familiarize tourers with the area and to answer questions.

COMMENTS:

Female, 20s: *My trip to Iceland included two journalists in their 70s, three men and one woman in their 20s, one single man in his 50s. Everyone was very friendly. There was very little teaching, but they showed you the secret photo spots. The pace was relaxed and unscheduled, the food was excellent, the accommodations were like ski huts. It is a great trip to take on your own.*

Female, 50s: *A fabulous trip with a nice, warm group of people ranging from their 20s to 60s, mostly couples. There was very little photographic instruction, but it was adequate. This was a hobby trip for me and I am not a beginner. It is fine coming alone—you don't remain alone.*

WILD HORIZONS PHOTOGRAPHIC SAFARIS, P.O. Box 5118-B, Tucson, AZ 85703; 602-622-0672. (E)

Years in business: 5
Age range: 35–65
Most common age: 35–65
Percent alone: 40
Number of participants: 8
Male/female ratio: 50/50
Will try to arrange shares.

This outfit caters to the amateur with small, personalized groups led by a professional photographer. The tours emphasize hands-on experience in places that have spectacular scenery. Destinations include Arizona ghost towns; the Tucson desert in spring; the Grand Canyon and Sedona in Arizona; Utah's Canyonlands, Bryce and Zion national parks; Mono Lake and the eastern Sierra Nevada mountains of California; the Canadian Rockies; and southwest Florida.

COMMENTS:

Female, 30s: *I happened to get a very small group, just two men, one in his 50s, another in his 30s. We were constantly on the move, sometimes had a picnic breakfast while we shot the sunrise. Accommodations were good; food varied according to where we were. The trip was an adventure, traveling by jeep away from the tourists. One day we went to an Indian reservation and the Indian guide cooked our lunch. The leaders knew the hidden great spots for photography. It was a very personal experience and I would especially recommend it for single travelers.*

Male, 40s: *Tours to Yosemite and the Painted Desert were fine, and I was very comfortable alone. Companions were ages 30 to 60, all on their own, equally divided between male and female. We shared all meals. The food and accommodations were the best available. I've been on similar tours—this one is quite professional, goes into more teaching detail, but is geared toward the experienced photographer. The instructors are very good, but can't spend too much time with one person, so it might not be enough for a beginner.*

For other U.S. and foreign photo tours, see the monthly listing in *Peterson's Photographic Magazine*, 8490 Sunset Blvd., Los Angeles, CA 90069; 213-854-2200. There are many tour advertisements in other photography publications such as *Modern Photography* or *Popular Photography*.

MUSEUM- AND UNIVERSITY-SPONSORED TOURS

Some of the best special-interest tours are organized by museums, universities, and college alumni groups. Although generally quite expensive, they are usually superior and may provide exceptionally knowledgeable escorts. Part of the cost often is considered a tax-deductible contribution.

To find such trips, start with the groups either in your own city or nearby large cities. You may also want to contact some of the following large institutions:

SMITHSONIAN INSTITUTION, c/o Smithsonian National Associates, 1100 Jefferson Dr. SW, Washington, D.C. 20560; 202-357-4700.

The Smithsonian has a long roster of both U.S. and foreign tours each year, accompanied by experts on nature, folklore, architecture, gardens, wildlife, theater, and many other special interests.

AMERICAN MUSEUM OF NATIONAL HISTORY DISCOVERY TOURS, Central Park West at 79th St., New York, NY 10024-5192; 800-462-8687 or 212-769-5700.

Tours of the world's greatest wildlife regions and archaeological sites, with expert lecturers. The "Market" section and other ads in the museum's publication *Natural History* includes a large number of additional specialized tours.

NATIONAL TRUST FOR HISTORIC PRESERVATION, 1785 Massachusetts Ave. NW, Washington, D.C. 20036; 202-673-4000.

A wide variety of tours, usually concentrating on distinguished homes, gardens, and architecture here and abroad.

NEW YORK BOTANICAL GARDEN, Education Department, Bronx, NY 10458-5126; 212-220-8700.

Gardens are the focus but sight-seeing is also included in the tours of this fine organization.

The companies below are among those that organize trips for museum, cultural, and educational groups. They can give information on upcoming tours, which individuals are welcome to join; you may be asked to enroll in the sponsoring organization, usually for a very modest fee.

LIMITED EDITIONS, c/o Travel Concepts, 373 Commonwealth Ave., Suite 601, Boston, MA 02115-1815; 617-266-8450.
VOYAGERS INTERNATIONAL, P.O. Box 915, Ithaca, NY 14851; 607-257-3091.

For more information on tours:

NATIONAL TOUR ASSOCIATION (546 E. Main St., Lexington, KY 40508; 606-253-1036) offers a list of names and addresses of its 550 members in the United States and Canada. They also publish a brochure describing how group tours are run, what to expect of an escort, and other matters. Both are free.

UNITED STATES TOUR OPERATORS ASSOCIATION (211 E. 51st St., Suite 12B, New York, NY 10022; 212-944-5727) issues a free list of its 45 member companies including details of programs and destinations, as well as a brochure on how to read a tour brochure and select a package tour.

7

GO TO SEA

MAYBE YOU DON'T WANT AN ACTIVE VACATION at all. Maybe what you'd really like to do is lie back and soak up some sun. Or maybe you can't decide. You'd like to relax, but you'd also like the excitement of seeing new places.

Cruises offer the best of two worlds—the chance to travel while you enjoy the pleasures of resort life at sea. The new superliners really are floating resorts, with a lineup of activities ranging from exercise classes and trap shooting to lectures, dance lessons, contests, and the chance to strike it rich in the casino. And few resorts can match the fantastic menu on a cruise ship, where something is being served almost nonstop from 7:00 A.M. until that fabled midnight buffet.

Best of all, this is a resort where you will never lack for company at dinner.

Ship travel is also easy and convenient. Accommodations, activities, entertainment, and lavish meals are all part of one package price, often even including transportation to the port of departure. And you can travel to a number of new places on one vacation without the hassles of making plane connections or dealing with baggage. No matter how many ports you visit, once you unpack, you need never face a suitcase again until you head home.

Recent changes in the cruise industry offer more good news for single people. No longer catering only to the wealthy or to older travelers, many cruise lines have updated their facilities and programs, shortened their itineraries, widened their offerings, and whittled their costs to appeal to a much wider audience—including singles. According to a study by the Cruise Lines International Association, thc number of single passengers signing on for cruises has doubled since 1986.

A SINGULAR DILEMMA

It is only fair to warn that a cruise vacation by yourself does present some special challenges. The new cruise liners keep getting bigger and bigger and it is harder to meet people on an enormous ship. In spite of the increase in numbers, singles remain a definite minority on most cruises, usually representing less than 20 percent of the passengers. And women are the very great majority of that small number. On a recent sailing aboard one of Carnival Cruise Line's "fun ships," which attract more single passengers than many other lines, the number who showed up for a get-acquainted singles mixer was less than 150 out of about 1,400 people on board—and the women outnumbered the men 10 to 1.

This may be welcome news if you are a male, but therein lies the dilemma for women. After dinner, couples naturally couple up. Evenings on shipboard are romantic, particularly on the two nights when everyone dresses up for dinner, and it isn't much fun to be alone. Yet that's exactly what you may be, and you should know it in advance. If you are a female who will feel like a wallflower without a dancing partner, don't go on a cruise by yourself. If, however, you can enjoy the pleasures of days at sea and be content to watch the evening's entertainment and then maybe read a good book at night, cruising is for you.

MEETING AND MINGLING

This is not to say that the odds are totally against single passengers. But with all those couples around, cruising is a situation where you really want to find compatible single company, even just a good buddy of your own sex. On a large ship, that takes a little luck and a lot of effort because it is easy to feel lost.

The only people you see regularly each day are the others at your dinner table, so your seating assignment is crucial. Ask to be placed at one of the largest tables, which usually seats eight, to increase your chances of meeting people you'll want to spend time with. And request the second, or later, seating. The first seating tends to attract those who are early to bed, and because the dining room must be cleared ahead for the next sitting, there is less time for lingering over conversation.

If you are not happy with your table, ask to have it changed—and do it right away.

Persistence and an outgoing attitude are needed to search out the other unattached passengers on board a big ship. Cruise lines do their best to help by holding singles get-togethers early in the cruise, but I don't know why they don't schedule more than one such gathering. On most ships, if you don't connect at that early mixer, there are no set places afterward to meet the other single passengers on board. To better your odds of meeting people, sign up for lots of daytime activities. And women should not be afraid to try the bar, which is easy and comfortable to do on a ship. A piano bar especially is often a particularly pleasant gathering place.

Florence Lemkowitz, a veteran cruise writer, suggests that it is a mistake to go to bed early the first night at sea if you want to meet people, since that's just when other solo travelers are probably checking the scene with the same thought in mind. The first night is the best night to visit the ship's lounges and bars, she says, before people give up on them because nobody seems to be around. She also recommends telling the social director that you want to make friends, putting him or her to work on your behalf.

Cruise author Antoinette DeLand adds that making up little cards with your name and cabin number is a good idea. These are not meant to serve as invitations to drop in. Ships' cabins have telephones, and on a large ship a card ensures that new acquaintances remember where to call you if they want to get together. You can't just assume you will run into one another again.

One way to ensure company is by signing on for a cruise with a singles group. Singleworld specializes in cruising, and has separate departures for passengers under and over age 35. But while a tour group guarantees people in your own age group, it won't necessarily affect the male/female ratio. I met one Singleworld passenger in her 40s who found she was boarding with a group of just four other women. All were literally in the same boat—their only consolation was being in it together.

Recognizing this problem, some lines have gone out of their way to make things pleasanter for single women at night. Royal Cruise Lines introduced a host program in 1982, inviting congenial single gentlemen in their 50s and 60s to come along as hosts to dance with the women, attend cocktail parties, act as a fourth for bridge, provide companionship in port, or sometimes just serve as someone to talk to. These men, mostly retired or semiretired businessmen and military officers, are carefully screened and receive explicit instructions to mingle, with no favoritism allowed to any one passenger or group.

To encourage more male guests, Royal recently added a Commodore Club that offers a 20 percent discount to single men on selected sailings, as well as discounts on shore excursions. Unlike the hosts, they have no specific obligations, though they are encouraged to mingle.

Other companies use the ships' officers to ensure that all women passengers get a turn on the dance floor. Veteran cruisers report that ships with Italian crews tend to have the most charming dance partners.

BOARDING THE RIGHT SHIP

If the lack of romance does not deter you, you can concentrate on the other pleasures of being at sea. And these are plentiful. There's nothing quite like the sense of freedom you feel standing on a breezy deck and gazing at the limitless horizon—or the excitement of watching a new port loom ever closer into view.

Your first decision when planning a cruise should be based on which ports you most want to visit, and that depends a lot on the season. In winter, the Caribbean is by far the most popular destination. The eastern ports of the Bahamas, Puerto Rico, St. Thomas, and St. Martin are the most frequently chosen because they are easily reached on 7-day cruises from Florida. Close seconds are Jamaica, Cozumel, and Grand Cayman. Cruises out of San Juan go farther afield to western Caribbean islands such as Barbados, Guadeloupe, Martinique, St. Lucia, or Antiqua. These harbors are less crowded with cruise ships and for that very reason are more appealing to many people.

In summer, Bermuda is a convenient port of call in the east while Alaska's Inside Passage, with its ice-blue glaciers and some of the continent's greatest scenery, make for an unforgettable cruise in the west. Unlike many trips where you see very little from port to port, the views of Alaska from shipboard are often so engrossing that many passengers need no other entertainment than watching the show from their deck chairs.

If you have the time and the fare, there are also wonderful itineraries to South America, the Mediterranean, the Greek Islands, the South Seas, and Asia, and a number of exciting and exotic expeditions to remote regions of the world. In fact, there's almost no place on earth you cannot happily explore on a cruise.

One problem you rarely have to consider any longer is seasickness. Today's ships are remarkably stable and there are plenty of over-the-counter remedies available, such as Dramamine, in case things get rough. If you are really concerned about rough seas, ask your doctor to prescribe the Transderm Scōp patch. The little patch, which looks like a small round Band-Aid, goes behind your ear and feeds the medication scopolamine slowly into your bloodstream. Each patch lasts for 3 days. Choose a cabin close to midship and near the waterline for the least amount of motion. And relax, knowing that if all else fails, the ship's doctor is ready with an injection that will quickly put you back on an even keel.

GETTING THE BEST DEAL

Once you have decided where you want to go, your next dilemma is choosing among the many companies offering similar itineraries. The makeup of passengers will vary from week to week, but here are a few general guidelines.

Your age may narrow your choices. Generally, longer cruises get older passengers, and many retired people. Three- and 4-day cruises to the Bahamas and Freeport from the East Coast and to Baja California from the West Coast tend to attract younger passengers. Seven-day Caribbean trips are perfect winter vacations for all, and get a good mix of people.

The nationality of the crew will affect the ambience of the ship. Greek cruise line operators such as Sun Lines are known for warmth, for example, and many enjoy the attentive service on such Italian lines as Costa. Individual ships in a company's fleet may differ in size as well as personality. Read a comprehensive guidebook to cruises to learn more about specific vessels you are considering.

Among the ships Antoinette DeLand recommends for younger single people in her excellent guide, *Fielding's Worldwide Cruises*, are the *Sun Princess*, the *Cunard Countess*, the *Cunard Princess*, and Norwegian Cruise Lines' smaller ships. For those who are outgoing and want the extra activities of a big ship, NCL's *Norway* and the Carnival Cruise Line ships may be good selections. Also look into the specialty cruises mentioned on page 166, since knowing there will be people who share your interest gives you a head start on making friends.

Information on rate policies for singles has been provided here by some of the major cruise line operators. However, verify that the data is still correct; the cruise industry is in the midst of merger mania, and many lines may have new owners by the time you read this. Incidentally, not a single cruise line would release reference names of past single passengers—maybe to avoid sad tales from disillusioned females?

CARNIVAL CRUISE LINES, 5225, N.W. 87th Ave., Miami, FL 33178; 305-599-2600. Popular-priced cruises to the Bahamas, Carribean, and Mexico.

Years in business: Since 1972

Most common age: 35–55

Average number of passengers: 1,400–2,600

Percent alone: 15–20

Cruise most popular with singles: No special favorites

Single supplement: 150 percent; guaranteed shares for cabins for 4.

NORWEGIAN CRUISE LINES, 2 Alhambra Plaza, Coral Gables, FL 33134; 305-447-9660. Popular-priced cruises to the eastern and western Caribbean, the Bahamas, and Mexico. Many theme cruises—jazz, country & western, magic, big bands, eras of 50s and 60s, etc.

Years in business: Since 1906

Most common age: 25–45

Average number of passengers: 700 except for the *Norway,* 1,794; and the *Seaward,* 1,534

Percent alone: Not available

Cruise most popular with singles: Weekend cruises

Single supplement: 150 to 200 percent. Quad shares on space-available basis—may wind up with 1 to 3 roommates.

ROYAL CARIBBEAN CRUISE LINE, 9035 S. America Way, Miami, FL 33132; 305-379-2601. Popular-priced cruises to the Caribbean and Bermuda.

Years in business: 18

Most common age: 35–55

Average number of passengers: 1,000 except *Sovereign of the Seas,* 2,000

Percent alone: of men, 20; of women, 30

Cruise most popular with singles: Fairly even; younger singles like the western Caribbean, older passengers seem to favor the eastern Caribbean and longer cruises.

Single supplement: 150 percent. Will try to match—no guaranteed shares.

CHANDRIS FANTASY CRUISES, 900 Third Ave., New York, NY 10022; 212-223-3003. Popular-priced cruises to the Caribbean, Bermuda, Mexico, the Mediterranean, and South America.

Years in business: 50
Most common age: 30–50
Average number of passengers: 850
Percent alone: 25
Cruise most popular with singles: Nassau and other shorter cruises

Single supplement: 150 percent; guaranteed quad shares.

ROYAL CRUISE LINES, 1 Maritime Plaza, Suite 660, San Francisco, CA 94111; 415-956-7200. Luxury cruises to the Far East, South Pacific, Panama Canal, Mexico, Mediterranean, Caribbean.

Years in business: Since 1974
Most common age: 50+
Average number of passengers: 460–1,000
Percent alone: 20
Cruise most popular with singles: No special favorites

Single supplement: 150 percent, less on selected sailings; guaranteed shares.

COMMODORE CRUISE LINE, 1007 N. America Way, Miami, FL 33132; 305-358-2622. Popular-priced cruises to the Caribbean.

Years in business: 23
Most common age: 35–55
Average number of passengers: 876
Percent alone: 20
Cruise most popular with singles: Western Caribbean because of the diving and water activities

Single supplement: 150 percent; will try to match—no guarantees.

REGENCY CRUISES, 260 Madison Ave., New York, NY 10016; 800-457-5566 or 212-972-4499. Popular-priced cruises to the Caribbean, West Indies, Panama Canal, and Alaska.

Years in business: 4
Most common age: Middle age
Average number of passengers: 717–950
Percent alone: Varies
Cruise most popular with singles: Caribbean

Single supplement: Varies with cabin category. Will try to match—no guarantees.

HOLLAND AMERICA LINES, 300 Elliott Ave. W., Seattle, WA 98119; 206-281-3535. Luxury cruises to the Caribbean, Alaska, Mediterranean, French Polynesia.

Years in business: 115
Most common age: 40+
Average number of passengers: 1,100
Percent alone: 20–30
Cruise most popular with singles: None in particular

Single supplement: 150 percent. Guaranteed singles shares; will match nonsmokers.

Holland America has been bought by Carnival Cruise Lines, so watch out for changes.

PRINCESS CRUISES, 2029 Century Park East, Los Angeles, CA 90067; 213-553-1770. Luxury cruises to Mexico, Caribbean, Transcanal, Alaska, Europe, Mediterranean, Orient, South Pacific, South America, New England

Years in business: 23
Most common age: 50+
Average number of passengers: 900
Percent alone: Varies
Cruise most popular with singles: Caribbean and Mexico

Single supplement: 125 percent; will try to match shares—no guarantees.

SUN LINE CRUISES, One Rockefeller Plaza, Suite 315, New York, NY 10020; 212-397-6400 or 800-872-6400. Moderate-priced and luxury cruises to the Mediterranean, the Greek Islands and Turkey, Egypt, the Black Sea, South America, and the Caribbean.

Years in business: 31
Most common age: 50+
Average number of passengers: *Stella Oceanis,* 300; *Stella Solaris,* 620; *Stella Maris,* 180
Percent alone: 10–15
Cruise most popular with singles: Mediterranean

Single supplement: 150 percent. Guaranteed singles shares.

CUNARD LINE, 555 Fifth Ave., New York, NY 10017; 800-5-CUNARD or 212-880-7500. Cunard operates the fabled liner *Queen Elizabeth II* across the Atlantic, as well as cruise ships to the Caribbean, Bermuda, the Mexican Riviera, Alaska, the Mediterranean, South America, and the Panama Canal; and makes crossings between Port Everglades, Florida, and either Acapulco or Puerto Caldera, Costa Rica. Their large fleet ranges from classic luxury liners such as the *Sagafjord* and *Vistafjord* to the more moderate priced *Cunard Princess* and *Cunard Countess.*

Years in business: 150
Most common age: Mid-50s
Average number of passengers: *QE2,* 1,800; smaller ships, 600–700
Percent alone: 15–18
Liner most popular with singles: *Cunard Countess*

Single supplement: 150 percent. Will try to match shares on world cruises only.

As you can see, there is variation in the share arrangements offered by various lines. It's not that the lines dislike single passengers, they just prefer to get double revenue from the same space. Single cabins are built only where the physical space on the ship is too constricted for two beds, and there are very few such quarters. Most of the time, when you ask for a single you are getting a double cabin to yourself.

To compare prices, divide the total cost by the number of full days on board. Arriving in home port at 8:00 A.M. hardly counts as a day at sea. In calculating the cost of any cruise, remember that you must figure at least $7.50 per day for tips. The recommended sums are $3.00 per day for room stewards and waiters, $1.50 for busboys. If you order drinks or use the barber shop or beauty salon, figure a 15 percent tip on each tab. Tips for other shipboard personnel who provide special services are at your own discretion. If you are traveling alone and plan to take group tours once ashore, figure in that cost, also—the more ports, the more you must allow for.

To save money booking a cruise, you are better off reserving very early or very late. Early birds get advance booking discounts. In the late 1980s, with the advent of many new mega-ships with huge capacities, some lines began offering better pricing for single passengers who are willing to wait until 30 to 60 days before the sailing date for confirmation. Half a fare, after all, is better than none.

For this reason, passengers are wise to deal with a travel agent who specializes in cruises and is up-to-date on all the current possibilities. Larger cruise specialists also can frequently offer their own discounts, passing along the reductions they get from the cruise lines for being favored customers who buy space in bulk.

Dealing with someone who is familiar with the industry will also give you an edge in choosing a ship where you will be happy, regardless of the price. Single passengers come in all demographics and tastes as do any other cruise passengers. Many will not be happy with ships that hold 2,000 or more, even though they may be the newest, liveliest, and most luxurious in the fleet. A lot of people, alone or not, simply feel more comfortable in a smaller group.

A company such as Carnival has become the largest afloat by going after first-time cruisers who may have little travel experience. They offer lots of participatory activities and costume parties such as male beauty contests for husbands wearing their wives' nightgowns. These are right on target for many of their passengers, who thoroughly enjoy the high jinks. But sophisticated travelers may prefer a more conservative ambience, even if the tab is higher. Paying extra usually means getting better food, as well.

Among the knowledgeable agencies that specialize in cruise travel and also offer discounts are:

GROSSMAN CRUISES OF DISTINCTION, 460 Bloomfield Avenue, Montclair, NJ 07042; 800-634-3445 or 201-744-1331.

WORLD WIDE CRUISES, 8059 W. McNab Rd., Fort Lauderdale, FL 33321; 800-882-9000. (They have a special division called "Singles Mean Business" devoted to serving single passengers.)

SOUTH FLORIDA CRUISES, 5323 NW 35th Ave., Fort Lauderdale, FL 33309; 800-327-7447 or 305-739-7447.

THE CRUISE LINE, INC., 260 N.E. 17th Terr., Suite 201, Miami, FL 33132; 800-777-0707. (This company publishes a free magazine, *World of Cruising*, with cruise news, tips, and listings of current discount offerings.)

INTERNATIONAL CRUISE CENTER, 185 Willis Ave., Mineola, NY 11501; 800-221-3254 or 516-747-8880.

TRAVELTIPS, INC., 163-07 Depot Rd., P.O. Box 188, Flushing, NY 11358; 800-872-8584 or 718-939-2400. (Also see page 169.)

Among the agencies offering discounts on late bookings are:

SPUR OF THE MOMENT CRUISES, 800-343-1991 or 213-839-2418.
POST HASTE TRAVEL, 305-966-7690.
CRUISE RESERVATIONS, 800-892-9929 or 305-759-8922.

SPECIALTY CRUISES

Specialty cruises are a boon for single passengers because they have a focus. These are regular sailings with the customary itinerary of ports, but with special guests on board to provide a drawing card. The singles percentages on these cruises may be no higher, but the chances of meeting people who share your interests probably will be. Knowledgeable travel agents and cruise specialists will know about these offerings, which vary each year. Some of the specialty choices in the past have included a jazz festival featuring Dizzy Gillespie and other all-stars on Regency Cruises' *Regent Sea* touring the Pacific Coast and ABC's "Nightline" anchor Ted Koppel as host aboard Princess Cruises' *Island Princess* from Miami to San Juan.

For the arts minded, NCL has sponsored an "Artists of the Southwest" cruise on its *Southward* with painting workshops and demonstrations by a number of area artists, and supervised sketching and painting on location. Arts and crafts was the lure also on Commodore Cruise Line's *Caribe* to the eastern Caribbean. Colleen Dewhurst, Richard Kiley, and Jason Robards are among those who have been aboard for the annual Theatre Guild "Theatre at Sea" aboard Cunard's *Q.E. II*, while many of Norwegian Cruise Lines' ships present full-scale Broadway musicals.

If you are worried about gaining weight from the nonstop meals on a cruise ship, you can choose a seagoing spa. Holland America's *Nieuw Amsterdam* and *Westerdam* both have added the Bonaventure Spa at Sea program for those who want to shape up while they ship out, and the *Queen Elizabeth II* and other Cunard ships offer the Golden Door spa program. Sheila Cuff, the fitness guru of The Oaks at Ojai and The Palms in Palm Springs, also conducts health holidays on selected cruises aboard NCL's *Norway* and Sun Line's *Stella Solaris*.

SMALLER SHIPS

Large cruise ships are not the only way to go to sea. Check out the interesting and offbeat itineraries offered by some of the following vessels:

BARGE CRUISES

For affluent travelers, a placid, luxurious way to see Europe is along its waterways, with congenial small groups and plenty of time to sightsee at each stop. The barges cruise at about 4 miles per hour, so it's easy to get off and bicycle, walk, or jog along towpaths or go into nearby villages and catch up with the ship at its next stop.

FLOATING THROUGH EUROPE (271 Madison Ave., New York, NY 10016; 800-221-3140 or 212-685-5600) offers deluxe tours on boats for 8 to 18 passengers along the Thames and through Shakespeare country in England; on the Lys River past Brussels and Ghent in Belgium; on the Bonjour and Anjodi rivers in the south of France; and along the Juliana in Holland. A special treat is the Dutch tulip cruise in spring. Many of FTE's ships have single cabins; the company reports that 15–20 percent of the passengers come alone, with most in their 50s and 60s.

HORIZON CRUISES (1600 Ventura Blvd., Suite 200, Encino, CA 91436; 800-421-0454; 800-252-2103 in California) takes pride in featuring deluxe cuisine and wines on its Royal Canal Cruises through Burgundy, Alsace-Lorraine, along the river Shannon in Ireland, through Belgium and Holland and in Britain's East Anglia. Ships hold 6 to 18 passengers usually ranging in age from 55 to 60 with 15 percent single. A few boats have single cabins.

CRUISES FOR NONSMOKERS AND OR NONDRINKERS

People with an aversion to cigarette smoke or alcohol may enjoy the eight-person minicruises in western Canada sponsored by *Cebu Cruises*, 1017 168th Ave. SE, Bellevue, WA 98008; 206-746-3414.

CRUISING THE U.S. WATERWAYS

Whether you sail the East Coast, the Colonial South, or the Mississippi River, domestic cruises are a change of pace.

CLIPPER CRUISE LINE (7711 Bonhomme Ave., St. Louis, MO 63105; 800-325-0010) sails the 102-passenger ships *Newport Clipper* and *Nantucket Clipper* on U.S. itineraries that include the New England coast north from Boston; the Hudson Valley; the southern coast to Fort Lauderdale and Florida's Keys and Intracoastal Waterway.

DELTA QUEEN STEAMBOAT COMPANY (30 Robin Street Wharf, New Orleans, LA 70130; 800-543-1949 or 504-586-0631) operates two of the rare paddle wheel riverboats left in the country, keeping alive a 150-year-old tradition of cruising the Mississippi River through the heartland of America. One- to 12-day cruises sail from New Orleans to Memphis, St. Louis, Minneapolis, and St. Paul, or branch out on the Ohio River to Cincinnati and Pittsburgh or on the Cumberland River to Nashville. The *Delta Queen,* listed on the National Register of Historic Places, recently was joined by the more luxurious *Mississippi Queen.* Both provide old-fashioned American-style entertainment, such as Dixieland jazz and barbership quartets, and many festive special events, such as the Great Steamboat Race or Mardi Gras or Cajun Christmas celebrations.

FREIGHTER CRUISES

If you have the time for long voyages, freighter travel is an adventurous way to visit foreign ports at a reasonable cost and in surprising comfort. Many retired people and others with long vacations sign on. Trips may range from 20 to 70 days.

Most cargo vessels accommodate no more than 12 passengers, so the experience is very personal. Staterooms are spacious and have views, and unlike cruise liners, many freighters do have large single cabins. This is travel for the self-sufficient, for there are no shipboard activities, and evening entertainment usually means conversation, cards, and games. Rates may average $100 a day, including meals shared with the ship's officers. Passengers may also use the lounge and deck. Possible destinations include Australia and New Zealand, the Norwegian coast, South America, the South Pacific, Africa, Europe, and the Orient. One of the more unconventional possibilities is the 55-passenger supply vessel *Amazing Grace*, which roams the West Indies and the Grenadines, provisioning the Windjammer fleet of sailing ships (see page 109). For the adventurous, this is a novel, low-cost way to do the Caribbean for about $75 a day.

TRAVELTIPS CRUISE & FREIGHTER TRAVEL ASSOCIATION, 163-07 Depot Rd., P.O. Box 188, Flushing, NY 11358; 800-872-8584 or 718-939-2400.

This group charges a modest membership fee, credited toward the first voyage. Members receive the *TravLtips* magazine, which includes firsthand accounts of other members' journeys and a listing of upcoming freighter itineraries. Discounts on special-value regular cruises are also listed (see page 165). A special introductory edition of the magazine is filled with personal accounts of past trips, answering many questions about these voyages.

SAILING CRUISES

The best bet if you are looking for single company on a ship is to board a sociable no-frills windjammer sailing cruise, where many passengers are unattached. (See page 109 under Adventure Vacations for more details.) Also note that Club Med now has its own sailing ship—the world's largest—with pools, restaurants, and bars, a fitness center, sauna, movie theater, casino, and computer workshop on board, plus classes in aerobics and calisthenics and plenty of equipment for windsurfing, waterskiing, snorkeling, and scuba diving off the ship.

CRUISE EXPEDITIONS

Small ships that are able to get off the beaten path to such exotic locales as Antarctica, the Amazon, Polynesia, Micronesia, Melanesia, and Indonesia offer another option for adventure-minded travelers. These trips are expensive, but they are also once-in-a-lifetime experiences, worth saving up for. Since the numbers of passengers are small and the visits are thrilling, the groups quickly become close, making these seemingly remote excursions very easy to go on alone. Operators report that it is not at all unusual for passengers to come by themselves. The following are among the great expedition cruises I can personally recommend:

CRUISING THE NILE

A trip on the Nile is an unforgettable experience, a chance to see life on the banks of the river and to visit the astonishing ruins and the tombs of the pharoahs with expert guides. The ships are small, carrying an average of 80 passengers, and the narrow ribbon of gentle river allows a close-up view of village life on the banks, at the same time providing a graphic illustration of the Nile's importance—beyond the border of green irrigated by the river, barren desert begins.

Longer cruises begin in Cairo, shorter ones in Luxor or Aswān, reached by plane from Cairo, The major sights lie between these two cities. Sight-seeing stops include the Temple of Luxor and the awesome ruins of the Temple of Karnak as well as the Valley of the Kings, where the tombs of Tutankhamen and other pharoahs were found; the Valley of the Queens, and the Tombs of the Nobles, which contain some of the most important art of ancient Egypt.

Besides the many international expedition cruise companies, a number of local Egyptian operators run cruises, as do the major Cairo hotels. Among the most popular operators for Americans are these familiar names:

HILTON INTERNATIONAL, P.O. Box 257, Cairo, Egypt, or phone 800-448-4782 or 212-697-9370.

SHERATON NILE CRUISES, c/o Sheraton Hotels, P.O. Box 125, Orman, Giza, Egypt, or phone 800-325-3535.

CRUISING THE SEPIK RIVER, PAPUA NEW GUINEA

Papua New Guinea is like nowhere else on earth, a fantastically varied island, a bird and flower lover's paradise still widely unblemished by man. The country's finest native art, such as masks, carvings, and bark paintings can be found in villages along the Sepik River. This route is served by two new and comfortable small boats, *The Melanesian Discoverer*, an aluminum catamaran accommodating 42 passengers that departs from the port city of Madang, and the *Sepik Spirit*, an 18-passenger vessel that leaves from the art-filled Karawari Lodge, the country's oldest and best-known tourist lodging. The *Sepik Spirit* comes highly recommended, being owned by Bob Bates, who does a superb job of running tours from his lodges, both Karawari and the newer Ambua Lodge in the highlands.

The serpentine Sepik River, the only means of transportation in this region, twists and turns, providing a new vista around every bend—birds, luxuriant vegetation, families traveling by dugout canoe, and thatched-hut villages where you can go ashore to see traditional ceremonies. Some itineraries also include the Trobriand Islands, whose culture is unique.

While Papua New Guinea is remote, it is a perfect add-on to a visit to Australia, and a truly exceptional travel experience. It is one of the few remaining places on earth where you can see tribes living as they have since the Stone Age. In many areas, they have had contact with Western man for less than 50 years. The cruise can be combined with a land package for further exploring in the beautiful highlands.

The best source of current tour and cruise information is Air Niugini, 5000 Birch St., Suite 3000, West Tower, Newport Beach, CA 92660; 714-752-5440. For additional cruise information, contact *The Melanesian Discoverer*, c/o UNIREP/Melanesian Tourist Services Pty. Ltd., Suite 105, 850 Colorado Blvd., Los Angeles, CA 90041; 800-621-1633 or 213-256-1991. Also, *Sepik Spirit*, c/o O.V.C. Pty. Ltd., P.O. Box 46227, Station G, Vancouver, BC V6R 4G5, Canada; 604-734-8707.

DARWIN'S WORLD: CRUISING THE ENCHANTED GALÁPAGOS ISLANDS

None of the photographs, none of the shipboard briefings prepare you for the reality of the Galápagos, an extraordinary configuration of islands formed by the peaks of million-year-old volcanoes. Isolated some 600 miles off the coast of Ecuador, the Galápagos are unusual in their lava-scarred landscapes as well as their tame wildlife. This is an enchanted world where rare birds and animals that have never been hunted by predators accept human visitors as just one more of nature's species—no more to be feared than a passing bird. Who lives here? Birds like none you've ever seen. Blue-footed boobies standing a foot and a half high, with feet and legs the color of a clear summer sky. Funny masked boobies, eyes framed in black, clucking over their tall, fuzzy chicks. Flapping albatrosses, graceful oystercatchers, exotic lava herons, all but sitting for the photographers furiously snapping in their midst.

In the Galápagos, you'll go swimming with sea lions, step around 2-foot-long iguanas, examine bright red sea crabs and the giant turtles that gave the islands their name. Still present are the finches that fascinated Charles Darwin—evolved into 13 distinct species, each with a beak shaped for most efficiently getting at food. Forty-five percent of the plants here are found nowhere else in the world, including the amazing Opuntia cactus that has evolved into a strange and sturdy tree. No matter how much film you bring it won't be enough.

To visit the Galápagos, you must travel to Guayaquil, Ecuador, and board a cruise ship or a sailing yacht. For someone traveling alone, the best bet is the *Santa Cruz,* run by Metropolitan Touring, Ecuador's leading tour company. It is the most comfortable of the ships, accommodating 90 passengers. Excursions to the islands are in small boats, each holding only about 20 people, so you will soon be friends with your fellow passengers, marveling together at what you have seen.

For information, contact Metropolitan Touring Galápago Cruises c/o Adventure Associates, 13150 Coit Rd., Suite 110, Dallas, TX 75240; 800-527-2500 or 214-907-0414.

SOURCES FOR EXPEDITION CRUISES

One excellent source for a number of expedition cruises is the DISCOVERY CRUISES program run by the American Museum of Natural History, Central Park West at 79th St., New York, NY 10024-5192; 800-462-8687 or 212-769-5700.

Other top operators who run some of the cruises described on pages 167 to 169 as well as a host of others from the Arctic to the Amazon include:

SOCIETY EXPEDITIONS, 3131 Elliott Ave., Suite 700, Seattle, WA 98121; 800-425-7794 or 206-285-9400.

OCEANIC SOCIETY EXPEDITIONS, Fort Mason Center, Bldg. E, San Francisco, CA 94123; 415-441-1106.

LINDBLAD TRAVEL INC./ SPECIAL EXPEDITIONS, P.O. Box 912, Westport, CT 06881; 800-243-5657 or 203-226-8531.

ABERCROMBIE & KENT/CONTINENTAL WATERWAYS, 1420 Kensington Rd., Oak Brook, IL 60521; 800-323-7308 or 312-954-2944.

SWAN HELLENIC CRUISES, c/o Esplanade Tours, 581 Boylston St., Boston, MA 02116; 800-426-5492 or 617-266-7465.

The following publications provide further information on cruising:

FIELDING'S WORLDWIDE CRUISES by Antoinette DeLand (William Morrow & Company, Inc., New York, 1989) gives in lively fashion the history of every company and details about the facilities and ambience of almost every ship afloat.

THE TOTAL TRAVELER BY SHIP by Ethel Blum (Travel Publications, Inc., Miami Beach, Florida, 1988) is another comprehensive report by a longtime cruise expert.

CARIBBEAN PORTS OF CALL by Kay Showker (Globe Pequot Press, Chester, Connecticut, 1987) is a useful guide to making the most of limited time in some of the more frequently visited Caribbean ports.

8

THE SINGLES SCENE

WITH THE NUMBER OF SINGLE TRAVELERS GROWING so rapidly, it was inevitable that enterprising folks would find ways to serve them. Club Med, the first to come up with a vacation formula where single people feel comfortable, now has plenty of company. Whether you want to find a traveling companion, a group tour, or a resort where singles meet and mingle, they are out there waiting for you. Let's look at some of the possibilities.

TRAVEL COMPANIONS

For many solo travelers, one of the happiest developments on the single scene is the appearance of "matchmakers," organizations dedicated to pairing travel-minded single people, allowing them to avoid the discriminatory supplement for singles and, hopefully, to meet new friends at the same time. These services flourish, as one brochure reminds, "because friends don't always want to go when or where you want to go, won't always care to spend the same money you spend."

THE TRAVEL COMPANION EXCHANGE (Box 833, Amityville, NY 11701; 516-454-0880), the largest matching organization, began in 1981. It has over 5,000 members across the United States and in Canada. Most are age 40 or over, but ages can range from 20 all the way to 85. The male/female ratio is almost even, the organization reports.

The Exchange works a bit like a dating service. Applicants fill out a profile form describing themselves and their travel interests, then place a "personal" ad in a newsletter that is circulated to all members, with a coded number for replies. Those who are interested in the ad can send for the longer profile, and, if the interest remains, can contact the person directly for a meeting before deciding to make travel plans. Even if the vibes are good, president Jens Jurgen recommends spending time together on a weekend or short trip before setting off on a long excursion.

While some members wish to be matched with members of their own sex, others are equally interested in meeting partners of the opposite sex, and Jurgen reports that more than one compatible traveling mate has turned into a lifetime companion. Here are samples of recent ads:

Ted: 41, 5'11", 175, SWM [single white male], NS [nonsmoker]. Quiet, practical professional w/sense of humor. Enjoy most fine arts, current events, good food, learning about other cultures. Seek MTC [male traveling companion] 20–70. Considering trip to Mideast or North Africa, but flexible. Home: So. California.

Marie: 32, 5'4", 140, SWF, NS. Banker. Easygoing, good sense of humor, well-traveled, love European sight-seeing, museums, castles, dining. Other int. tennis, reading, classical music, making new friends, weekend trips. Home: Philadelphia.

"L": 65, 5′10″, 148, DWM [divorced white male], NS. Enjoy tennis, reading, hiking. Seek F/MTC 40–70, college grad with enthusiasm for life. Good conversational skills a must. Pix. Home: Grosse Pointe, MI.

There is also a shorter listing for specific travel plans such as:

DWF, 45, NS. Seek MTC 50–65 to explore Spain/Portugal, rent condo and use as home base. No. California.

DWM, 51, NS. Seek M/FTC 25–45, NS, for Rome–Athens 2/88, 1 week Phoenix, 3/88, 3 weeks Europe 5/88. Budget travel. CT.

Other smaller matching services include:

TRAVEL MATES, INC., 49 W. 44th St., New York, NY 10036; 212-221-6565.

After members complete a profile form, the service culls its files and sends information about prospective companions who may be compatible. It is up to the member to make contact, arrange a meeting, and decide whether to plan a trip. A yearly membership fee includes one search. There is a minimal charge for additional searches. This company also plans singles tours and packages, so they hope newly matched partners will sign on. See page 180.

ODYSSEY NETWORK, c/o Charles River Travel Inc., 118 Cedar St., Wellesley, MA 02181; 617-237-2400.

Spawned by a 15-year-old travel agency with a female owner and staff, this 1988 network for women grew to 200 members in its first two months, and is increasing rapidly. Members pay annual dues and fill out a questionnaire on their travel preferences and budgets. Along with searching for compatible roommates for independent travel, the agency plans trips according to members' interests. Some early offerings: Soviet Union Sampler, an expedition to the Seas of Ulysses and the Black Sea, a shopping trip to Portugal and a trip to Canyon Ranch Spa. Age range of members is 20 to 85; most common range is 40 to 60.

SHARED ADVENTURES—A WOMAN'S TRAVEL NETWORK, Fairview Travel Service, Fairview Plaza, 420 W. 75th St., Downers Grove, IL 60516; 312-852-5533.

Once again a travel agency was the catalyst for a club to help women find compatible traveling companions. Founded in 1987, the group quickly gained more than 100 members, mostly from the Chicago area. As word spreads, the numbers are growing and the reach has spread from Florida to California. When members request travel partners, a "network alert" goes out in the form of postcards and direct calls to those who have already indicated interest in the destination. There is no fee to join, but the agency does expect to make the travel arrangements for those it pairs. All ages have enrolled; the majority are between 30 and 55.

TRAVEL PARTNERS CLUB, INC., 4146 N. Concord Dr., P.O. Box 2368, Crystal River, FL 32629; 904-795-1117.

No age limit, but mostly widows and widowers 50 plus. The club began in 1984 and has several hundred members in 50 states, according to the directors.

GOLDEN COMPANIONS, Box 754, Pullman, WA 99163; 208-883-5052.

A 500-member organization formed in 1987 to assist travelers ages 50 and up to find travel partners. Members pay annual dues, receive a bimonthly travel newsletter. They also list vacation home exchanges, and hold regional get-togethers.

SAGA HOLIDAYS CLUB, 120 Boylston St., Boston, MA 02116-9804; 1-800-441-6662.

Saga is a large tour organization for travelers over age 60. Those who pay the small fee to join the Holidays Club can use the member magazine *Connections* to run "want ads" for roommates or travel companions. Some areas also hold club meetings where you may find likely companions.

SINGLES TOURS

One way to assure meeting other single people is to sign up for a tour designed expressly for singles. There are such tours today for all ages, ranging from budget to deluxe. All of these groups will arrange for shares, usually at no charge, but unless noted all do have a surcharge if you request single occupancy. Here are some of the possibilities:

SINGLEWORLD, 401 Theodore Fremd Ave., Rye, NY 10580; 800-223-6490 or 914-967-3334. (M–E)

The oldest and largest organizer of tours for singles has been in business since 1957, and handles about 15,000 single travelers per year. It operates as a club, with a small annual membership fee, and offers trips in two categories: all-ages and under-35. Those traveling alone are guaranteed shared accommodations based on double, triple, or quad occupancy. They try to match according to age, gender, and smoking preference. If there is no roommate available, the share rate is guaranteed. Singleworld specializes in cruises, booking a variety of cruise lines and destinations. There are never guarantees about the male/female ratio (usually heavily female), or even the number of fellow passengers. The brochure warns that groups can range from 6 to 60, and reminds that this is "not a lonely hearts club . . . not a tour with equal numbers of men and women." Escorted trips include several European itineraries.

THE SINGLE GOURMET, 133 E. 58th St., New York, NY 10022; 212-980-8788. (EE)

This nationwide organization dedicated to good eating and sociability started in 1982, and now has chapters in a dozen U.S. locations and four Canadian cities, with over 2,500 members. Restaurant outings are arranged regularly in each city, and a few trips are offered to all members each year. The trips include a full sight-seeing agenda, but concentrate on dining, visiting the very top restaurants in each location. Lodgings are also deluxe. Recent trips included a long New Year's Eve weekend in Toronto, and a tour of Australia, New Zealand, and Fiji. Travelers are paired at no charge. Members may attend dinners in other member cities when they travel. The age range of the membership is from 20 to 60, with most age 40 or older. Women outnumber men 5 to 2. Many of the trip participants are from the Northeast, but there is a representation from all the chapters. Members say the trips are well run and sociable, and the days are flexible enough to allow for free time.

TRAVELING SINGLE STYLE, Travel Designs of Connecticut, Inc., 16 Squirrel Hill Rd., West Hartford, CT 06107; 203-521-4386. (M–E)

East Coast single vacationers from 30 to 60 are the most common participants in tours arranged by this nine-year-old organization. The majority are female and around age 40. Groups are quite small—averaging seven to ten. Recent destinations have included New Orleans, a Caribbean cruise, Spain, and England. A variety of activities is included, as on the England tour which featured London sightseeing, a literary outing to Oxford and Stratford, and a mystery weekend at a country manor house. Shares are arranged and the double rate guaranteed whenever possible. Participants say the programs are very well managed with good accommodations, enough time on your own, and a nicely balanced itinerary.

TRAVEL MATES, INC., 49 W. 44th St., New York, NY 10036; 212-221-6565. (M–E)

For almost 50 years, this Manhattan organization has planned singles trips for all ages to Europe, the Caribbean, the West Coast, and Mexico. Their roommate-matching service makes it easy to find traveling companions. Most (though not all) participants are from the New York metropolitan area. There are many weekend offerings for New York area singles ages 28 to 45 or 40 plus as well, to Catskills resorts, and other destinations such as Vermont, Lake George, and Quebec City.

AMERICAN JEWISH CONGRESS, 15 E. 84th St., New York, NY 10028; 800-221-4694 or 212-879-4500. (M–E)

This highly respected cultural organization offers 2-week vacation tours of Israel for singles in three age categories, under 40, ages 39 to 55, and over 55, as well as a few tours to Europe and the Orient for singles under 45. They will also attempt to match roommates on the rest of their extensive travel program which covers most of the world. Participants say the groups are large, so you don't get to know everyone, but you do get to know the people on your tour bus. As is usual on tours, women outnumber the men. There is little "singles" pressure. These are mostly professional people with similar interests who simply prefer to travel with people their own age. The trips to Israel get high recommendations; guides are said to be excellent.

GRAND CIRCLE TRAVEL, 347 Congress St., Boston, MA 02210; 800-221-2610 or 617-350-7500. (M–E)

Special singles departure dates for escorted tours to Europe, China, and the Orient for travelers over age 50, "offering both independence and companionship with peers," are offered by this 30-year-old travel company. They also report 54 percent single registration on their regular tours. Many participants are females who have been widowed, says a company representative.

SAGA INTERNATIONAL HOLIDAYS, 120 Boylston, St., Boston, MA 02116-9804; 1-800-343-0273. (M–E, includes transportation)

A selection of singles-only departures for travelers over age 60 is included in the extensive itinerary of this long-established travel group. (See more information on Saga tours on pages 177 and 141 to 142.)

TOURS WITH MANY SINGLE PARTICIPANTS

The following tours are not limited to single travelers, but at least half of their participants are single. They are listed from youngest to oldest age groups.

CONTIKI HOLIDAYS, 1432 E. Katella Ave., Anaheim, CA 92805; 800-626-0611; in California, 800-624-0611 or 714-937-0611. (I)

For 27 years, Contiki has served adventure-minded passengers ages 18 to 35 with trips to Europe, Australia and New Zealand, the continental United States and Hawaii. Most participants are in their 20s; 70 percent are single, and they come from English-speaking countries all over the world. The average male/female ratio is 40/60, but according to one insider, males outnumber females on most U.S. and South Pacific tours, while European trips tend to be more heavily female. The trips are by motor coach; U.S. accommodations are in hotels, motels, and cabins; European lodgings may be in hotels as well as French châteaus and 13th-century Italian villas, or aboard Greek island schooners. Some trips include cruises. For budget travelers, there are camping tours and Contiki Villages of cabins or frame tents already set up at selected campsites. Participants may also stay at Club Contiki facilities on Corfu in the Greek Isles or in the Austrian Tyrol to relax and enjoy sports facilities. Travelers are paired whenever possible, but there is no single supplement regardless. Said one young woman recently returned from her first trip to Europe: "I can't think of a better way to go."

STUDENT TRAVEL INTERNATIONAL, 8619 Reseda Blvd., Suite 103, Northridge, CA 91324; 800-225-2780 or in California, 818-637-7687. (I)

An eight-year-old organization with tour packages to Europe, Australia, China, and Mexico, the group serves some 3,000 travelers annually, ages 18 to 30, with the most common age range between 20 and 24. Most of the travelers are from California, the Northeast, Florida, and Texas. Ninety percent are single and 60 percent are female. Motor coach groups average about 40 people. The first-class programs stay in better hotels; supersaver trips use budget hotels but always with private baths. Singles are placed in double, triple, or quad rooms, depending on availability.

AMERICAN YOUTH HOSTELS, INC., P.O. Box 37613, Washington, D.C. 20013-7613; 202-783-6161. (I)

AYH and its affiliate, International Youth Hostel Federation, are nonprofit organizations supported by membership dues, tour fees, and tax-deductible contributions. They are pioneers in low-cost travel, and their modest annual dues entitle members to a wide variety of trips. The adult category ranges from ages 18 to 54; several trips are divided into age groups. Accommodations are mostly in hostels, spartan dormitory-style lodgings with separate bed and bath facilities for men and women. The tours range from bicycle and hiking jaunts to motor trips and adventure outings. They also are included under these categories in the book.

TRADEWIND TRAVELLERS CLUB, 40 E. 49th St., Suite 1602, New York, NY 10017; 800-223-0567 or 212-832-9072. (I)

A newcomer to the budget travel field, this club offers low-cost camping tours of Europe for two age groups: 18 to 30 and 30 plus. Trips are from Amsterdam, and run for 2, 3, or 4 weeks; fees include tents in campgrounds near major European cities. Participants spend 2 or 3 days in each location. They may prepare their own food or eat at local restaurants.

CLUB 21-35, Trafalgar Tours, 21 East 26th Street, New York, NY 10010; 800-854-0103 or 212-689-8977. (I)

"Fast-paced coach tours through Europe for younger travelers who want to see as much as possible on a budget," say the managers of this program, which has offices in Canada and New Zealand, providing an international mix to the group. Itineraries range from a 12-day "Sights of Europe" to a 24-day "Southern Globetrotter." The male-female ratio is close to even.

50 PLUS CLUB, A.J.S. Travel Consultants, Inc., 177 Beach 116th St., Rockaway Park, NY 11694; 800-221-5002 outside New York or 718-945-5900. (I–M)

Some 70 percent of the travelers on A.J.S. tours are single people over age 50, with the average age of travelers 60 and up. Small group trips of 10 to 15 people are offered to Israel, Switzerland, and northern Italy. Past participants report that the guides are excellent, itineraries well designed to give lots of time in one location, thus avoiding constant packing and unpacking, and that along with sight-seeing there are nice surprises, such as picnics beside scenic lakes.

RESORTS RECOMMENDED FOR SINGLES

CLUB MED

Club Med is the place where swinging young singles go for wild partying, right? When the first North American club was born in Guadeloupe in 1967, that image might have been accurate, but well over two decades later, it is strictly out-of-date. Club Med's original guests have grown up and so has the club. Listen to today's statistics for the North American membership:

- 50 percent of Club Med members are married.
- 40 percent have children.

- 8 percent *are* children.
- 75 percent of the membership is between the ages of 25 and 44.
- Median age is 35.
- 68 percent hold professional or managerial positions.
- Median income is $60,000.

Does that mean Club Med is no longer a good choice for young vacationers? Not at all. Singles still make up half the membership, and many of them welcome the fact that the social pressure at most clubs is less than it used to be. If anything, Club Med now holds more appeal for more people. Those who knew the Club Meds of old will be pleasantly surprised at new and remodeled clubs with larger rooms—some even with carpeting and air-conditioning—and a variety of small dining rooms offering a choice of cuisine. Several clubs now have fitness centers with exercise equipment. And you can learn anything from scuba diving and windsurfing to tennis and skiing, to walking a trapeze. Instruction is usually included in one all-inclusive price, along with three meals a day and wine or beer for lunch and dinner.

Lately, the club has relaxed its rules about 7-day stays in some cases, allowing guests to come for weekends or extend their visits, and while it is still more usual for everyone to have a roommate assigned, at certain clubs during certain times of year, you can request a single room for a surcharge. Because Club Med is such a well-known choice for single vacationers, it deserves special space and description, pro and con.

LIFE AT CLUB MED

Life at Club Med villages is meant to be carefree. There's no cash to worry about—it goes into the safe and you pay for everything with poppit beads bought when you arrive. Nor are there room keys or clocks, though old hands know to bring a watch, because lessons are scheduled and if you don't get there on time, you'll miss out. While rooms are improving, they are still spartan compared to those in a resort hotel.

With the many activities offered, days tend to be busy. Meals are plentiful. How's the food? One guest put it aptly, "Not so good—and not so bad." Some of the newer clubs are said to be better. Breakfast and lunch are buffet style, and the rush to the dining room at lunchtime resembles an athletic competition. Dinner is more orderly. Single diners usually start out in the main dining room where you are seated at tables for eight by the hostess, making it very easy to meet people. If you make friends, you can make reservations for the smaller and calmer dining rooms. And therein lies the greatest appeal of Club Med. Here's a warm-weather vacation where you can be absolutely comfortable alone, and always be sure of plenty of company at mealtime.

But Club Med is not for everyone. The locations are isolated, and you won't see much of the place you are visiting unless you sign up for extra tours. If you hated summer camp, and you are not turned on by the idea of group lessons, sign-up sheets, "Crazy Signs" songs with hand motions, or a "color war" between guests, you may not be Club Med material. In fairness, no one forces you to do anything—you can stay under a palm tree with a book, if you like—but you can't always avoid the distraction of all the activity around you, or the sound of the French accent on the loudspeaker announcing things like "See-lee games at the pool."

The voice belongs to a G.O. (*gentil organisateur*), one of the bouncy, good-looking young men and women who do everything they can to make their enthusiasm contagious to their flock of G.M.'s (*gentils membres*). The G.O.s work hard, giving sports instruction, being sociable, and putting on the amateur entertainment after dinner each night—tricky stuff like dressing up in silly costumes and mouthing words to a record. Sophisticated? Hardly. Some people absolutely love the G.O.s, others think they are a nuisance. You'll have to judge for yourself.

After the show, the disco opens and dancing goes on well into the night.

CHOOSING A CLUB

If you decide to give Club Med a try and look at their big catalog, it's difficult making a choice. A recent count tallied 110 villages in 33 countries. All of the properties look tempting, because two of the club's main attractions are great locations and interesting architecture. Among the newcomers are Huatulco in Mexico and a ski village near Sapporo in Japan.

Multimillions of dollars' worth of major renovations recently have transformed some of the older clubs such as Playa Blanca, Paradise Island, Caravelle, and Punta Cana. Old hands suggest that you wait a year before visiting a new location, to allow time for the staff to settle in and work out any problems, but all of these should be running smoothly by the time you read this.

Some recent additions to the Club Med agenda may help determine your choice. Certain locations offer more sight-seeing excursions. A combined package with Walt Disney World is available in Florida; small villas have been built at areas such as the Mayan ruins in Mexico; and the world's largest sailing vessel, a 610-foot sloop, offers cruises in the Caribbean.

So which Club Med is for you? Getting the "inside scoop" on the ambience at the various clubs from former guests proved difficult, because so many varying reports came in on the same club. What you find depends entirely on the makeup of the guests, which changes from one week to the next. So here are a few generalizations taken from former visitors—but to be taken as guide only, not as gospel. The week you choose may have an entirely different crowd.

- Bermuda's club tends to attract more couples, a slightly older and more conservative group.
- Ixtapa, said to be a terrific club, is on a beautiful unspoiled part of the west coast of Mexico. There are many couples. Here and elsewhere, golf seems to attract an older group.
- All the clubs on Mexico's Pacific coast enjoy almost guaranteed good weather most of the year.
- Paradise Island gets a sports-minded younger crowd and lots of singles.
- While guests come from all over, the majority choose a nearby location. There usually are more guests from the East Coast in the Caribbean and Bahamas, more from the West in Mexico.
- Turkoise (Turks and Caicos) has beautiful facilities, gets an older crowd in winter, a young, heavy-drinking group in summer.

- Guadelupe in the French Caribbean has an outstanding beach.
- Guaymas in northern Mexico can have unpleasant winter weather.
- Guaymas gets many younger singles, but Buccaneer's Creek (Martinique) is the youngest, wildest, and most hard-drinking of all the clubs, the one place said to still fit the old swinging image of Club Med.
- Huatulco is said to be the most magnificent club yet.
- Mooréa (Tahiti) and Marrakesh (Morocco) are the most popular foreign destinations with Americans. The Marrakesh location just outside the major souk (marketplace) allows for getting the real flavor of the country—but bring your French dictionary.
- School vacation weeks are not the best choices for singles, since they are overweighted with families.

One final bit of advice—don't choose a club that requires complicated travel such as plane changes or long bus rides. The journeys are tiring and use up valuable vacation time. Ask about connections in advance.

PICKING YOUR SPORT

If you have a particular sport or activity in mind, a more reliable guide is to look for the Club Med villages that make it a specialty. Here are some possibilities:

SCUBA DIVING: Turkoise (Turks and Caicos) and Sonora Bay (Mexico) are the places to go if you are new to the sport and want certification. Other villages with scuba programs include Buccaneer's Creek (Martinique), Eleuthera (Bahamas), Mooréa (Tahiti), Cancun (Mexico), and Maldives (Indian Ocean).

GOLF: Bermuda, Sandpiper (Florida), Caravelle (Guadelupe), Paradise Island (Bahamas), Eleuthera (Bahamas), Sonora Bay, Ixtapa (Mexico).

TENNIS: Sonora Bay, Paradise Island.

HORSEBACK RIDING: St. Lucia (Caribbean), Sonora Bay, Playa Blanca (Mexico).

FITNESS CENTERS: Sandpiper, Bermuda, Turkoise, St. Lucia, Buccaneer's Creek, Huatulco, Sonora Bay, Cancun.

CIRCUS WORKSHOPS: Turkoise, Punta Cana (Dominican Republic), Eleuthera, Playa Blanca.
WINDSURFING: St. Lucia, Sonora Bay.
SKIING: Copper Mountain (Colorado), plus ski villages in France, Switzerland, and Japan.

If you don't want kids around, or want to better your chances of finding more single adults, you'll find no one under the age of 12 at Turkoise, Cancun, or Paradise Island, and nobody under 18 at Buccaneer's Creek or Playa Blanca.

Mostly, you take your chances when you choose a Club Med location, simply hoping to find congenial friends—and judging from the enormous number of people who return, the chances are good. The club reports that more than 40 percent of their guests are repeaters and 70 percent have come on the recommendations of their friends.

To enroll in any Club Med, you must pay a one-time initiation fee and there is an annual fee thereafter. The travel sections of major newspapers frequently carry ads from tour operators who buy space in bulk and promise discounts on rates, so check before you reserve.

For more information and a catalog, contact any travel agent or Club Med direct at 800-CLUB MED.

SUPERCLUBS: HEDONISM II AND JAMAICA, JAMAICA

Beautifully located in Negril, Jamaica, along a 7-mile strip of beach, Hedonism II lures many singles with attractions similar to those offered by Club Med—rates that include all meals plus tennis, sailing, waterskiing, windsurfing, volleyball, a Nautilus gym, squash, snorkeling, scuba diving, bicycling, horseback riding, aerobics, and arts and crafts classes. In addition, they offer an open bar all day and night, and better nighttime entertainment, including top local bands and performers. Unlike Club Meds, the club is not isolated. The beach is shared by several hotels, and you can take a walk into town to sample the local nightlife as well.

Hedonism's unique lure is the freewheeling Jamaican spirit and contagious reggae beat that permeate the island. "Let's party" is the motto, right from the rum punch you are handed as you arrive. All this attracts a young crowd, averaging between 21 and 35, and about 65 percent single. There is a nude beach and a "prude" beach. One observer noted with surprise that it was the young who tended to be covered; older guests, who ranged into their 60s, seemed to be on the nude beach, unconcerned with appearances.

Much of the food is grown locally, and menus feature a lot of native fruits and vegetables. All-you-can-eat meals include grilled lobster; some who have visited both resorts say the food here is better than at Club Med.

The same owners operate Jamaica, Jamaica, a resort on Runaway Bay, near Ocho Rios, another all-inclusive resort with a slightly more sophisticated ambience. Though the single population may often be as high as 50 percent, there are more couples here. Tennis clinics are a resort specialty. For more information, contact International Lifestyles, 800-858-8009 or 516-868-6924.

The single scene offers many options, but not every single traveler wants or needs to be limited to a group or a resort vacation. For many, a more rewarding adventure is independent travel, the topic of the chapter ahead.

9

TRAVEL ON YOUR OWN

GROUP VACATIONS MAY PROVIDE WONDERFUL companionship, but many independent souls prefer to set their own pace and schedule. If you've always wanted to see the Statue of Liberty or the Eiffel Tower or the Duomo in Florence, there's no reason why you cannot blaze your own path, design your own dream trip, and happily do and see exactly what you please. One of the special privileges of solo travel is that you can tailor a trip to your own special likes and dislikes. Sleep as late as you please. If you love antiques or book shops or offbeat museums away from the main tourist track, you can indulge to your heart's content. If you hate cathedrals, you need see nary a one! Or you can zip in and out in 5 minutes instead of having to listen to a 45-minute spiel.

It will take more planning to go your own way, yes—but often that very planning is a large part of the fun of travel. Pretrip research is the best way to start learning about your destination. And the more you know, the more you will get out of your trip.

What are the best destinations for a first trip on your own? Whenever anyone asks me that question, my answer is, "Head for a city." Every great city has its own intriguing rhythms and personality, and often you can actually sense these best when you are alone, when you have no distractions and plenty of time to stroll, eyes wide open and antennae turned on high. Staying in one place also gives you a chance to get your bearings and begin to feel confident about getting around.

The best time to plan a city trip alone is during warm weather, when sociable outdoor cafés are in high gear. But, if you can avoid it, never travel alone during the peak vacation season in July and August. Hotels and restaurants are least happy to see single guests during these months when they are most crowded. Late May, June, September, and early October are the ideal times to enjoy good weather without meeting up with hordes of tourists.

Pick your city carefully. Choose one with a vital center and plenty of intriguing neighborhoods that can be explored on foot, plus an efficient and inexpensive public transportation system to get you from one place to another so that you won't need a car. Cities fitting this description usually meet another important criterion that makes for easier travel on your own—they have large single populations and an abundance of informal neighborhood restaurants to serve them. These restaurants are ideal for single visitors.

Among the cities in the United States that meet these qualifications well are Boston, New York, Philadelphia, Chicago, Seattle, and San Francisco. The best bets in Canada are Montreal, Toronto, and Vancouver. Almost any major city in Europe is a likely candidate, though places where English is spoken are probably the best choices for a first foreign venture. This doesn't mean you must limit yourself to London, wonderful city though it is. Think also of Dublin or Edinburgh, where English comes with a delightful brogue, Amsterdam, where the multilingual Dutch will welcome you in your own tongue, or cities in Scandinavia, where English is the second language. I'll zero in on four of my favorite cities shortly, but first let me share some techniques that work for me when I get ready to visit any new town.

SIZING UP A CITY

If you allow yourself to arrive alone in a new city without specific plans, you can feel lost and confused. To feel in control, your days should be mapped in advance. Start at home by contacting the local tourist office for information and city street and transit maps. Next, get the best guidebooks you can find as well as a copy of the city's local magazine. If you don't have access to a newsstand that sells out-of-town publications, get the address and phone number of the magazine from the tourist office and order a copy by mail. If your community does not have a good travel bookstore, order by mail from those in the resource list on page 269.

When you have assembled your materials, read the brochures and books to learn about the character of the city and its special attractions for tourists. Use the magazine to find out what the people who live there are doing and where they are going right now.

Using both sources, make a list of places you most want to see, and circle them on the street map. Though it is hard to get an accurate sense of scale from a map of a strange city, you can easily see which attractions are close together and plot your days accordingly, grouping places in the same general geographic area. Check the transit map against the street map to see which attractions can be reached by bus or tram or subway and in which order to see them makes the most sense.

Now make a tentative day-by-day schedule of what you hope to do and see, ranking the sights each day from most to least important. That way, if something proves fascinating, you can find extra time by dropping the least important items on the agenda. If a top choice turns out to be a disappointment, you have plenty of options to fill your time.

In a brand-new big city, I always fill part of the first day with the local sight-seeing tour. This gives you a quick sense of where things are actually located, and often takes in inconvenient sites that you may not get back to easily on your own. Sometimes when I actually get a look at a place that sounded wonderful in the guidebooks, I realize it is not so great in reality, and I strike a further visit off my list.

I also like to leave time for guided walking tours in interesting or historic areas of the city. Walking tours are made up of fewer people than bus tours and are far more personal and interesting; and they are also a perfect way to meet people. In foreign cities walking tours with English-speaking guides are the best way to seek out fellow travelers as well as a welcome respite from struggling to speak the language. And, with a really knowledgeable local guide, you'll get colorful inside information that isn't found in any book. The best current walking tours aren't always listed in guidebooks, but they are usually included in city magazines. Or you can check with your hotel or the local tourist office after you arrive.

Schedule plenty of time just to wander when you explore a new city. As long as you stay in safe neighborhoods, don't worry about getting lost. Some of the best discoveries may lie on little side streets that don't show on the map. Even in a foreign city, if you write down the name of your hotel and mark it clearly on the map, you will be able to get directions or find a cab when you want to return.

When you go exploring, you might just pretend that you are a travel writer who will want to bring the place alive for your readers. Take your time, look closely, window-shop, talk to people, ask questions, take mental notes or make written ones, make lists of the unusual shops and galleries you pass, take photos, and keep a nightly journal of your impressions. A journal is fun—it keeps you company—and it will vividly bring back the pleasures of your trip every time you open the pages back home.

How much time you allot to shopping beyond souvenirs for friends and family depends on your own disposition. If you are like me and seldom find time for relaxed shopping at home, an afternoon to yourself for browsing stores in a new city is a treat and a great luxury. And when I buy clothing or unique local handcrafts on a trip, they come with a bonus of happy memories. Some of my favorite souvenirs have been paintings or posters purchased on my travels. Looking for them invariably means talking to people and learning a lot about the local art scene.

CHOOSING A PLACE TO STAY

The circles you've marked on a city street map will help you choose the most convenient area for your lodging. There are a few ways to go when you are alone, the choices dictated by budget and personal preference—and whether you are in the United States or abroad.

U.S. LODGINGS

If you can afford the splurge, it's a special pleasure to stay at a top hotel when you are traveling alone. Being surrounded by luxury is even more of a treat when you are by yourself, and the better hotels offer an important practical advantage as well: the concierge.

Now found widely in hotels in the United States as well as Europe, the concierge is there purely and simply to make your stay pleasanter. Besides taking care of all your transportation and ticket arrangements, a good concierge should know the city inside out—the best places to shop, the best ways to sightsee, *and* the best places for single diners to feel comfortable. Well-connected concierges provide a lot of business to the city's restaurants, and when they phone in a reservation and say a good word, you can be sure that you won't be shunted to a cramped corner or ignored by your waiter. A good way to determine the quality of the concierge service is to find out whether the head concierge wears the golden keys of Le Clé d'or, the prestigious international concierge association.

At the other end of the scale, the small, charming budget hotels available in Europe just don't exist in the United States. Our budget lodgings in cities are at best impersonal and at worst dreary. Luckily, now that the bed-and-breakfast craze has moved into big American cities, there is a cheerier choice when funds are limited. A bed-and-breakfast apartment or a home in a pleasant neighborhood provides an insider's advice on the city from your host, plus someone to talk to at breakfast and when you get home at night. You get a better sense of the real life of the city away from the business district. Dining is almost always more reasonable in the neighborhoods than in the business center of town—and if you have fellow-lodgers, you may even wind up with company for dinner.

Bed-and-breakfast reservations can be made through services that handle a large number of locations in each city. You'll find a sampling of these services on pages 195 to 196, and there are plenty of books with further suggestions. Lodgings vary from lavish to modest, with either private or shared baths. Be very specific about your wants when you make your reservation. Most of all, be sure the location is convenient to public transportation. If you think there may be times when you will be coming back to your lodging late at night, find out whether cabs are readily available from midtown and the approximate fare to your destination.

Another plus for bed-and-breakfast accommodations is that, unlike hotels, they often give a generous rate break to single travelers. It isn't that hotels don't like to accept singles, but the overwhelming majority of their rooms are designed for two people, and they seem to feel it is not good business to lose the extra revenue. That means one guest pays almost at the same rate as two.

When you do get a single room in a hotel, it may be the smallest and least attractive in the place. Don't be afraid to speak up and ask for a better one.

The single supplement remains the biggest gripe of solo travelers, so perhaps if enough people write to complain, some savvy hotels will begin to change this discriminatory policy.

While they may not have done much about improving their single rates, a number of U.S. hotels have begun offering a few services for their guests who are traveling alone. These amenities are aimed at attracting business travelers, but they are equally welcome to vacationers. One innovation commonly available in large chain hotels (even at some big-city Holiday Inns) is a special "executive floor" where continental breakfasts and complimentary cocktails are served in a special lounge. You pay extra for a room on this floor, but the lounge is a very easy setting for finding company, and the complimentary breakfast is pleasant and a money-saver. Executive floors also tend to provide extra security, with concierges on duty and special elevator keys.

Compri Hotels, a relatively new chain, has designed sociable "club" facilities to serve all their guests. Each club is equipped with lounge chairs, a bar, a library stocked with books and periodicals, work desks, and a large-screen television set. They are very comfortable places for single guests to relax. Compri and Embassy Suites are also among a number of lodgings that have instituted free breakfasts for all guests, once again in sociable settings.

Selected Marriott, Four Seasons, and other hotels are also experimenting with a dining option known as the "captain's table" or the "networking table" where single diners can get together. A Marriott in Fort Lauderdale recently took another approach, setting up a section of the dining room with tables specially set for one, complete with brass reading lamps and a selection of reading materials. Because these dining innovations are the projects of individual hotels rather than uniform throughout the chains, it is not easy knowing where you will find them, but it is certainly worth having your travel agent do some checking or making some phone calls on your own. Where they exist, they are a pleasant plus.

Don't forget that if you work for a company that gets special corporate rates at hotel chains, those same rates are available to you if you show your company identification.

U.S. BIG-CITY BED-AND-BREAKFAST REGISTRIES

NEW YORK

CITY LIGHTS B & B LTD., P.O. Box 20355, Cherokee Station, New York, NY 10028; 212-737-7049.

URBAN VENTURES, P.O. Box 426, New York, NY 10024; 212-594-5650.

NEW WORLD BED & BREAKFAST LTD., 150 Fifth Ave., Suite 711, New York, NY 10011; 212-675-5600.

BED & BREAKFAST (& BOOKS), 325 West 92d St., New York, NY 10025; 212-865-8740.

BOSTON

BED & BREAKFAST ASSOCIATES, BAY COLONY LIMITED, P.O. Box 166, Babson Park, Boston, MA 02157; 617-449-5302.

BED & BREAKFAST, BROOKLINE/BOSTON, Box 732, Brookline, MA 02146; 617-277-2292.

GREATER BOSTON HOSPITALITY, P.O. Box 1142, Brookline, MA 02146; 617-277-5430.

HOST HOMES OF BOSTON, P.O. Box 117, Newton, MA 02168; 617-244-1308.

CHICAGO

BED & BREAKFAST, CHICAGO, P.O. Box 14088, Chicago, IL 60614-0088; 312-951-0085.

WASHINGTON, D.C.

BED & BREAKFAST LEAGUE, LTD., 3639 Van Ness St. NW, Washington, D.C. 20008; 202-363-7767.

BED 'N BREAKFAST, LTD., P.O. Box 12011, Washington, D.C. 20005; 202-328-3510.

PHILADELPHIA

BED AND BREAKFAST OF PHILADELPHIA, P.O. Box 630, Chester Springs, PA 19425; 215-735-1137.

BED AND BREAKFAST, CENTER CITY, 1804 Pine St., Philadelphia, PA 19103; 215-735-1137.

SAN FRANCISCO

AMERICAN FAMILY INN/BED & BREAKFAST SAN FRANCISCO, P.O. Box 349, San Francisco, CA 94101; 415-931-3083.

EUROPEAN ACCOMMODATIONS

Bed-and-breakfast homes have long been available in Europe, but, unlike in the United States, there's also a far better chance of finding small and reasonable hotels in European cities that have local character and at least a modicum of charm. Also, in a city where I don't speak the language, I feel more secure staying in a centrally located hotel. Most tourist offices, as well as many guidebooks, offer listings of both small hotels and bed-and-breakfast associations.

By choosing smaller accommodations, you can hold down the cost of traveling on your own. But if you go this route, you may have to do it yourself by mail or phone. Travel agents are business people, after all, and these time-consuming reservations usually pay no commission. It's a simple matter to make your own arrangements, but allow plenty of time for mail to make its way across the ocean.

If you are willing to make a move after you arrive, you can try another technique. Make a hotel reservation for the first night or two, and then take a morning to check out a list of small, less-expensive hotels in person, reserving your favorite for the rest of your stay. If you find that you have booked a hotel that is disappointing, do the same—pay for the first night and look for a pleasanter alternative. Having the option to look around for lodgings is another reason to avoid traveling during busy peak seasons.

When you are hotel-shopping, don't hesitate to ask to see rooms—or ask if there is anything less expensive available. Contrary to what many people think, room prices are often negotiable if the hotel is not filled.

TRAVEL ARRANGEMENTS

SAVING ON AIRFARE

If you are making your own travel arrangements, one way to save on transportation costs is to investigate some of the consolidators who offer bargain airfares. You'll see ads from these companies in almost any big-city newspaper listing fares to major cities that are far below the going official rate. How do they do it? They buy blocks of seats—

mostly on international routes—that the airlines do not expect to be able to sell themselves. Some may specialize in specific regions such as Hawaii or the Orient, others sell only to travel agents. But many do offer flights to the public, as well. Rates and dates vary from one firm to another, so comparison shopping is essential.

There can be drawbacks to dealing with a consolidator. It is more difficult to get a refund and you may not be transferred to another carrier in case of cancellation or delay of a flight. And you may have to juggle your dates to coincide with the flights that are available.

Consolidators are not recommended for the inexperienced traveler who might panic if complications arise, but for those who feel confident about coping in case of emergencies, consolidators do offer flights on regular scheduled airlines at a very substantial saving.

Dealing with a reputable company is important. Two large consolidators who come well recommended are:

ACCESS INTERNATIONAL, 250 E. 57th St., Suite 511, New York, NY 10107; 800-333-7280 or 212-333-7280.

TFI TOURS, 34 W. 32d St., New York, NY 10001; 800-TAKE TFI or 212-736-1140.

Remember also that many tour operators offer independent tours that do not involve traveling with others. They simply give you the benefit of a group rate for airfare and hotels, and sometimes a free sight-seeing tour. The hotels tend to be commercial, but you may want to compare these group rates with those you are quoted on your own.

FARTHER AFIELD

Once you feel confident staying in a new city, you may well want to take in some of the scenic countryside and perhaps visit nearby towns as well. Having done a lot of driving, my best advice for stress-free sight-seeing is: *Don't* drive. Instead, take a short sight-seeing tour or take a train. Long periods alone in a car can be lonely. Reading maps and watching for signs alone is nerve-wracking, and finding your way in a strange city can be a nightmare. The only way I ever found my hotel in Dublin was to pull up to another hotel and hire a taxi to lead me!

Trains, on the other hand, are a pleasure, a way to relax and see the sights and to arrive at a central location where both taxis and public transportation are usually available. There are no guarantees, but trains can sometimes be a way to meet people, as well.

TRAIN TRAVEL IN EUROPE

European trains are a pleasant surprise for first-time American travelers. They are fast, comfortable, run frequently, and are almost always on time.

The Eurailpass is one of Europe's best buys. For a specified period, it allows from 15 days to 3 months of unlimited first-class travel on speedy trains that go almost everywhere in 17 countries. Since distances are small and trains run often, you can cover a lot of ground in a short time.

If you want to base yourself in cities and do day or overnight trips, the Eurail Flexipass is ideal, allowing 9 days of first-class travel within a 21-day period. For those under age 26, the Eurail Youthpass offers economy second-class travel. But there is nothing second class about those second-class seats—they are perfectly comfortable and recommended for anyone who wants to save a bit on travel.

You can adapt a train trip to almost any kind of European itinerary. I had a wonderful journey recently, seeing Swiss mountain villages on day trips from Lausanne, then whizzing to Paris in 3½ hours on the TGV, the amazing high-speed superliner. After several days in Paris, a 1½-hour train ride took me to Blois, which became my home base for an excursion into the Loire Valley château country. I didn't need a car in Blois—there were daily bus excursions to the great châteaus of Chambord, Chenonceau, and Amboise, and Blois itself was a charming medieval town with its own famous château within walking distance of my hotel.

Stays in the countryside are also a way to ease your budget, since hotels and restaurants are far less expensive than those in big cities. In Blois I stayed at the L'Horset La Valliere, a stylish, modern 3-star hotel where three-course gourmet dinners were half the price of comparable services in Paris.

Each European country has its own national railroad featuring special money-saving passes, which you can learn about from the local tourist office. Because trains in Europe run more frequently than they do in the United States, it is possible to tour short distances with almost as much flexibility as you would by car, and train stations are often ideally located for sight-seeing in the old parts of the cities.

My first European travel on my own was a 1-week low-budget train trip through Holland, a compact country that is ideal if you want to see a lot in a short time. I used a suitcase small enough to fit into station lockers, and traveled much the way I might have by car. Fifteen minutes out of Amsterdam, I got off the train, checked my bag, and spent a few hours in the charming little town of Haarlem, walking the old square and visiting the Franz Hals Museum. (Finding your way is a cinch in Holland, since the VVV, the local information office near each train station, provides walking maps and has an English-speaking staff.)

After lunch in the square, I reboarded the train for the old university town of Leiden, another short ride away, where I did more browsing. Later, I headed for The Hague for a couple of days. From there, day trips by train took me to Delft, Gouda, and Rotterdam, and a trolley ride brought me to the seaside resort of Scheveningen. The entire journey was cheap and easy and I never felt nervous for a minute.

There are also famous scenic tours to be taken by train. The Bernina Express and the Golden Pass Route in Switzerland, the Bergen Express in Norway, and Loisirail in France follow magnificent routes that you can sit back and enjoy from your picture window. Most long-distance trains have either a dining car or will serve meals at your seat. And you can reserve a sleeper—your own little bedroom—and use the train as your hotel, making the most of your travel time.

You'll find that train travel is not intimidating in most foreign countries. Signs in stations are easy to read, since there are pictures pointing out lockers and checkrooms. Reservations offices are marked with a big *R* and information offices with a big *I*. In larger cities there is always someone in either of those offices who speaks English. The trains and their tracks and departure times are clearly listed on big boards. In countries where you can't understand loudspeaker announcements, you need only to spot the track number, line up at the right place, and you'll know when to board when you see the crowd starting to move.

With most major trains, it's hard to make a mistake, since the side of each car bears an identification panel showing the name of the city where the train originated, the final destination, and the major stops in between. Trains sometimes switch cars en route so always check the destination on your car. First- and second-class cars are identified with large numbers, and a smaller number clearly identifies the cars with reserved seats.

A few tips about European train travel:

- Most trains can be boarded without reservations, but the TGV and certain other special trains do require advance seating. These are clearly marked with an *R* on Eurail timetables so be sure to check.
- Porters may not turn up when you need them, but many stations have an ample supply of luggage carts. It takes exact change to get one, however, so find out in advance what coins are required and have them ready.
- Some European cities have more than one train station. Paris, for example, has six. Be sure to find out from which station your train is leaving.
- Avoid travel on Friday and Sunday afternoons when weekending Europeans jam trains.

For more information on train travel and reservations, see a travel agent or write to Eurailpass, Box 325, Old Greenwich, CT 06870-0325.

AMERICA'S AMTRAK

Amtrak is an underrated resource for people traveling alone in the United States, particularly on the eastern corridor. Boston, New York, Wilmington, Philadelphia, Baltimore, Washington, Fredericksburg, and Richmond are a straight run from conveniently located midtown stations and the trains run often. Getting to and from the stations is much easier than the hassle of traveling to the various airports, the train seats are wide and comfortable, and you can walk to the club car for refreshments if you get restless. Amtrak also offers its own tour packages using local hotels. So if an eastern U.S. tour is on your agenda, consider doing it by rail.

MEETING LOCAL PEOPLE ABROAD

Spending time in a new country is always far more meaningful if you are able to meet and really talk to the people. When you are traveling alone, the chance to visit with local residents is doubly welcome. A few organizations help make such visits possible.

U.S. SERVAS COMMITTEE, INC., 11 John St., New York, NY 10038; 212-267-0252.

This is a nonprofit, interracial, and interfaith group affiliated with the United Nations as a nongovernmental organization. Its purpose is to promote peace through person-to-person understanding and friendship, which they do by opening doors for travelers to "homes and hearts" in over 100 countries.

Servas maintains a roster of approved hosts abroad and throughout the United States, who welcome foreign visitors for a stay, usually for 2 nights; no money is exchanged. To apply for membership, each applicant fills out a detailed form, which subsequently serves as a letter of introduction to hosts. This form must be submitted with two letters of recommendation. A personal interview by a volunteer is required before a new applicant is accepted for the program. If approved, members pay an annual fee plus a refundable deposit for host directories in specific countries. Travelers then write or phone these hosts to ask for hospitality, giving each reasonable notice.

Members are asked to learn as much as possible in advance about the customs and cultures of the places they plan to visit. They are also requested not to stay only in major cities since hosts in suburbs and smaller communities often have more time to welcome visitors. The purpose of visiting is to share yourself, your country, and your interests, and travelers are urged to be respectful of their hosts' values and customs. When the program works well, lifelong friendships can be formed, and many hosts eventually visit former guests.

FRIENDS OVERSEAS, 68-04 Dartmouth St., Forest Hills, NY 11375; 718-544-5660 (please phone after 5 P.M. Eastern Time).

Scandinavian visitors can contact this organization which arranges contacts between Americans and residents of Oslo, Copenhagen, and Stockholm. Members receive the names and addresses of Scandinavians who are eager to meet compatible Americans and the two parties then correspond to make whatever arrangements they wish—dinner in the homes of the Scandinavians, an evening out, or a day of sight-seeing. Sometimes accommodations in homes may be arranged.

Tourist offices in some cities abroad also keep lists of local people who are willing to meet with visitors. One longtime program exists in Zurich, c/o the Zurich Tourist Office, 15 Bahnhofplatz, 8023 Zurich, Switzerland, 01-211-40-00. Another is in Brussels, where the Chatterbus tour organization, 12 rue des Thuyas, 1170 Brussels, 02/673-18-35, has a list of English-speaking residents who will either join you on foot or drive you on a sight-seeing tour of the city, free of charge. The French tourist office also maintains a list of organizations that foster visits. They are listed in the Paris section (page 219).

DINING ALONE

The one feature of solo traveling that people seem to dread most is dining alone. Even the most worldly travelers seem to hate it. Some people refuse to travel by themselves to avoid it.

In part, this is understandable since it is undeniably a lot pleasanter to share a meal. But often the reluctance is strictly a matter of point of view. When *Travel & Leisure* talked to business people who frequently travel alone, many of them said that after a hectic day it is actually a relief to be able to relax and not have to make conversation with strangers. Many also considered a room service dinner a wonderfully indulgent luxury.

The same is true after a busy day of sight-seeing. It really isn't so bad relaxing over a drink by yourself and thinking back over the day—unless you think it is. Some diners are so self-conscious they bury themselves in a book, thereby missing out on the pleasure of people-watching in the restaurant—or maybe even starting up a conversation with someone at the next table. The best way to ease this awkward feeling is to choose your dining times and places carefully.

One of the reasons for feeling ill at ease is that busy restaurants don't always seem pleased to see a solo diner. It's that same old problem—most tables are designed for two. The smaller tables inevitably seem to be stuck back near the kitchen. And, understandably, it may be true that waiters would be happier getting tips from two instead of one. However, if you make the effort to be friendly, explain that you are traveling alone, and enlist the waiter's advice about the menu and even about the city, you may find you can win him over into a staunch ally.

It annoys me that I can't always be sure of a welcome when I dine alone, but since I don't know how to beat the system, often I join it. I shift my schedule so I can eat early before restaurants are filled and when I know they are happier to seat me. Often I'll have an early meal in the neighborhood where I spent the afternoon, which gives me a chance to try places I might not venture into on my own later in the evening.

When I want to eat at a really posh place by myself, I usually go for lunch. I've also found that if you stop by in advance and explain to the captain that you are in town alone and ask which day they might best be able to accommodate you for lunch or dinner, you'll likely get a more cordial reception—and a reservation. And of course, a tip never hurts. However, don't try this visit during the height of the lunchtime rush.

I have a female friend with another technique. She phones to reserve tables for one under the name of "Dr. Glenn." Somehow the title seems to do the trick.

As a rule, when you travel alone, it is a lot more comfortable going to smaller, more casual restaurants. The less formal dining rooms in large hotels are always a good bet for single travelers, since management is quite used to serving them; you'll notice that these rooms tend to have a lot of small tables. You don't have to be staying in a particular hotel to take advantage of its dining facilities, so you can have a number of comfortable evenings simply by surveying the local hotel scene.

If I want variety, when there is no concierge to guide me, I always scout the blocks around my hotel during the day to seek out promising little places within walking distance. This may or may not be successful, depending on the neighborhood and the city.

A surer technique is to seek out the trendy city neighborhoods that attract a lot of browsers. Usually as you stroll along you can count on finding small cafés in these areas. Watch for outdoor terraces with empty tables or little cafés with lots of small tables by the windows or along the walls. These are often used to serve single diners; you will probably spy some who have arrived before you.

Other best bets in every city are restaurants with serving counters. These are not necessarily boring coffee shops or luncheonettes, as you'll see from some of the places listed beginning on page 206. Sushi bars are always fine for dining alone, as are restaurant lounges or the wine bars in many cities that also serve light meals at the bar. Good sources of ideas are the Zagat restaurant surveys, which are made up of opinions from local residents, and always include suggestions for dining alone as well as listings of places where the local singles gather. The Zagat guides are available for New York, Chicago, Boston, Philadelphia, San Francisco, Washington/Baltimore, New Orleans, Phoenix/Scottsdale, Dallas/Fort Worth, and Houston. For ordering information contact Zagat Survey, 45 W. 45th St., New York, NY 10036; 212-302-0505.

Wherever you go, you'll be better received in a restaurant if you are reasonably well dressed. I met one traveler who told me she always dresses up when she goes out to dine by herself. She also carries a notebook and asks lots of questions about the restaurant and the menu. She hopes she will be mistaken for a food critic, and so far, she says she has been treated well wherever she has tried her little game.

Another way to find dining companions in a strange city in the United States is to look into the meeting dates of the local chapters of any professional organizations or alumni club you may belong to, or the scheduled dinners of the local Single Gourmet group. Contact the national Single Gourmet organization listed on page 177 for local addresses. And don't hesitate to look up friends of friends.

The best way to find nightlife is to read the local publications. If you are 35 or under, look for alternative papers such as the *Boston Phoenix*, or the *Village Voice* in New York. If you are hesitant about venturing out alone, check into nighttime tours.

Singles bars still exist, but they are far less attractive to travelers in this age of AIDS. A brief romance in a strange city once might have seemed romantic, but today it is a bit like playing Russian roulette. A good rule for females always is to pay your own way at bars or in restaurants. Then you are free to say good-bye with no hard feelings.

For those who prefer specific dining destinations to browsing, here are some solo suggestions from knowledgeable residents in a few major U.S. cities, with my own comments added for the East Coast cities I often visit. Remember, these are not gourmet choices, but places where you'll eat decently and feel at ease.

BOSTON

From Janice Brand, former Service Features Editor of *Boston Magazine*, who frequently writes about the local restaurant scene:

DARTMOUTH STREET, 271 Dartmouth Street, a popular Italian restaurant off Newbury Street, with many small tables in the front.
ROCKO'S, 5 S. Charles Street (in the Massachusetts Transportation Building, facing Park Square) is "in," a good place to get a corner table and watch the action.
COTTONWOOD CAFÉ, 1815 Massachusetts Avenue (in Porter Square Exchange), Cambridge, has easy ambience and a friendly bartender.
CAFÉ DE PARIS, 19 Arlington Street, is all old-world lace and mahogany, perfect for lunch or tea.
29 NEWBURY STREET, (at that address), has a big, friendly outdoor terrace, great for watching the world go by.
THE BLUE DINER, 178 Kneeland Street, has its ups and downs, but is an easy place to be and is often very good.
JACOB WIRTH, 33-37 Stuart Street, an old German restaurant that has been around forever, is perfect before a performance at the nearby Wang Center or theater district—or for a beer at a front table when

the sun is shining in. The neighborhood isn't great, however, and the crowd changes later in the day.

QUINCY MARKET. In warm weather, the restaurants here serve at outdoor terraces, or you can get your food inside and take it to one of the outdoor tables.

SERENDIPITY, a Faneuil Hall branch of the New York ice cream parlor, has super desserts as well as burgers and is a prime place for people-watching.

THE NORTH END. You can poke your nose into almost any of little Italian restaurants and pick one you like. The waitress will fuss over you just like mom.

COMMENTS:

E.B.: *When I am in Boston alone, I always head for the bar/counter at* Legal Seafoods, *27 Columbus Avenue, behind the Park Plaza Hotel. There are waiting lines, but a single sometimes gets a seat while couples wait. The seafood is super, the chowder is heaven.*

Other places I have found pleasant are Rebecca's, *a little café at 21 Charles Street, near Beacon Hill;* Back Bay Bistro, *565 Boylston Street, an informal place on Copley Square, and the* Harvard Book Store Café, *190 Newbury Street. One other possibility is* Durgin Park, *a longtime landmark in the North Building in Quincy Market, where diners are seated at long communal tables and served big portions by waitresses renowned for their grumpiness. It's touristy, but do it once anyway. Do* not, *however, go to the new branch in the Westin Hotel—it's not the same.*

St. Botolph, 99 St. Botolph Street, and St. Cloud, 557 Tremont Street, are two other popular restaurants with serving bars.

PHILADELPHIA

From R. C. Staab, Vice President, Communications, Philadelphia Convention & Visitors Bureau:

"I often used to visit the city on my own before I lived here, and these are the places I found most comfortable":

THE COMMISSARY, 1710 Sansom Street, with both Edens, 1517 Chestnut Street and particularly the one at International House, 3701 Chestnut Street. You buy the food, which is excellent, from a cafeteria line, and seat yourself. On any given night there are many single travelers.

CHINATOWN. There are lots of tourists and locals, as well as business people. Just walk in and pick a place. No one questions a customer alone.

STROLLI'S in South Philly (on Dickinson, just west of Broad) forces you to eat elbow to elbow. It's Italian, cheap, friendly, and fun. In fact, most of the smaller family restaurants in South Philly are good places to meet people and have a homey dinner.

REMBRANDT'S in Fairmount Park, and Friday, Saturday, Sunday, at 261 S. 21st Street, offer good food and a pleasant, friendly environment where you will be left alone or can join in.

COMMENTS:

E.B.: *No one should miss a lunchtime visit to Philadelphia's* Reading Terminal Market, *12th & Arch streets, a bustling landmark selling all manner of produce and with food stands of all descriptions, from seafood to barbecue.* South Street, *where young Philly hangs out, is lined with a variety of little ethnic restaurants—just browse and take your pick.* Jim's Steaks, *at 400 South, is one of the best places in town to sample that only-in-Philly specialty, a cheesesteak sandwich. This is truly the haute cuisine of junk food.*

CHICAGO

From Carla Kelson, Dining Editor of *Chicago Magazine:*

BERGHOFF, 17 W. Adams, German food, a local landmark.

HATSUHANA, 160 E. Ontario, top-rated sushi bar.

RESTAURANT SUNTORY, 13 E. Huron, another prize sushi bar.

ED DEBEVIC'S SHORT ORDERS, 640 N. Wells at Ontario, a back-to-the-'50s diner, complete with rock 'n' roll.

FRONTERA GRILL, 445 N. Clark, the best Mexican food in town.

RUE SAINT CLAIR, Richmont Hotel, 640 St. Clair Street, a Parisian-style sidewalk café.
LA CREPERIE, 2845 N. Clark, bistro decor, dozens of kinds of crepes.
METROPOLIS, 163 W. North Avenue (between Wells and LaSalle), warm neighborhood ambience, great eclectic menu.
BLUE CRAB LOUNGE, 21 East Hubbard, part of Shaw's Crab House, an old favorite seafood standby, with lots of oyster-bar seats. Shaw's is also fine if you prefer a table alone.
CAFÉ SPIAGGIA, 980 N. Michigan, all the pleasure of the top northern Italian cooking of the main restaurant without having to dress up. The menu has lighter choices such as pizza and pasta.
GORDON, 500 N. Clark, whimsical decor, enjoyable, popular.
RITZ CARLTON CAFÉ, Ritz Carlton Hotel, 160 E. Pearson, lovely atmosphere but less formal than the main dining room.
SCOOZI, 410 W. Huron, jammed bar, good Italian food.
CAFÉ BA-BA-REEBA, 2024 N. Halsted, Spanish with an oversize tapas bar.
BISTRO 110, 110 E. Pearson, good choice for light dining.
HARD ROCK CAFE, 63 W. Ontario, chili, burgers, etc., at the bar—if you can stand the noise.
BENUCCH, Bloomingdale's Building, new and "hot."

COMMENTS:

E.B.: *I don't know Chicago well, but I do know* Giordano's, *747 W. Rush Street or 1840 N. Clark Street, the place that made "stuffed pizza" famous—and it's the best* I've *ever tasted. See what you think.*

SAN FRANCISCO

From Patricia Unterman, respected restaurant reviewer for the *San Francisco Chronicle:*

CHINA MOON, 639 Post Street, a stylish Chinese café with a counter; owner Barbara Tropp has a loyal local following.
IL FORNAIO, Levi Plaza, a bustling Italian trattoria with a comfortable counter.

LITTLE JOE'S, 523 Broadway, a busy old-fashioned Italian restaurant known for its pasta and veal; inexpensive, and there is a counter.

HAYES STREET GRILL, 320 Hayes Street, specializes in fish and has a number of smaller tables for singles (Zagat calls this the best fish in SF).

STARS, 150 Redwood Alley between Polk and Van Ness, offers both counter seating and an informal café in a large *au courant* restaurant in the Civic Center; owner Jeremiah Tower is a culinary star.

VICOLO PIZZERIA, 201 Ivy Street, an upscale pizzeria with counter seats and small tables.

VIVANDE, 2125 Fillmore Street, a wonderful Italian deli and café with a counter and small tables, but note that it is open only until 7 P.M.

COMMENTS:

E.B.: *Recommended by an S.F. friend is* Isobune Sushi, *1737 Post Street, where everyone sits around a big oval counter—and the food glides by on little Japanese boats. People love it; expect a line.*

10

FOUR FAVORITE CITIES

EVERYBODY HAS HIS OR HER OWN FAVORITE CITIES for different reasons. I've chosen Amsterdam, Montreal, Paris, and New York, not only for their beauty or excitement but because I have found them to be especially easy cities to be in by yourself. The descriptions are not meant to be used as a substitute for a comprehensive guidebook—they are simply personal impressions of what I've found most enjoyable on my own.

AMSTERDAM

There's a fairy-tale quality to the tilty gabled town houses on the tree-lined canal streets of Amsterdam. Though apartments, boutiques, and cafés may hide behind the historic facades, the beautiful old city has not changed since the 17th century. No matter how many times you walk along the canals, they are always enchanting, even in busy midday when traffic and whizzing bicycles dispel the old world illusion. The loveliest times for walking are on a silent Sunday morning or on a summer evening, when the old facades are floodlit.

The contrasting aspects of this city equally well known for its Rembrandts and its red-light district are endlessly fascinating. Amsterdam is small, so you can cover most of it on foot, savoring such details as the charming, no-two-alike gables atop the houses, the growing number of kicky boutiques, the many art galleries, the tempting bakeries, and the masses of flowers in the colorful floating flower market. Outdoor markets for everything from postage stamps to parakeets to junk-tique are another intriguing part of the cityscape. Two excellent books to guide your walks are *On Foot in Surprising Amsterdam* by Tom Vincent and *Amsterdam Canal Guide* by Tom Killiam. Both are available in the city's bookshops.

Amsterdam's polyglot population is another part of its appeal. The freewheeling atmosphere makes everyone, young and old, feel at home, which you can sense by the street music. On one recent stroll in the heart of the city I counted six kinds of music from various musicmakers: a classical violinist outside the concert hall, a folksinger-guitarist near the Van Gogh museum, a rock group in front of the train station, a carillon serenading from a church steeple, an organ concert wafting from an open church door, and the tinkly tunes of a barrel organ in Dam Square. All are typically Amsterdam.

Several things make Amsterdam particularly easy if you are on your own. First, everyone speaks English. Second, if you stay within the confines of the old city, you can easily walk to see the Rembrandts in the Rijksmuseum and the priceless collections in the Vincent van Gogh Museum, as well as to concerts and restaurants. And if you tire, cheerful clanging trolley cars are waiting on every major street. To save, instead of paying for individual rides, buy trolley tickets for one, two, or three days, or get a strip of tickets good for ten rides.

Because the center of the city is small, almost any hotel is conveniently located, but two with particularly sociable bars are the AMERICAN HOTEL, an art deco landmark at 97 Leidsekade, and the PULITZER, an amalgam of 17th-century town houses at 315 Prinsengracht. Among less-expensive hotels with special charm are the AMBASSADE, 341 Herengracht, made up of six patrician canal houses, and the more modest CANAL HOUSE, 148 Keizersgracht, which is exactly what the name suggests.

What's best of all about Amsterdam when you are by yourself is that it is a city where people like to "hang out"—in sidewalk cafés in summer, in coffee shops and local taverns, known as "brown bars," in winter. There's always a place where you can comfortably have a cup of coffee or a drink or a meal without feeling out of place because you are alone. And if you need to, it is easy to watch your budget. At dozens of restaurants, you'll see the knife and camera symbol indicating a tourist menu, a price-fixed three-course meal for around $10. You'll no doubt make your own dining discoveries as you wander, but here are some recommended spots:

LEIDSEPLEIN

This busy square, the center of the city's nightlife, together with the side streets running off it, offers a wide range of cafés from casual to chic.

Special recommendations:

CAFÉ-RESTAURANT AMERICAIN, American Hotel. A high-ceilinged art deco rendezvous for everything from reading a newspaper over a cup of coffee to indulging in a full dinner menu. Theatergoers, actors, musicians, and tourists all can be found here or on the big terrace café outside. One of the city's most popular gathering spots, it's perfect for when you are alone.

OESTER BAR, 10 Leidseplein. A top seafood restaurant upstairs with an informal tiled dining room on the street level with tables and a counter.

SPUI

A busy little intersection called Spui has more than its share of dining possibilities nearby.

HAESJE CLAES, 275 Spuistraat, is small, narrow, wood-paneled, atmospheric, and inexpensive.

CAFÉ ELVONNE, 413 Singel at the corner of Singel and Spui, serves everything from omelets to steak in a wine cellar with wooden tables.

Other suggestions:

DE KNIJP, 134 van Baerlestraat, not far from the Concertgebouw, serves up good food on wooden platters.

BRASSERIES VAN BAERLE, 158 van Baerlestraat, run by two former KLM stewardesses, offers a range of choices from quiches to six-course feasts in a pleasant spot with a garden.

CAFÉ HANS & GRIETJE, 27 Spiegelgracht, is a quaint place, with an upstairs restaurant and a downstairs bar/café.

PULITZER COFFEE SHOP, in the Pulitzer Hotel, corner of Keizersgracht and Reestraat, has rattan furnishings, contemporary art, and a menu that runs the gamut from snacks to substantial meals.

CONTINENTAL SHERRY BODEGA, 246 Lijnbaansgracht, a timbered place known mainly as a wine-tasting spot, serves light meals or tapas on the street level, rises floor by floor to more expensive fare. The bar is a popular watering hole.

PANCAKE BAKERY, 191 Prinsengracht, a restored canalside warehouse with 50 kinds of Dutch pancakes—great for lunch or a light dinner, and very light on the pocketbook.

L'OPERA, 27 Rembrandtsplein, a split-level art deco restaurant-café and bar with a big, popular terrace.

LE RELAIS, 2 Nieuwe Doelenstraat, the clubby smaller restaurant in the elegant Hotel de l'Europe, has atmosphere, good food, and surprisingly moderate prices.

SALAD GARDEN, 75 Weteringschans, near the Rijksmuseum, has much more than salads—light meals downstairs, formal dining above. A perfect place for afternoon tea.

HOLLANDS GLORIE, 220 Kerkstraat, a longtime local favorite, serves up popular-priced food in a wonderful Old Dutch setting of copper and tiles.

For further information on Amsterdam, contact the Netherlands Board of Tourism (NBT) at 355 Lexington Ave., New York, NY 10017; 212-370-7367.

The best guidebook for boning up before you go is *KLM's Holland* by Ian Keown, published by KLM Royal Dutch Airlines, New York. Another well-written guide is *Frommer's Guide to Amsterdam and Holland* by Linda Burnham (Prentice Hall Press, New York).

MONTREAL

Here's a touch of French *joie de vivre* right next door—and you don't even have to know the language. Montreal is an easily manageable city of 1.6 million people with the life and charm and sophistication of a city many times its size. Promenaders on the streets and laughter in the sidewalk cafés last well into the night.

The setting is unusual and scenic, an island in the middle of the St. Lawrence River, with a little mountain, Mont Royal, providing acres of greenery right in the middle of town. The street and shop signs, much of the food, and the ambience are strictly French and foreign, yet everyone in Montreal is bilingual, so you'll never have to open your phrase book unless you want to.

The marvel of Montreal is its Metro, a subway system that is not only clean, safe, and speedy but a tourist attraction in itself. Miles of wide, well-lit, attractive corridors connect the city's main shopping complexes and offer hundreds of shops on their own. The system provides you something to do no matter what the weather. The entertainers who make your strolling and waiting time tuneful are top-rate musicians who have auditioned to compete for their spots. The excellent train system also makes it easy to visit far-flung attractions such as the former site of Expo 67, now a complex of gardens and museums, or the Olympic Stadium. The guided tour of the Olympic Park includes a shuttle bus to the city's fine Botanical Garden. Buy eight metro tickets at a time for a discount, and ask for a free pocket-sized map card.

Quaint Old Montreal is the city's tourist mecca. Browsing is pleasant but the shops are decidedly commercial. For a fascinating non-touristy history of the area, take a walking tour with an English-speaking guide, held daily May 15 to September 15 by Les Montréalistes, 514-744-3009.

Self-guided walking tours printed in the free official Tourist Guide take you through some of the city's other neighborhoods—the elegant Sherbrooke Street area that boasts the city's top hotels and boutiques and the handsome McGill University campus; Saint-Denis, the "Latin Quarter" of student life; Boulevard Saint-Laurent with its mix of nationalities; and Avenue Laurier, a burgeoning area of upscale shops. Everywhere you go, you'll find sidewalk cafés for a rest and a view of the passing scene.

Shopping is one of this city's greatest pleasures, and one you need no company to enjoy. The fashions are French and the prices are Canadian, a great combination for travelers with American dollars. Boutiques and department stores on Sainte-Catherine Street vie with the most elegant of those to be found at city shopping centers anywhere. Ogilvy's, for one, is an old-world treasure filled with five floors of lovely boutiques and is not to be missed.

Two of the newest centers are modernistic dazzlers and good places for informal meals, as well. Les Cours Mont-Royal, a former hotel on Peel Street, has been converted to a 14-level elegant mall of interior courtyards, skylights, fountains, and glittering chandeliers. The mall is shared by 125 fine shops, movie theaters, a condominium-office complex, and a black-and-white food court of counters and restaurants known as Noir et Blanc. Among the tenants are the first Gianfranco Ferre outside Italy, and an outpost of Harry's New York Bar.

Place Montreal Trust, between McGill College Avenue and Mansfield, boasts a number of cafés and 120 boutiques on its 5 multicolored levels, including such familiar names as Fendi, Rodier, Bally, Abercrombie & Fitch, and Crabtree and Evelyn, as well as dozens of shops featuring exclusive designer creations.

And if you have dreamed of buying a fur coat for yourself or to give as a gift, Montreal is definitely the place. The selection and the prices are superior, and the American dollar goes far. The fur district is centered around Mayor Street; a knowledgeable and friendly couple I enjoyed meeting are the Le Blancs who run a shop called oslo at 5149 Saint-Laurent Boulevard.

Where to stay? The top-of-the-line hotels are on Sherbrooke West, the Ritz-Carlton at 1228 and the Four Seasons at 1050. They are top-notch and conveniently located near the cafés on convivial Crescent Street. The more moderately priced Holiday Inn Crowne Plaza is about 6 blocks away at 410 Sherbrooke West. Château Versailles, 1659 Sherbrooke West, a small hotel comprising four Victorian houses, is also a good value.

The safe and efficient Metro makes this an ideal city for bed-and-breakfast lodgings. For reservations, contact Montreal Bed and Breakfast, 4912 Victoria Street; 514-738-9410.

When it comes to restaurants, you can hardly go wrong in Montreal, which is all but dedicated to wining and dining. This is a sophisticated city, and no one raises an eyebrow when you enter a restaurant alone. Take your pick of the places in the following suggested areas:

CRESCENT STREET

Crescent, between Sherbrooke and Sainte-Catherine, is a favorite area of Montreal's over-30 smart set. A host of good, informal choices await, many with outside terraces. (Les Halles at 1450, one of the city's gourmet landmarks, is probably a better bet at lunchtime if you are alone.) Nearby streets such as Bishop and Stanley have their own share of charming cafés. A few recommendations:

THURSDAYS, 1449 Crescent; French, with a lively young crowd.

LE CHRYSANTHEME, 1208 Crescent; interesting Chinese.

LE MAS DES OLIVIERS, 1216 Bishop; French.

L'AUTRE SAISON, 2180 Crescent; a good lunching spot with super salads.

SAINT-DENIS STREET

The lower part of the street near the University of Quebec draws the younger patrons to its wall-to-wall lineup of cafés of all nationalities. The farther up the hill you go, the more sophisticated the restaurants and the older the crowd. During the late-June Jazz Festival, the lower street sings with impromptu concerts. Suggestions:

LA SILA, 2040 Saint Denis; Italian.

LES MIGNARDISES, 2035 Saint Denis; French (this one is "in"—come early).

PRINCE ARTHUR STREET AND DULUTH AVENUE

Both streets, not far from the Saint-Denis area, are filled with Greek and other ethnic restaurants with big outdoor patios. They're all inexpensive and strictly BYOB (bring your own bottle [of wine]). Prince Arthur is also a pedestrian mall where guests enjoy street entertainment along with the modest dinner tabs. Just pick the place with an empty spot out front.

OLD MONTREAL

More tourists than locals here, but you'll find street musicians and a host of outside cafés. It's not my favorite part of the city, but one place I did enjoy was

LES FILLES DU ROY, 415 rue Bonsecours; with typical Quebecois menus and charming atmosphere.

Other good bets:

THE ALCAN BUILDING (Maison Alcan), 1188 Sherbrooke Street West. In the inner court of this interesting building are the

MOBY DICK BAR, where local journalists meet after work;

LE PAVILLON DE L'ATLANTIQUE, a good seafood restaurant; and

LA TULIPE NOIRE, a perfect place for lunch, light suppers, or desserts.

THE RITZ GARDEN, 1228 Sherbrooke Street West. Don't miss this beautiful outdoor setting and delicious food. The gracious Ritz staff will make you comfortable, but if you are shy about dinner, come for lunch or a fabulous breakfast.

THE FOUR SEASONS, 1050 Sherbrooke Street West, offers L'Apero off the lobby for a pleasant buffet luncheon and Le Café for informal meals.

For further Montreal information: The free Tourist Guide and other materials put out by the Greater Montreal Convention and Tourism Bureau are excellent. Contact Delegation Generale du Quebec, 17 W. 50th St., Rockefeller Center, New York, NY 10020-2201; 212-397-0200. Or contact Tourisme Quebec, 1-800-443-7000 from eastern United States or call collect 514-873-2015 from western United States. *Birnbaum's Canada,* Houghton Mifflin Company, Boston, also has a good chapter on the city.

PARIS

Can the most romantic city in the world really be a good place to be alone? I know none better. Paris is dazzling, incredibly beautiful, and interesting at every turn. There are never enough days to begin to cover all the neighborhoods to be explored, all the fascinating shops for browsing, and all the incredible museums to be visited. No matter how many times you go, there is always something new to see. The two latest museums, the soaring d'Orsay, filled with Impressionist works, and the charming small Picasso Museum, are visual treats, and the old Place de Vosges neighborhood grows more beautiful by the year. And since there is always some controversial modern building going up, it's fun to have a look and form your own opinion about places you keep reading about such as the Pompidou Center, the new Les Halles, the pyramid entrance at the Louvre, and the Bastille Opéra.

By the time you've walked your feet off all day, you will likely be content to turn in early, eager to start all over the next day.

Of course, it helps if you speak a modicum of French. Some lessons before you leave home are helpful, and a phrase book is a necessity, although on my last visit I noticed that a remarkable number of Parisians now speak some English and many are now as helpful to strangers as the residents of any other city. The 3-star restaurants may not be overly warm to American-speaking guests, but in the less-rarified stratas of the city, in my opinion, Paris no longer deserves its longtime reputation for coldness.

Those you can't always count on to speak English are the cab-drivers. When I travel around Paris, besides writing down the address of my destination, I always carry the indispensable street guide, the little red Cartes Taride which locates every single address in each of the city's *arrondissements* or districts. It also includes a detailed map of each arrondissement as well as maps of the Métro subway system and the bus routes. All you need do is add an *X* to mark your spot. You can find the Cartes Taride in larger U.S. bookstores or buy one when you arrive in Paris.

The Métro is simple to figure out. Buy *un carnet* ("uhn karnay"), a book of ten tickets good for train or bus at a discount. The lines are named for their first and last stops, and switching is made easy by an electronic board next to the ticket booth in most Métro stations. Press the button next to the name of the station you want to reach and the board will light up the names of the lines you need to take.

You might prefer to take your time and ride the bus, since every route in this city makes for a scenic tour. The clearest guide is the big map available free from the tourist office on the Champs-Elysées, but at many intersections around town there are also machines to guide bus riders. Type in your destination and out comes a paper tape listing the number of the bus line, the direction, and the approximate time the trip will take. Just a few of the outstanding sight-seeing routes are:

- Line 24, which crosses the Seine four times and passes most of the city's famous sites.
- Line 29 from the Opéra to the Bastille.
- Line 38 from Les Halles across Ile de la Cité and up Boulevard Saint-Michel to the Luxembourg Gardens.
- Line 63, a Left Bank route through the Saint-Germain-des-Prés area.
- Line 84 from the Madeleine up rue Royale, around the Place de la Concorde through the heart of the Left Bank to the Luxembourg Gardens and around the Place de Panthéon.

Just remember that bus service is limited Sundays and evenings.

Not even the most magnificent ride will satisfy for long in a city made to order for walking. One of the best ways to get to know Paris on a first visit is on the Bonne Journée walking tours. There is a different one every day, taking in the Marais; the Ile de la Cité; Montmartre; the Père-Lachaise Cemetery where Oscar Wilde, Edith Piaf, and Jim Morrison are buried; and theme tours such as The History of Crime in Paris, which leads from prisons to gallows to the Police Museum, and "A Movable Feast" that follows in the steps of Hemingway and explores the expatriate scene of Paris in the twenties. Bonne Journée can be contacted at 6, place Charles-Dullin, 75018 Paris; (33) (1) 46.06.24.17.

It's also nice for those of us who haven't mastered French that the Louvre offers regular tours in English. Check at the information desk for the time schedule.

Besides tours, the many English-language bookshops afford an excellent way to find English-speaking companions in Paris. BRENTANO'S, 37, avenue de l'Opéra, is the largest and a good place to pick up information through the little paper called *American in Paris*, which lists activities of interest to Americans, including such events as a "quintessential July 4th party." Restaurants advertising in this paper are those where Americans living in the city are likely to be found. For a list of such places, see page 224.

My favorites of the English-language bookstores are W.H. Smith's combination restaurant, tea-room, and bookshop, 248, rue de Rivoli (also a fine place for a meal or a snack), and Shakespeare and Company, 37, rue de la Boucherie, an atmospheric gem of a used-bookstore on the Left Bank, where you can borrow a copy of *Pariswalks*, one of the best guides to walking tours on your own (they'll ask you to leave a deposit) and have free tea upstairs on Sunday afternoons at 4 P.M. If you are staying in the city long enough, you might want to sign up for language lessons at the Alliance-Française, 101, blvd. Raspail, another place to meet your countrymen.

Of course you haven't come all the way to Paris only to meet other Americans, but when you have no companion in a city where few people speak your language well, it is a relief to take a break occasionally and talk freely to someone from home.

If you want to meet French people while you are visiting, the French Tourist Office offers the following list of organizations that will help:

FRANCE ETATS-UNIS, 6, boulevard de Grenelle, 75015, Paris; phone 4273-0348.
FRANCE-AMÉRIQUE, 9–11, avenue Franklin D. Roosevelt, 75008, Paris; phone 4359-4516.
ACCUEIL FRANCE JEUNES, 23, rue Cherche-Midi, 75006, Paris; phone 4222-5034.
ACCUEIL DE FRANCE, 7, rue Balzac, 75008; Paris; phone 4359-4800.
AMERICAN CHURCH, 65, quai d'Orsay, 75007, Paris; phone 4705-0799.
AMERICAN CATHEDRAL, 23, avenue George V, 75008, Paris; phone 4720-1792.

While you're in Paris, read all you can about the city to discover some of the special small pleasures that you might overlook, such as the concerts held at Sainte-Chappelle, illuminated by daylight through the church's glorious stained-glass windows. Check the "Bests" section in the guidebook *Paris Access* for other treasures favored by a number of noted Paris visitors.

It would require a separate book to even begin to name all the small Parisian hotels where you can be comfortable by yourself without spending a fortune. Since many other guidebooks are quite helpful in this area, I'll mention just two hotels that I enjoyed recently—the ASTOR, 11, rue d'Astorg, a reasonably priced 4-star hotel in a lovely Right Bank location near the Madeleine, and the Hotel Verneuil Saint-Germain, 8, rue de Verneuil, a cheap and tiny charmer on the Left Bank. Both can be reserved in the United States, the Astor through Mondotels, 800-847-4249 or 212-757-0225; the Verneuil through Jacques de Larsay, Inc., 800-366-1510 or 212-477-1600. De Larsay is an excellent resource, specializing in small personal hotels in desirable areas of Paris as well as in France, Italy, Germany, and Switzerland. His hotels range from economy, 2 stars, to deluxe, 5 stars.

Unless you are determined to try the famous culinary palaces of Paris, dining alone in this city is a snap. There are brasseries in every neighborhood, most with big outdoor terraces, and dozens of tiny eateries where solo diners are commonplace. Attractive tearooms are perfect places for lunch, as are wine bars. And though the street has become tacky, the Champs-Elysées offers a lineup of reasonably priced cafés offering the traditional steakfrites (beef and French fries), and lone diners are not at all unusual.

An expensive but wonderful way to enjoy French cuisine with company—and to take home the ability to cook it yourself—is to sign up for a 1-week "visitors series" cooking course at La Varenne, 34, rue Saint-Dominique, the famous culinary school run by Anne Willan. The lessons are in French, but English translators are on hand. There are demonstrations by famous chefs, with tastings, but even better are practical classes that can be taken in the morning or the evening, with small groups sharing the meal prepared either for lunch or dinner. If the whole course is too much, you may be able to purchase individual tickets for demonstrations. The famous school Le Cordon Bleu, 24, rue de Champs de Mars, may also have demonstration tickets for certain classes.

Atmospheric neighborhoods where you can roam and almost take your pick of comfortable spots to dine are, with a few specific recommendations:

THE MARAIS

BOFINGER, 5, Rue de la Bastille; a lively and pretty landmark brasserie dating back to 1864.

LE GRENIER SUR L'EAU, 14, Rue du Pont Louis Phillippe; with a well-priced *prix fixe* menu.

MA BOURGOGNE, 19, Place des Vosges; under the arcade in one of the most beautiful squares in Paris, and the most informal and least expensive on the block.

L'EBOUILLANTE, 6, Rue des Barres; an outdoor lunching spot near the Place des Vosges.

CAFÉ COSTES, near the Pompidou Center, a place to see and be seen.

JO GOLDENBERG'S DELICATESSON, 7, Rue de Rosier; on the main artery of the atmospheric old Jewish ghetto, a local landmark.

ILE DE LA CITÉ

NOS ANCETRES LES GAULOIS, 39, Rue Saint-Louis-en-l'Ile; minute, charming.

AU GOURMET DE L'ISLE, 42, Rue Saint-Louis-en-l'Ile; simple and pleasant, with a *prix fixe* dinner.

SAINT-GERMAIN

AUX DEUX MAGOTS, 170, Boulevard Saint-Germain; possibly the most famous of the city's cafés, the place where Sartre, Hemingway, and other literary lions once assembled.

LA COUPOLE, 102, Boulevard du Montparnasse; another legend, recently redone and more popular than ever.

BRASSERIE LIPP, 151, Boulevard Saint-Germain; another famous and still lively gathering place for the intellectual community.

OTHER RECOMMENDATIONS

LA TABLE DE L'ASTOR, Astor Hotel, 11, Rue d'Astorg, 8th arrondissement; quiet, gracious, and a good value.

RESTAURANT DE PALAIS D'ORSAY, 62, Rue de Lille; in the marvelous d'Orsay Museum, open until 10 P.M.

CAFÉ DE LA PAIX, 12, Boulevard des Capucines, 9th arrondissement; a restored national landmark; come for meals or tea between 3 P.M. and 6 P.M.

FAUCHON, 26, Place de la Madeleine, 8th arrondissement; the best cafeteria in Paris; you'll eat standing up, but it's still a "don't miss" for lunch.

DRUGSTORE, 133, Champs-Elysées and l, Avenue Matignon; a tourist attraction, but you might as well join the lineup at the counter at least once for a hamburger or other reasonably priced fare. Open late.

LA FERMETTE MARBEUF, 5, Rue Marbeuf; good to know about because it is open on Sunday in a neighborhood where most places are closed. Ask for a seat in the winter garden.

RUE DE LA HUCHETTE, a Left Bank street near the Shakespeare & Company bookshop, is lined with inexpensive small Greek restaurants, good to know about if your budget is running low.

MORE RECOMMENDATIONS FROM RESIDENTS AND FREQUENT VISITORS TO THE CITY

1ST ARRONDISSEMENT

LE SOUFFLE, 36, Rue du Mont-Thabor; with souffles the house specialty.

AU PIED DE COCHON, 6, Rue Coquillière; the last remnant of the old Les Halles market district, filled with nostalgia.

LE PAVILLON BALTARD, 9, Rue Coquillière; cuisine of Normandy.

2ND ARRONDISSEMENT

DROUANT, Place Gaillon; art deco decor and friendly waiters.

5TH ARRONDISSEMENT

BRASSERIE BALZAR, 49, Rue des Ecoles; long a favored student gathering place.

LE TAVERNE DE CLUNY, 51, Rue de la Harpe; French cuisine and a piano bar at night.

6TH ARRONDISSEMENT

LE MUNICHE, 27, Rue de Buci; summer *terrasse* and jazz.

VAGENENDE, 142, Boulevard Saint-Germain; classic cuisine in a historic monument.

LE PETIT ZINC, 25, Rue de Buci; known for good food and always busy. (The block of rue Gregoire-de-Tours between rue de Buci and boulevard Saint-Germain has about 15 other, similar cafés.)

LE PROCOPE, 13, Rue de l'Ancienne-Comédie; said to be the world's oldest operating café and still a favorite.

7TH ARRONDISSEMENT

LE GALANT VERRE, 12, Rue de Verneuil; one of the best in a charming neighborhood.

8TH ARRONDISSEMENT

LA FERME ST. HUBERT, 21, Rue Vignon; next door to a cheese shop of the same name and specializing in cheese dishes.

CHEZ EDGAR, 4, Rue Marbeuf; popular, noisy but well priced.

BRASSERIES MOLLARD, 115, Rue Saint-Lazare; sumptuous turn-of-the-century decor.

LE CELADON, Hotel Westminster, 15, Rue Daunou; busy at lunch but not at night.

LA COURONNE, Le Warwick Hotel, 5, Rue de Berri; elegant but good value *prix fixe* dinner.

PLACES WHERE AMERICANS GATHER

If you want to hear English spoken, here's where *Paris Magazine* says you will find Americans living in Paris:

CACTUS CHARLY, 68, Rue de Ponthieu; country-western bar.

CAFÉ PACIFICO, 50, Boulevard Montparnasse; Mexican food.

CONWAYS, 73, Rue Saint-Denis; "Style New-Yorkais" says the magazine.

FRONT PAGE, 56, Rue Saint-Denis; said to have great hamburgers.

HARRY'S BAR, 5, Rue Daunou; legendary; open 10:30 P.M. to 4:00 A.M.

HOLLYWOOD SAVOY, 44, Rue Notre Dame des Victoires.

JOE ALLEN, 30, Rue Pierre Lescot; in the new Halles, serving chili, salad, steak, apple pie.

MARSHAL'S BAR AND GRILL, 63, Avenue Franklin D. Roosevelt; California cuisine and wine.

MOTHER EARTH'S, 66, Rue des Lombards; live music.

RIVOLI COFFEE SHOP, 6, Rue Poucher.

THE STUDIO, 41, Rue du Temple; Tex-Mex.

If you are really homesick, there are dozens of McDonalds and Burger Kings, plus scores of sound-alikes all over Paris. What is the culinary world coming to?

Some of the better guides to Paris:

THE BEST OF PARIS, by Gault/Millau (Prentice Hall Press, New York). The best for restaurants and hotels, good for shopping also.
PARIS ACCESS, by Richard Saul Wurman (AccessPress, Ltd., 59 Wooster St., New York, NY 10012). Detailed neighborhood walking tours that include sights, shops, and dining places where you need them.
CROWN INSIDERS' GUIDE TO FRANCE, by Helmut Koenig (Crown Publishers, Inc., New York, 1987). Very personal guide by someone who obviously knows the city well.
MICHELIN GUIDES, Paris. The old standbys, green for sight-seeing, red with those much-desired star ratings for dining. The guides stay pop-

ular because they tell you what you need to know quickly and the narrow size is easy to carry in your pocket or purse.

NEW YORK

This is my city. Almost all of us who live here have a love-hate relationship with the place. We grumble about the traffic, the subways, the rents, the prices, and the crowds. What keeps us here, however, are the same things that make New York a fabulous place to visit: It is one of the most diverse and exciting cities in the world, overflowing with cultural riches, theater magic, marvelous food and wares from around the globe. The old saying is true: If you can't find it in New York, it probably doesn't exist.

The pace and pulse of the city are tangible, maybe daunting at the start but eventually drawing you in to pick up your step and share the excitement. If you can't have a wonderful time here, you just aren't trying.

The New York subway is intimidating to strangers, sometimes even to natives. To feel secure getting around the city, familiarize yourself with the bus system. Buses are slow but sure and a great way to see the sights as well as the natives, for just $1.15 per ride. You won't mind the traffic nearly so much if you aren't watching a taxi meter tick. You'll need exact change before you board, and no bills are accepted, so bring lots of change with you. Better yet, go down into any subway station and buy a batch of tokens, which are also accepted on the buses.

Getting your bearings is easy because most of Manhattan is laid out on a straight grid, with avenues running north to south, streets running east to west. The central business district is only about 16 blocks wide, and you'll spend most of your time within 8 to 10 of them. Bus transfers are free if you need to change from a "crosstown" (east-west) bus to one heading uptown or downtown (or vice versa), but you have to ask for a transfer when you *board* the first bus, not when you are getting off.

Bus routes are clearly marked on maps at most bus stops. A bus map is also printed on the back of the subway maps available free at token booths at the main city stations, or you can write ahead to the New York Convention and Visitors Bureau (see page 239) for their comprehensive Big Apple Guide, which includes maps.

No one should miss a heart-stopping skyscraper-high view of the city at night. Nothing else shows you so vividly why New York is unique. The Empire State Building observatory is open until midnight and the top floor of the World Trade Center until 9:30 P.M., or you can have a drink in the lounge of the Rainbow Room on the 65th floor of the RCA building, at City Lights on the 107th floor of the World Trade Center, or atop the Beekman Tower Hotel, First Avenue and 49th Street.

Some favorite city dwellers' pleasures that can be shared by visitors include:

- Biking the car-free roadways on the weekend, or jogging around the reservoir any day in Central Park (both activities recommended for daylight hours only).
- Sitting on the steps of the Metropolitan Museum of Art on Sunday afternoon and watching the street performers and the passing parade.
- Visiting the farmer's Green Market in Union Square on Wednesday, Friday, or Saturday.
- Weekend brunching and gallery-hopping in SoHo along Broadway, West Broadway, and the cross streets between.
- Wandering Eighth Street, West Fourth Street, Bleecker, and other Greenwich Village streets along with young and young-at-heart New York.

New Yorkers are champion walkers and they like exploring their city as much as visitors do, so when it comes to seeing specific neighborhoods on foot, you'll find a great choice of walking tours around almost every part of the city each weekend from late spring through fall. Some of these groups also offer bus excursions that make it easy to visit nearby suburban attractions. Here are some of the organizations that offer guided walks and tours:

MUNICIPAL ART SOCIETY, 457 Madison Ave. at 50th St., New York, NY 10022; 212-935-3960.

92ND STREET Y, 1395 Lexington Ave., New York, NY 10128; 212-996-1105.

WALKING TOURS OF CHINATOWN, 70 Mulberry St., 2d floor, New York, NY 10013; 212-619-4785.

NEW YORK WALK-ABOUT, c/o Lister Travel Service, 30 Rockefeller Plaza, New York, NY 10022; 212-582-2015.

NEW YORK WALKS, New-York Historical Society, 170 Central Park West at 77th St., New York, NY 10024; 212-873-3400.

MUSEUM OF THE CITY OF NEW YORK, 1220 Fifth Ave. at 103d St., New York, NY 10029; 212-534-1672.

ADVENTURES ON A SHOESTRING, 300 W. 53d St., New York, NY 10019; 212-265-2663.

URBAN PARK RANGERS CENTRAL PARK TOURS, New York City Department of Parks and Recreation; 212-860-1353. (Continuous slide presentations on park history are given at *The Dairy*, in the park near 64th Street.)

Two organizations that sponsor many walks and day tours that attract lots of younger city singles are the Discovery Center (245 W. 72d St., Suite 21, New York, NY 10023; 212-877-0677) and the Learning Annex (2330 Broadway, New York, NY 10024; 212-580-2828). You'll notice their flyers in sidewalk dispensers and stacked in many small stores.

On a first trip, Little Italy and Chinatown can be confusing, and might well be better seen with a guide. But here are some suggested neighborhoods to roam on your own to get a sense of the city and its diversity:

- The posh Upper East Side residential streets, roughly between 70th and 90th streets from Fifth to Park avenues.
- The charming West Side neighborhoods from Central Park West to West End Avenue between 68th and 86th streets.
- The chic Madison Avenue shops from the 60s to the 90s.
- The overpriced but enticing young boutiques on Columbus Avenue from 68th to 81st streets.

Shopping is a favorite New York pastime. Besides the special merchandise carried by the hundreds of small shops, out-of-towners often find the variety of wares in the big department stores such as Macy's, Saks Fifth Avenue, and Bloomingdale's a revelation. Most of the branches in major cities can't compare with the home stores.

If you are brave and you know your labels, you can venture down to bargain hunt on the Lower East Side. Note that stores are closed on Saturday in this Jewish neighborhood, and Sunday is the busiest shopping day. It is a good idea to go armed with one of the little special shopping guides to the area sold in most bookstores.

Another pleasure not to be missed by book lovers is the city's trove of wonderful bookstores. Among the many stops providing hours of happy browsing are the beautiful Rizzoli store at 31 West 57th Street, specialty shops such as The Biography Bookshop, 400 Bleecker Street; Applause Theater Books, 211 West 71st Street; Kitchen Arts & Letters, 1435 Lexington Avenue between 93d and 94th streets; The Military Bookman, 29 East 93d Street; E. Wyhe Art Books, 794 Lexington Avenue, and Murder, Inc., a store full of mystery novels at 271 West 87th Street. Remaindered bargains can be found at Barnes and Noble, 105 Fifth Avenue and 600 Fifth Avenue, and used-book treasures are available at the Strand, 828 Broadway at 12th Street, the Argosy, 116 East 59th Street, and the Gotham Book Mart at 41 West 47th Street. The Yellow Pages will guide you to dozens of other specialists for everything from comic books to collectors' volumes.

No trip to New York is complete without a visit to the theaters and concert halls. To avoid spending a king's ransom, take advantage of the various half-price ticket booths in the city. These are:

TKTS (Times Square Ticket Center), 47th Street and Broadway. Half-price tickets for Broadway and Off-Broadway shows are sold on the day of the performance starting at 3 P.M., and at 10 A.M. for matinees on Wednesday, Saturday, or Sunday. If you happen to be sight-seeing downtown, there is a branch of TKTS, usually with much shorter lines, on the mezzanine at 2 World Trade Center.

MUSIC AND DANCE TICKETS BOOTH, Bryant Park, near the corner of Sixth Avenue and 42nd Street. Tickets are available Tuesday, Thursday, and Friday noon to 2 P.M.; Wednesday and Saturday 11 A.M. to 2 P.M., 3 P.M. to 7 P.M.; and Sunday noon to 6 P.M. Tickets to Monday performances are available on Sunday.

AFTER 6 TIX, Avery Fisher Hall, Lincoln Center, Broadway and 64th Street. Unsold tickets for New York Philharmonic concerts go on sale at 6 P.M. on the night of the performance, at noon for Friday matinees. To check availabilities, phone 212-799-9595.

For a highly personalized visit to Lincoln Center, sign up for the "Meet-the-Artist" series held during the "Mostly Mozart" summer season. Once a week, small groups assemble before the concert for a light summer supper and the chance to chat with key artists of the series. For information on current dates and rates, contact "Meet the Artist," Lincoln Center, 140 W. 65th St., New York, NY 10023; 212-877-1800.

Contrary to popular belief, everything in New York does not cost money. Television shows are one favorite free pastime, but you must get your request in early, at least one month in advance, and often as much as six months ahead for the hot shows. Some networks will mail out ticket requests received by phone, others ask you to send in a postcard. At times, standby tickets may be available the morning of the show. Singles have a good shot. You can also pick up same-day tickets on occasion at the New York Visitors Bureau, Two Columbus Circle. For up-to-date information on your favorite show, it's best to phone. Network numbers are: ABC, 212-887-3537; CBS, 212-975-2476; NBC, 212-664-3055.

There are numerous free concerts as well in building atriums, museums, and outdoor plazas around the city. Check *New York* magazine or phone the Convention and Visitors Bureau, 212-397-8222.

Any guidebook will list the city's leading hotels. My favorite in the top echelon is the warm and gracious MARYFAIR REGENT, Park Avenue at 65th Street. If you can't afford the best, but prefer a small hotel to bed-and-breakfast homes, a few good choices include:

DORAL PARK, 70 Park Avenue; classy.

DORAL COURT, 130 East 39th Street; attractive and good value.

ALGONQUIN, 59 West 44th; old-fashioned and cozy.

WYNDHAM, 42 West 58th Street; big, pretty rooms, dated plumbing, and the best values in town. This is a favorite with show biz people; reserve far ahead to get in.

But do consider leaving the high-priced midtown business center and seeing New York like a native by taking advantage of the city's bed-and-breakfast registries. They'll show you what real life is like in the Big Apple, where in warm weather people sunbathe in the parks on Sunday and sit around in sidewalk cafés. Having checked out a number of these lodgings for a recent article, I was amazed at the lovely apartments available as B&Bs. It says a lot about the price of housing in New York that so many people are welcoming paying guests.

Where to dine alone in New York? There are plenty of options—in fact, this is one of the few cities I know where single diners are remembered in one of the prominent restaurant guides, *The New York Times Guide to Restaurants* by Bryan Miller. You'll no doubt make your own discoveries, but some suggested havens for dining alone, by neighborhood, include:

MIDTOWN

THE OYSTER BAR, lower level in Grand Central Station, 42d Street and Lexington Avenue, provides counter service and a number of small tables; tops for seafood.

THE BRASSERIE, 100 East 53d Street (between Park and Lexington), has a long counter as well as small tables, a menu from onion soup gratinée to steak, 24 hours a day.

CHINA GRILL, 60 West 53d Street (corner of 6th Avenue), is a trendy favorite with a French-Chinese menu and long dining bar.

CARNEGIE DELICATESSEN, 854 Seventh Avenue between 54th and 55th streets, a New York landmark with wise-cracking waiters, long, cramped tables, legendary corned beef and pastrami sandwiches.

AURORA, 60 East 49th Street, and Palio, 151 west 51st, are two quite elegant restaurants offering light dining at a convivial bar. Palio is a knockout.

THE PEMBROKE ROOM, Lowell Hotel, 28 East 63d Street, is a gracious hideaway serving a lavish tea that can double as supper. Hours are 3:30 P.M. to 7:00 P.M., with the last serving at 6:30 P.M.

A few other places recommended by Bryan Miller as having small tables or banquettes suitable for one:

CAFÉ DES SPORTS, 329 West 51st Street.
CHEZ NAPOLEON, 365 West 50th Street.
LA BONNE SOUPE, 48 West 55th Street.
PRIMA DONNA, 50 East 58th Street.

UPPER WEST SIDE

Browse Columbus Avenue and its side streets between 65th and 81st streets for limitless possibilities—just pick a café that doesn't have a line spilling out the door! If you aren't going to Lincoln Center, come after 8 P.M. and the crowds are smaller. A few recommendations:

PIZZERIA UNO, 81st and Columbus, part of a chain, but the food isn't bad; sit at a table or at the counter.

MUSEUM CAFÉ, Columbus at 77th; pleasant ambience.

VICTOR'S CAFÉ, Columbus at 71st; a longtime favorite for Cuban food.

RIKYU, Columbus between 69th and 70th streets; Japanese with a choice of small tables or a Sushi bar.

LINCOLN SQUARE COFFEE SHOP, RESTAURANT AND BAKERY, Columbus Avenue between 65th and 66th streets; varied menu and the best salad bar in town.

Other possibilities near Lincoln Center

O'NEAL'S BALLOON, 48 West 63d Street; food okay and a can't-beat location across from the State Theater.

THE FOUNTAIN CAFÉ, Lincoln Center Plaza, Broadway at 64th; pleasant outdoor dining in front of the fountain.

CAFÉ LA FORTUNA, 69 West 71st Street (between Central Park West and Columbus) for desserts, espresso and cappuccino, served in the garden in summer.

UPPER EAST SIDE

Browse Second Avenue between 74th and 86th streets, and 86th Street east or west of the avenue, a mini world tour of cuisines. Recommendations:

PAMIR, 1437 Second Avenue, between 74th and 75th streets; a pretty little spot with Afghanistan specialties, a delicious and delicate blend of Indian and Middle Eastern fare.

ISTANBUL KABOB, 303 East 80th Street, just east of Second Avenue; a minute Turkish restaurant with rugs on the walls and wonderful dishes that taste homemade.

CAFÉ DIVINO, 1544 Second Avenue, between 80th and 81st streets; a breezy, busy café with good, moderately priced Italian food.

DIVINO GASTRONOMIA, 1542 Second Avenue, with the take-out counter/café next door the best bet when the main café is busy; its small tables are perfect for (and often occupied by) singles.

MOCCA, 1588 Second Avenue, between 82d and 83d streets; European-style Hungarian café, great goulash, great prices.

EMPIRE SZECHUAN, 1649 Second Avenue at 86th Street; one of the neighborhood's better Chinese choices.

CAFÉ GEIGER, 206 East 86th Street, west of Second Avenue; a long-time favorite in a German neighborhood.

ESTIA GREEK TAVERN, 308 East 86th Street, east of Second Avenue; a pleasant old-fashioned choice.

GIORGIO'S EXPRESS, 310 East 86th Street, east of Second Avenue, a tiny outpost of Estia for when you are in a hurry or on a tight budget.

GREENWICH VILLAGE

Pick any block and you'll likely find tiny, welcoming restaurants. Here are some possibilities:

MANHATTAN CHILI COMPANY, 302 Bleecker Street; best described as Texas east.

CUCINA STAGIONALE, 275 Bleecker Street; Italian food that pleases both palate and pocketbook.

JOHN'S PIZZERIA, 278 Bleecker Street; generally agreed to be New York's best, as attested by the long lines. Come at an off-hour.

BEATRICE INN, 285 West 12th Street; old-fashioned and homey Italian.

WHITE HORSE INN, Hudson and 11th streets; a 106-year-old neighborhood classic.

CHEZ BRIGETTE, 77 Greenwich Avenue; a hole-in-the-wall with counters—and incredible French food. Great for onion soup at lunch.

BLEECKER LUNCHEONETTE, Bleecker Street at Carmine; another no-frills place, famous for Italian food magic.

Don't leave the Village without sampling its coffee houses. Among the best:

CAFÉ REGGIO, 119 MacDougal Street.

LE FIGARO, 186 Beecker Street.

PATISSERIE LANCIANI, 271 West 4th Street, between Perry and 11th streets (this one also has a light menu).

THE EAST VILLAGE

Here's where young New York eats on a budget. A few favorites:

"LITTLE INDIA," covering all of 6th Street between First and Second avenues, and spilling over onto First, is lined with tiny Indian restaurants, most BYOB. There are at least a dozen to choose from. Try **GANDHI** at #345, **ANAR BAGH** at #338, **GAYLORD** at 87 First Avenue, or just read the reviews in the windows.

CHRISTINE'S, 438 Second Avenue at 25th Street, a bit uptown but noted for inexpensive and good Polish home cooking.

TERESA'S, 103 First Avenue at 6th Street; a downtown Polish choice.

SUGAR REEF, 93 Second Avenue between 5th and 6th streets; Caribbean fare, very happy happy hour from 4 to 7 P.M.

UNION SQUARE CAFÉ, 21 East 16th Street, is farther uptown, a stylish café with an innovative menu and a long bar where singles dine comfortably.

A final tip about tips: Most New Yorkers find it easiest to just double the tax (8¼ percent) on their restaurant bills and leave a 16.5 percent tip. The difference from the usual 15 percent is negligible, and it saves lots of mental arithmetic.

Recommended guides to New York:

THE BEST OF NEW YORK by Gault/Millau (Prentice Hall Press, New York, 1988). Best for restaurants and hotels.
THE PENGUIN GUIDE TO NEW YORK CITY (Penguin Books, Viking Penguin Inc., New York, 1990).
NOOKS AND CRANNIES: A Walking Tour Guide to New York City by David Yeadon (Charles Scribner's Sons, New York, 1979).
NEW YORK: THE BEST PLACES by David Yeadon and the Best Places team (Perennial Library, Harper & Row, New York, 1987). A fun survey of special spots.
AIA GUIDE TO NEW YORK CITY by Elliot Willensky and Norval White (Harcourt Brace Jovanovich, San Diego; New York, 1988). Knowledgeable architectural guide for walking tours.
THE CITY OBSERVED: New York, A Guide to the Architecture of Manhattan by Paul Goldberger (Vintage Books, New York, 1979). Written by the *New York Times* architecture critic.
THE NEW YORK TIMES GUIDE TO RESTAURANTS IN NEW YORK CITY by Bryan Miller (Times Books, New York, 1988). Reliable advice in every category.
EATS: THE GUIDE TO THE BEST LITTLE RESTAURANTS IN NEW YORK by Sylvia Carter (New American Library, New York, 1988). Highly recommended; her choices are great.

For a big, excellent, and free "Big Apple Guide," write to New York *Convention and Visitors Bureau Inc.*, Two Columbus Circle, New York, NY 10019.

11

BRING THE KIDS

BUSY SINGLE PARENTS WHO TAKE DOUBLE RE-sponsibility for their kids most of the year really deserve a vacation. They often want to share that vacation with the children. They look forward to rare relaxed and unscheduled time to have fun together, family time to really talk and share. Having kids for company actually solves certain travel problems, such as solitary meals.

Yet, while shared family vacations can be wonderfully rewarding, single parents also need a break. In fact, each generation benefits from time off for relaxing and socializing with people in their own age group. For parents, that doesn't necessarily mean looking for romance—just for a bit of adult companionship and conversation.

So the most successful single-parent outings offer both the opportunity for togetherness and time to be apart.

For that reason, some traditional family vacations aren't really great for single parents. One parent trying to keep up with two or three kids at Walt Disney World might be exhausted instead of exhilarated. Car trips can be miserable with no one to share the disciplining of the children or the driving. And resorts with children's programs can be populated mostly by couples who are relishing time together while *their* kids are busy, and they are therefore not much company for a parent alone.

Luckily, there are options that offer togetherness and still provide a chance for separate activities.

SOME PRACTICAL POINTERS

Start by planning something *you* really want to do, regardless of the kids. If you hate the idea of getting on a horse, life on a ranch isn't going to be any more appealing just because the children are along.

As with any family outing, things generally work out better if the youngsters are involved in the planning and are excited about the trip. If there are choices to be made, even preschoolers can look at color brochures and have some say in what looks great to them. Let the children help write for brochures and information, using their own names so that the mail comes back addressed to them. When you decide on a destination, have them participate in making lists of what you hope to do each day. Readers can make a trip to the library to get books about the area you will be visiting.

A productive pretrip activity is to have children put together a scrapbook with space for preplanning and a day-by-day diary with room to paste in souvenirs as you travel. It helps build anticipation beforehand and keeps them busy along the way.

Older kids can also help put together those tried-and-true travel games, such as making a list of states that can be checked off when their license plates are spied. Another family favorite is printing the alphabet down the side of a sheet of notebook paper for each child, with space to fill in objects spotted for each letter, starting with A.

Don't forget to bring favorite books, toys, and games to keep everyone happily occupied, as well.

When you pack, choose comfortable fast-drying clothing in dark colors so you needn't nag about keeping clothes clean on vacation. And be sure to include rain gear in case of bad weather.

Two things that make for crabby tempers on family vacations are fatigue and hunger, so do your best to avoid both.

- Keep traveling time to a minimum.
- Pack a small bag for each child with pajamas, toothbrush, toothpaste, and a favorite blanket and toy, so they can settle into a new place fast.
- If you need cribs and high chairs, call ahead to double-check that they are available and in place.
- Be prepared with snacks during travel times and in hotel rooms.
- Strange beds, unfamiliar schedules, and the excitement of new places wreak havoc with bedtimes, so plan time out for rest each day.

You'll find many more practical suggestions for traveling with children in the book *Great Vacations with Your Kids* by Dorothy Ann Jordon and Marjorie Adoff Cohen (E. P. Dutton, New York, 1987). The book also includes many vacation suggestions.

SINGULAR PARENT CHOICES

Some of the vacation choices recommended for single adults are equally comfortable for single-parent families. Active adventure vacations are wonderful for youngsters who are old enough to enjoy them. Almost all are appropriate for teens, and some can accommodate much younger children. Ask the operator about the ages recommended. Some groups that explicitly welcome children are listed below, along with learning options that have separate programs for youngsters.

Ranch vacations are made to order for single parents, and all the guidance on page 19 is appropriate.

If you want to go to a resort, check for tennis, sailing, or golf schools that are resort-based. If there is also a supervised children's program, you will have found a focus where parents can make new friends while the children are enjoying their own brand of fun. Cruising from a family point of view also is covered below.

Here are a variety of vacation suggestions for single parents.

CLUB MED, 40 E. 57th St., New York, NY 10019; 800-CLUB MED. **(M–E)**

Club Med doesn't just tolerate children—they welcome them (says the brochure) with open hearts and arms. Among the clubs that now have "mini-club" areas set aside for kids ages 2 to 11 are Caravelle (Guadeloupe), Punta Cana (Dominican Republic), Eleuthera (Bahamas), Ixtapa (Mexico), Huatulco (Mexico), The Sandpiper (Florida), Saint Lucia (Caribbean), and Copper Mountain (Colorado).

There are separate facilities within the Club Med village with activities, meals, and amusements designed just for children, supervised and coordinated by a special staff, all at no additional cost. They are open from 9 A.M. to 9 P.M. daily.

Activities vary from village to village, but lessons in scuba diving (with minisized equipment in the pool), sailing, snorkeling, waterskiing, swimming, practice golf, archery, painting, and dramatics are among those available for kids. Lots of children love Club Med circus workshops where they learn juggling, magic, miming, makeup application, how to use a trampoline, and how to walk a trapeze (with a net right below, of course). There are separate activity programs for the 2-to-5 age group and for the older children.

The Sandpiper club in Florida even offers a "Baby Club" for tots and toddlers 4 to 23 months. It is equipped with cribs, playpens, toys, and a special restaurant with hot and cold buffets, just for baby. The club is open from 9 A.M. to 6 P.M. and children may be left for a morning, an afternoon, or all day long. Bottle warmers, mixers and sterilizers, strollers and cribs for use outside the club are also available. The club boutique sells diapers—how family-minded can you get?

At certain times of the year, some clubs are free to younger children accompanied by a parent. Time periods and specific clubs vary from season to season, so it's best to check for current information. Those under one year travel free when sitting on their parents' laps; ages 2 to 11 pay three-quarters of the adult plane fare.

Teenagers can also have a ball trying out the many sports activities that are part of the package at every Club Med, where they can have a go at windsurfing or sailing or any other activity they've always wanted to try.

PARENT/CHILD WEEK, ALL-AMERICAN SPORTS TENNIS CAMPS, 116 Radio Circle, Mt. Kisco, NY 10549; 800-223-2442 or 914-666-0096. **(E)**

With separate programs offered for adults and children, the All-American Amherst camp is a good prospect for tennis-minded families anytime, but for the special Parent/Child Week held each July, parents get a special discount on rates for the Junior Camp. The daytime programs separate ages to work on their tennis games, but families can be together at night.

VAN DER MEER TENNIS CENTER, P.O. Box 5902, Hilton Head Island, SC 29938; 800-845-6138 or 803-785-9602. **(I;** does not include meals)

Besides teaching clinics for juniors ages 9 to 16, there are "Munchkin" activities for those 3 to 5 years and 6 to 8 years, keeping the kids happy while parents brush up on serves and strokes. Kids like the beach at Hilton Head also.

NICK BOLLETTIERI TENNIS ACADEMY, 5500 34th St. W., Bradenton, FL 34210; 813-755-1000 or 1-800-USA-NICK. **(M)**

There are tennis programs here for both juniors and adults, though no special designated family week.

GOLF DIGEST INSTRUCTION SCHOOLS, 5520 Park Ave., Box 395, Trumbull, CT 06611; 800-243-6121 or 203-373-7130. **(EE)**

Once a year, this large golf program offers a special parent/child week. Open to youngsters age 12 and up; instruction is geared to each age group, a sharing and learning experience that builds closeness as well as golfing prowess. The group is limited to 16 parent/child teams. In the past the week has been held at Amelia Island, Florida, and Sea Island, Georgia; check for the current locations.

BOSCOBEL BEACH, Jamaica, c/o International Lifestyles, P.O. Box 534, Freeport, NY 11520; 800-858-8009 or 516-868-6924. **(M–E,** depending on season)

It must be a sign of the times. This resort property near Ocho Rios once was the Playboy Club. Now it is part of the Superclubs all-inclusive resort group, and it has extended a special welcome to single parents. The offer of "single parent" months that do away with the single supplement and allow two children 14 or under to stay in a parent's room free has been so successful that this policy has been extended to the whole year. The hotel's origins now mean extra-large rooms and big baths, with plenty of space for families. All rooms have refrigerators.

Included in the rates are meals, drinks, airport transfers, and all activities, including water sports, scuba, snorkeling, tennis, squash, use of Nautilus equipment, two Jacuzzis, glass-bottom boat rides, and shopping excursions to Ocho Rios. While parents are enjoying all this, children are attended by "Supernannies." Toddlers have their own wading pool and petting zoo; older kids go to computer classes, learn arts and crafts and how to reggae. There are excursions for all ages. Parents can leave the kids as long as they like, until children's mealtime from 5 to 6 P.M., when they are asked to be on hand. Families who prefer to share dinner can do so. Cribs, booster seats, and other paraphernalia are provided.

SIERRA CLUB FAMILY OUTINGS, c/o Sierra Club, 730 Polk St., San Francisco, CA 94109; 415-776-2211. **(I)**

Introducing families to the joys of camping and the outdoors is one of the missions of the Sierra Club. Half a dozen outings each summer are designated especially for families, and the catalog notes that single parents as well as uncles, aunts, and grandparents are welcome. The difficulty of the trips varies; some are lodge-based, others are at campsites. All offer opportunities for nature study, day hikes, fishing, swimming, and solitude. The group meets for breakfast and supper; lunch for outings is packed at breakfast. Most activities are informal and unstructured, and the group usually makes its own fun in the evening.

Among recent offerings were "Toddler Tramps" in state and national parks appropriate for children ages 2 to 5, and other adventures designated for children over 5 years. The Sierra Club catalog also notes other types of trips that are suitable for families.

FAMILY GOES TO CAMP, SHERI GRIFFITH EXPEDITIONS, P.O. Box 1324, Moab, Utah 84532; 800-332-3200 or 801-259-8229. **(M)**

The most exciting river runs are recommended for ages 10 and up, but this special family trip of about 94 miles on the Green River through Desolation Canyon is full of big, rolling waves that are fun but not difficult and is open to children from age 5. Camping is on sandy beaches with plenty of beach toys, and shovels and buckets for sand-castle building. There are hiking excursions into side canyons, some with ancient Indian writings on the walls. Meals take pint-size tastes into account by including hamburgers as well as steak. After dark there are campfires, roasted marshmallows, and plenty of talk and song.

During these 5-day, 4-night excursions offered monthly in the summer, guides also take the children on separate outings. Parents can join in or take this time for themselves—for quiet relaxation beside the river, a leisurely walk, or a demanding hike. According to the operators, many of the adults usually are single parents, sometimes as many as half of the group.

FAMILY RAFTING, O.A.R.S. RAFTING ADVENTURES, Box 67, Angels Camp, CA 95222; 209-736-4677. **(I)**

For families who want to be introduced to the fun of river-rafting, special discounts are offered on selected dates for trips on the Rogue and South Fork rivers. Trips range from 2 to 5 days.

The regular trips offered by this group also welcome children of specified minimum ages, starting at 7 years for many of the trips and at 12 years for the more rugged rivers.

FAMILY RAFTING, Dvořák's Rafting Expeditions, 17921-B U.S. 285, Nathrop, CO 81236; 800-824-3795 or 719-539-6851. **(I–M)**

On specified family weeks, this outfitter invites one child under 16 to come along free with an adult. These trips on the Green and Dolores rivers are planned with kids in mind. Reserve early—they fill up fast.

Other short trips suited to introducing families to river-running offer discounts for families of three and up.

FAMILY TRIPS, American Wilderness Adventures, American Wilderness Alliance, 7600 E. Arapaho Rd., Suite 114, Englewood, CO 80112; 800-322-9453 or 303-771-0380. **(I)**

Wilderness rides combined with camping in the Colorado high country, canoe trips on Minnesota's lakes, and outings in the majestic canyons of the Green River in Utah are offered by this national nonprofit conservation group. Trips include guided walks to explore plants and wildlife, paddleboat floats, and plenty of water play. On water trips, kids with guides sometimes go off in separate rafts, leaving adults to do their own thing. Trips range from 3 to 5 nights. This is an ideal camping introduction, since guides take care of all camp chores and food preparation. Some trips also include stays at comfortable lodges.

CONSERVATION SUMMIT YOUTH PROGRAMS, National Wildlife Federation, 1400 Sixteenth St. NW, Washington, D.C. 20036-2266; 703-790-4363. **(I–M)**

Most of the programs for adults outlined on page 60 offer separate supervised activities for children of all ages. "The Big Backyard," running from 8 A.M. to noon for 3- and 4-year-olds, is a nature discovery program including micro-hikes, touch-and-feel expeditions and fun-with-nature crafts. "Junior Naturalists" ages 5 to 12 divide into age groups for nature hikes, stream studies, wildlife investigations, bird walks, folk tale hours, outdoor games, and arts and crafts. Their day runs from 8:30 A.M. to 3:00 P.M. A separate Teen Adventure program is adventure-oriented, with the chance to learn hiking, orienteering, and rope skills.

CORNELL ADULT UNIVERSITY, 626 Thurston Ave., Ithaca, NY 14850-2490; 607-255-6260. **(I–M)**

Though the title says adult, kids are far from forgotten here. About 150 youngsters from all over the United States enroll in the Youth Program, having fun while their parents are learning on their own level. Families always have breakfast and dinner together, but child supervision is available from 8:30 A.M. to 11:15 P.M. for those who want it.

Programming is provided for five age groups. Infants and tots under 3 years have no formal schedule but qualified baby-sitters are available. Li'l Bears, ages 3 to 5, learn and play in a Cornell preschool facility. Art, music, crafts, expeditions across campus, and time to rest are all part of their fun. (Children enrolled must be potty trained.)

Sprouts, kindergarteners, and first-graders have a learning program as well as hikes, games, sports, crafts, and cookouts. Junior Cornellians from second and third grade meet in the morning for a choice of classes, have recreational activities, outings to state parks, bowling parties, and other fun during supervised afternoon and evening programs. Fourth-, fifth-; and sixth-graders choose from a variety of classes, including art, animal behavior, horse care, tennis, and racquet sports and outdoor adventures such as rappeling, using ropes, wilderness hiking, orienteering, and canoeing.

Teens up to tenth grade have an even wider selection, including theater and windsurfing. They have their own reserved dormitory floor and dining hall.

CHAUTAUQUA INSTITUTION, Chautauqua, NY 14722; 716-357-6200. **(I–M)**

While parents enjoy the multitude of classes and cultural events during the summer at Chautauqua, youngsters can enroll in the diverse children's programs offered. Programs are for one week to a full season.

Children's School, held from 9 A.M. to 12 noon daily, is an early childhood center for preschoolers from 2½ to 6. It includes language enrichment, pre-reading, early math concepts, and exposure to the arts as well as creative free play. An afternoon Pre-Club for 5- and 6-year-olds who have attended the morning program includes beach activities, group games, arts and crafts, music, creative dramatics, and field trips. About 1,000 youngsters each summer take advantage of the Boys' and Girls' Club for ages 6 to 15. It is organized as a day camp where children get a full schedule of summer recreation such as swimming, sailing, canoeing, arts and crafts, drama, music, archery, basketball, soccer, volleyball, and baseball. The group is divided into smaller sections according to age.

For teenagers, there is a Youth Activities Center open daily from noon to 11 P.M. It has its own beach with diving board, snack bar, amusement machines, Ping-Pong equipment, swimming pool, table games, and color TV. Dances, cookouts, guest speakers, and movies are offered at night. The center also is headquarters for the High School and College Clubs, each with activities planned by its own members.

FAMILY ADVENTURE TRAVEL

These organizations present opportunities for group travel with children to exciting destinations that single parents might not undertake on their own.

JOINT ADVENTURE—A Journey for Parent and Child, c/o Malcolm Musicante, Westport Travel Services, 136 Main St., Westport, CT 06881; 800-243-3335 or 203-226-3555. **(E–EE)**

Activity-centered adventures for families, including white-water rafting in Alaska, sailing in the Virgin Islands, hiking through the Maine wilderness, and horseback riding through the Canadian Rockies are planned for groups consisting of several one-parent, one-child couples by founder Malcolm Musicante, who feels this is the best way to foster parent-child closeness even in two-parent families. Trips are open to all ages and combinations—father-daughter or mother-son are as welcome as father-son or mother-daughter.

INTERNATIONAL FAMILY ADVENTURES, THE AMERICAN INSTITUTE FOR FOREIGN STUDY, 102 Greenwich Ave., Greenwich, CT 06830; 203-863-6106. **(EE)**

This long-established organization specializing in travel abroad for students also runs tours suggested for adults traveling with children in grades one to nine. The escorted groups are limited to 25, making for congenial ambience, and special activities are planned for the kids. Recent destinations have included China, Africa, and Europe. On the China trip, activities such as a puppet show, a visit to the zoo and a school, and a boat outing were included, and bikes were rented on one day. Often, the children become friendly with one another, choosing to eat together at their own table, and leaving the adults to socialize.

RASCALS IN PARADISE, c/o Adventure Express, 185 Berry St., Suite 5503, San Francisco, CA 94107; 415-442-0799 or 800-443-0799. **(EE)**

Diving in Fiji, visits to Papua New Guinea, Australia, Belize, Jamaica, East Africa, the western United States, the British Virgin Islands, India, Ecuador, China, Egypt, and Mexico are among the family offerings of this California-based group. Age minimums vary with the difficulty of the trip and are as low as 4 or 5 years for many destinations. To make the experience easier for families, the group establishes one home base and goes exploring on day trips. Babysitters are available as needed. Kids have a separate menu and mealtimes bring familiar foods even in remote climes. Groups are usually composed of one to six families; if four or more families sign up, a teacher-escort goes along. The operators also book family-oriented resort vacations.

FAMILY CRUISES

Children love cruise ships. They love climbing the steps or riding the elevators from one deck to another; they like the pools and the gyms and all the activities and entertainment on board; they adore scampering down the gangplank to see a brand-new port. The constant parade of food is a treat, especially since it usually includes familiar favorites like hamburgers and ice cream as well as more sophisticated fare. Teens enjoy it too—provided they find company aboard. Some ships provide special video/disco centers where they can meet one another.

Cruising certainly is not a cheap family vacation, but it can be a memorable one, and many of the problems of cruising alone are solved when you have your family along.

Almost any itinerary seems exciting, but Premier Cruise Lines (400 Challenger Rd., Cape Canaveral, FL 32920; 800-327-7113 or 407-783-5061) is of special interest to families because it is the official cruise line of Walt Disney World. Their 7-day combination packages allow you to rest up from a visit to Disney World and a tour of the Kennedy Space Center with a 3- or 4-day cruise to the Bahamas. Big family-sized cabins can hold up to 5 people. There are always plenty of kids on board and activities are planned for them. Premier also has special single-parent rates.

Most cruise lines today recognize that families are good business, and more than 50 ships now offer varying kid-size amenities, from baby-sitters to foreign language lessons. Norwegian Cruise Lines runs a popular program known as "Circus at Sea" where kids learn to juggle and perform circus routines, showing off their prowess in an onboard performance for the adults. Young passengers also get their own edition of "Kids' Cruise News" with schedules of special activities such as story hours, arts and crafts programs, and movies.

Regent Cruises organizes children's talent shows and takes young passengers on tours of the Captain's steering quarters on the bridge. Costa Cruises also passes out a "What to play today" information sheet, with a coloring page on the back. Kids on Royal Caribbean ships can attend pizza parties and take part in athletic contests just for them, as well as participate in a special ritual: tossing a bottle containing a message into the sea. These bottles have been found by beachcombers all over the world.

Activities are usually divided according to age, with nurseries for children ages 2 to 6, separate programs for ages 7 to 12 and teens. Many cruise lines allow children under 3 to share their parents' staterooms free of charge, and others have special children's rates or reduced fares for the third and fourth passengers in a cabin.

Reduced rates and children's programs vary with the seasons, and some lines offer them only during school breaks.

It is wise to ask a few pertinent questions when you compare cruises.

- Are there cabins large enough to comfortably accommodate families? Are there any connecting cabins? Is there room for a crib if you need one?
- What are children's rates? Are there periods when these go down? (One child traveling with a single adult is usually charged the going double rate, but rates should go down for additional children.) Some lines are now making special concessions for single parents, and others have special children's rates during off-peak periods.
- When can you count on supervised activities for children? How large is the children's staff? What is the average size of the group they supervise?
- Is there a children's center on board? What does it offer?
- Is there a separate center for teens?
- Are children's meals offered during the early sitting if parents are signed up for the later serving?
- Are booster chairs available in the dining room?
- Are any evening activities planned for young passengers?
- Are baby-sitters available in the evening?
- Is there any provision for baby-sitting for young children while the ship is in port?
- Are there any special shore excursions for youngsters? Any special children's rates on regular excursions?

Choose carefully, and you can look forward to smooth sailing on a family vacation at sea.

WINDJAMMERS

Teenagers love the adventure of the big sailing ships listed beginning on page 109. They aren't well suited to restless younger folks, however.

SKI WEEKS

Skiing is a wonderful family sport. Even the youngest children take to the slopes with glee, and thanks to nurseries and lessons for children, parents can find free time to take off at their own ability level. The bigger ski resorts typically have centers that accommodate children from infants to ages 6 or 8, so parents can still get in some extra runs after the small fry retire. You can leave the children there for an hour or two or for the day.

As the kids get older, skiing allows for plenty of independence. After one or two family runs, everyone usually goes off to his or her own challenges, reuniting for lunch and at day's end. If the weather is uncooperative, parents can stay by the fire or read a book in the lodge while gung-ho youngsters brave the elements. In our case, skiing was the one family vacation that remained popular even after my children were in college and traveling on their own.

If you can afford it, the ideal situation for families is a lodge within walking distance of the slopes or one that has shuttle service to the mountain. This means eager beavers can be first on the slopes while parents get needed rest, and everyone can quit and go home when they are ready.

Another good bet is Club Med at Copper Mountain in Colorado, where special lessons are available for children ages 3 to 12. Younger ones get a basic initiation, those 6 to 12 have 2 hours of lessons morning and afternoon. Besides skiing, the Mini Club is open from 9 A.M. to 9 P.M. with staff-supervised activities and meals for the kids.

Every ski area offers money-saving ski week packages with or without lessons, and many have additional savings for children who stay in parents' rooms. Families also may choose less-expensive, less-crowded smaller ski areas while children are still young and need less challenge. The best plan is to pick several areas that interest you and write for current programs.

SINGLE GRANDPARENTS

Single grandparents and their grandchildren can make great traveling companions. Each generation widens the other's perspective, and a trip affords them a wonderful chance to get to know each other better and bond affection for life. Grandtravel was founded to make it easier to arrange this type of trip. These escorted tours take care of all travel arrangements, leaving grandparents free to enjoy themselves without worry. And they provide compatible companions for each age group as well. Small groups number no more than 20. The grandparents typically are in their 60s or early 70s, the grandchildren ages 7 to 14. Among the U.S. destinations are the western national parks, Washington, D.C., Colorado, southern California, the desert Southwest, and Alaska. Foreign itineraries include New Zealand, China, England, and Scotland, barging in Holland, and safaris in Kenya. For more information, contact Grandtravel, c/o The Ticket Counter, 6900 Wisconsin Ave., Suite 706, Chevy Chase, MD 28015; 800-247-7651 or 301-986-0790.

The American Association for Retired Persons also offers a few tours for grandparents who are members and children ages 10 to 18. Information is available from A.A.R.P. Travel Service, 4801 W. 100th St., Overland Park, KS 66211; 800-365-5358.

CITY SAFARIS

Parents who prefer an outing solely for their own family would do well to think about visiting a city. Kids really wax enthusiastic about picking a city and planning what to see and do. All you have to do to keep everybody happy is to allot a fair share of time for activities that appeal to youngsters as well as grown-ups. You might try making an itinerary, alternating your choices with those of the children.

Intersperse museum visits with trips to the zoo, the beach, or an aquarium, for example. If you insist on shopping with children along, reward them with a performance at a children's theater. Look for boat rides, major league baseball games, and other sure-to-please treats everyone can share. While you are researching reasonable family-priced dining, look out also for the best local ice cream emporiums. Above all, provide plenty of breaks such as excursions to city parks where kids can run and play or use up excess energy on a rented bike. Parks offer a bonus for parents, for while the smaller members of the family are letting off steam, adults can gain a special perspective watching everyday local life they might otherwise have missed.

The growth of all-suite hotels with two rooms for the price of one is a real boon for families. These are equivalent in price to standard hotels, and offer space, privacy, refrigerators, separate TVs, and some even have cooking facilities. While you may not want to spend your vacation cooking, having snacks, drinks, and breakfast ingredients on hand is a real money saver. Many of the all-suite chains also include a free breakfast.

Most bed-and-breakfast facilities, however, are not good choices for families with young children. Wriggly, noisy little ones often feel much too restricted in someone else's home. And somehow, even a budget motel seems more exciting, more of a special outing.

Almost any major city presents opportunities for family adventures, but those with easy and inexpensive public transportation systems offer a special advantage.

WASHINGTON, D.C.

This city is a guaranteed child-pleaser, and the Tour Mobile allows you to get on and off all day, seeing the many monuments and sights without wearing out shoe leather. The FBI tour is a special treat for most young visitors, and the Mall allows for stretching young legs. Every kid loves climbing on the prehistoric animals outside the Museum of Natural History.

BOSTON

Another of my favorite places with children is Boston, home of the New England Aquarium with its exciting dolphin shows as well as a fabulous Children's Museum and the country's only Computer Museum, a sure-fire hit with most youngsters. In Boston, kids can have a lively history lesson walking the red line of the Freedom Trail, tossing their own chest of tea overboard on the Boston Tea Party ship, and boarding "Old Ironsides," the USS *Constitution.* A visit to Paul Revere's home and the Old North Church in the North End can be followed by dinner at one of the area's many Italian restaurants, with unbeatable cannoli for dessert. The famous swan boats are still out in the Public Garden in warm weather, offering rides near the spot made famous by the classic children's story "Make Way for Ducklings." Read the book before you go.

Kids also love visiting the food booths at Quincy Market, where lavish choices for every taste include pizza and brownies as well as a whole world of ethnic fare, all to be enjoyed at outdoor tables to the tune of free entertainment by street musicians. And this is a great city for sports lovers, with two of the country's classic arenas, Fenway Park and the Boston Garden. Don't overlook the Esplanade beside the Charles River, a great place for watching roller skaters, joggers, rowing crews, and sailboat in action. And a walk up Beacon Hill is a wonderful way to see what cities were like in America a long time ago. Trolley tours and double-decker buses also allow on and off privileges around the city.

PHILADELPHIA

Children love Philadelphia—and vice versa. Besides the perennial attraction of the Liberty Bell and Independence Hall, this city makes youngsters welcome with some of the most innovative attractions in the country, including the "Please Touch" Museum, the first in the nation designed especially for children under age 7. Another award-winning attraction is the imaginative Treehouse at the Philadelphia Zoo, where kids can find out how it feels to climb through a 35-foot-high honeycomb or hatch out of a giant egg in the Everglades Swamp. The nation's oldest zoo also offers a separate Children's Zoo, where kids can board Noah's Ark to pet the furry passengers, see how cows are milked, ride a pony, or watch a sea lion show.

History, Philadelphia-style, becomes a hands-on experience at Franklin Court, a fabulous little museum devoted to Benjamin Franklin where a telephone hotline allows you to call anyone from George Washington to John F. Kennedy to hear what they had to say about the remarkable Mr. F. At Dial-A-Witticism, you can call up a Franklin quip on almost any subject. And not far away on the river, you can board historic ships.

The big Franklin Institute ranks as one of the nation's great science museums. It is full of participatory exhibits that let you climb aboard a steam locomotive or take a walk through the chambers of a giant walk-through heart. Adults are as fascinated as the kids. Philadelphia also offers the nation's largest city park, filled with diversions. And there is good eating both at the family restaurants near South Philly's colorful Italian Market and at Reading Terminal Market, where generations of Philadelphians have shopped for fresh produce and meat—and where knowing locals come for lunch at stands offering everything from freshly carved turkey sandwiches to Greek gyros or hot enchiladas.

CHICAGO

Chicago's many lakeside parks are ideal for families, offering all-star cultural attractions as well as beaches and boat rides. Among the special family favorites are the Children's Museum and Zoo in Lincoln Park, the Field Museum of Natural History, Adler Planetarium and Shedd Aquarium in Grant Park, the Junior Museum of the Art Institute, and the wonderful Museum of Science and Industry on the city's south side, with its Omnimax Theater, fabulous dollhouse, and such imaginative exhibits as a working coal mine. Brookfield Zoo, located just outside the city, is outstanding.

The special excitement of a great city makes for meaningful shared memories for everyone in the family—which is what family vacations are all about.

12

TRAVEL SMART

WHETHER YOU WILL BE JOINING A GROUP OR traveling on your own, with or without children in tow, when you set out without another adult along, it is doubly important to be a smart traveler. Traveling alone carries some built-in stresses: no one to help watch the bags or read a map, no one to share the aggravations. But there are practical things you can do to keep yourself feeling confident and in control.

PRACTICAL PACKING

Redcaps never seem to be around when you need them most, so remember when you pack your suitcase that every item inside is something *you* may have to carry. Use the smallest suitcase you can get along with and pack a folding tote bag to hold any extras you might acquire on your trip. If you need a lot of clothing, two smaller bags or a small case and a garment bag may be easier to manage than a giant suitcase.

A soft-sided bag with a frame is the best combination I've found for both light weight and protection; Cordura, which looks like canvas but is as strong as nylon, is an excellent choice as a luggage material. Sturdy wheels make a bag easy to transport. If the luggage lacks wheels, a wheeled carrying cart can be a lifesaver. Other helps are shoulder straps or straps that turn a bag into a backpack, freeing your hands for finding tickets or change.

Be merciless when it comes to paring down your travel wardrobe. Unless you are going to a resort where dressing up is the rule, all a woman really needs for a week of normal travel is three dark skirts or pairs of slacks, three daytime tops and three tops for evening, a sweater, a jacket, and a raincoat (preferably one that easily folds up). A similar basic wardrobe suits men, who may add also ties for evening. One pair of comfortable walking shoes (already broken in) and one pair of dress shoes complete the picture, unless you need to add a warmer coat for colder climates. If the temperature is unpredictable, try bringing silk long underwear, the kind skiers wear; it is lightweight, keeps you warm, and can be rolled up into almost nothing when you pack.

So many hotels have indoor pools these days that you may want to take along a bathing suit no matter what the season. Packing a couple of plastic bags to hold wet or dirty clothing is another good idea.

Before you set off on your trip, be sure your luggage is locked securely and clearly tagged, and remember to put your name, home address, and next destination address inside your suitcase, as well. Tags sometimes do get detached and if your bag gets lost, inside identification will help locate you.

It's also not a bad idea to jot down the brand, size, color, and any other aids for identifying your luggage in case it is delayed or lost by an airline. They will ask you to write a description and sometimes memories play tricks under stress.

Another helpful tip: Make copies of your tickets, confirmations of hotel reservations, passport, and other important documents. The copies will be a big help should you need replacements.

EASY ARRIVALS

If you are getting into a strange city from the airport alone, you'll feel a lot more confident if you know what to expect. Find out from your travel agent, tour operator, or hotel, or the airport or airline how long it takes to get into the city and the options for getting there. Is there a convenient bus or limo to your hotel? Does the hotel have courtesy service? Are cabs plentiful? What is the difference in cost between public transportation and usual cab fare?

If you take a cab, you can save hassles by knowing in advance the going rate to town. Ask the driver what the fare will be before you get in, and if it is out of line, wait for another cab.

One little thing I've learned that helps abroad and even sometimes in the United States is to write down the name and address of your destination clearly before you get into a cab and to mark the spot on a street map. You can't assume that foreign drivers know English or that all cab drivers know their cities well.

The more you know, the more you will have that all-important feeling of control in a strange place.

MONEY MATTERS

Nobody likes to think of bad things happening on vacation, but the surest way to prevent them is to be prepared. Money holders to guard against pickpockets give great peace of mind when you travel. Overladen single travelers juggling bags and bundles can be a tempting target.

Protection comes in many forms. Some money holders are slotted to fit on a belt, others have straps that either hang around your neck or across your shoulder like a holster, or fit around the calf of your leg under trousers. Some travelers like hikers' day packs that fit around the waist. Pick whatever seems easiest for you; all allow you to stash cash, tickets, and passports without worry. There's even a waterproof plastic money holder on a neck cord that solves the problem of where to put your cash if you go swimming alone.

You probably know to keep traveler's check receipts separate from the checks, in case you have to make a claim. It is also a good idea to keep your credit cards and cash separate, so that if your wallet disappears, you have another resource.

Another little money suggestion before you set out: Be sure you have small bills ready for tips and enough change on hand to use the telephone. If you are traveling to a foreign country, "trip packs" of foreign currency for this purpose can be bought in major U.S. airports. If you exchange money in the airport on arrival, remember to ask for small bills and change; the tendency is to hand out larger bills.

Obviously, it's safer to carry traveler's checks than a lot of cash. The one place you may want to bring more cash than usual is to Canada, since there is a service charge for converting traveler's checks to Canadian currency but no charge to change dollars.

The practice of tipping puzzles many travelers. If you are going to a foreign country, read up on local customs before you leave home. In many countries, the tip is included in the price of the meal. In the United States, the usual amounts vary in different parts of the country.

HANDY COMPANIONS

There are some terrific gadgets around to help you feel and look cool and collected on the road. One valuable traveling companion is a compact clothes steamer to remove wrinkles in a hurry when you unpack; they really work. Just remember to have the right adapter plugs if you are traveling in a foreign country. To get a free guide to the voltages in 200 countries around the world, send a stamped self-addressed envelope to Franzus Company, c/o Customer Service, Murtha Industrial Park, P.O. Box 142, Deacon Falls, CT 06403.

Other handy travel gadgets include inflatable hangers for drip-dry clothes; tiny sponges that expand in water when you find yourself without a washcloth; portable clotheslines and individual packets of laundry soap; portable alarm clocks; and tiny calculators that help you figure foreign currency rates in a flash. I love my Banana Republic unisex Gore-Tex hat that packs flat but can be popped into shape to ward off both sun and rain. Folding umbrellas may also come in handy when the weather is uncooperative. It's expecting too much to think a thundershower will wait until you're within convenient reach of a store.

Shop your own department store notions department for these and many other intelligent travel items. If you don't have access to a good selection, here are three mail-order companies that specialize in travel gear; write for their catalogs:

LE TRAVEL STORE, 295 Horton Plaza, San Diego, CA 92101; 1-800-854-6677; in California, 619-544-0005.
EAGLE CREEK TRAVEL GEAR, 1665 South Rancho Santa Fe Rd., San Marcos, CA 92068; 1-800-874-9925; in California, 619-471-7600.
TRAVELER'S CHECKLIST, 335 Cornwall Bridge Rd., Sharon, CT 06069; 203-364-0144.

STAYING HEALTHY

When you are tired or not feeling well, minor problems loom twice as large, so to maintain a feeling of calm and control, it's wise to do what you can to minimize the fatigue of traveling and to take sensible precautions to keep yourself healthy.

Air travel is particularly tiring because seating space is tight. Experienced travelers make the best of it by asking for seat assignments as soon as they make plane reservations—and they know which seats to ask for to get the most leg room on board. Always avoid the squeezed-in middle seats if you can. Aisle versus window is a matter of preference—the aisle makes it easier to leave your seat, the window provides a headrest for napping. Inflatable pillows contoured to support the neck are a smart investment to rest better on plane, train, or bus, without a stiff neck as a souvenir of your trip.

On most planes, the lower-numbered seats near the front get the quickest meal service, and the best chance of getting your meal of choice; sometimes the most popular dish is no longer available by the time the meal cart gets to the back. Rows 10 to 20 are often the best choice for a quick exit; on many planes they are closest to the door. If you are serious about getting the best seat for seeing the movie or stretching your legs, you can invest in the *Airline Seating Guide*, a reference that comes in U.S. and overseas editions. For information contact Forsyth Travel Library, Box 2975, Shawnee Mission, Kansas 66201-1375; 800-FORSYTH.

As for jet lag, no one has solved the problem. Only time really helps your body clock to resynchronize when you cross several time zones. But there are some strategies that may help to reduce the fatigue. Begin a few days before departure to gradually shift your meal and sleep times to fit the new time zone. Adopt the new time immediately when you arrive at your destination, and spend time out of doors—daylight somehow seems to help readjust the body's rhythms. Avoid overeating or excessive drinking on the plane—as well as at your destination. Whether you are better off traveling by day or night depends a great deal on how well you sleep on a plane. Some travelers find that taking a mild sleeping pill helps them rest better and feel fresher at journey's end.

Don't leave your sunglasses and suntan lotion behind just because you are heading for a city; sight-seeing often puts you out of doors for long periods.

Bring along medication from home for the most common travel maladies such as headaches and diarrhea. You'll be thankful you did if the need arises when pharmacies are closed. And, just in case, remember to look for extra blankets or pillows as soon as you check into your hotel room. The middle of the night may be too late.

If you are traveling to countries where hygiene is a problem, you no doubt have been warned to drink only bottled water, but remember to avoid drinks with ice as well. Eat only cooked fruits and vegetables or those that can be peeled, and only meat that is well done. Many people even play safe by using bottled water for brushing their teeth.

Time for rest should be a must in your travel schedule. Travelers generally are better off seeing one less sight and getting more out of what they do see. And being tired is a special problem when you are alone. It magnifies the difficulties and gets you down, makes you less willing to reach out to meet other people. So allow plenty of time for sleep and plenty of rest breaks in your day. And if you are traveling to a high-altitude destination, remember to allow extra rest time until you adjust.

Be good to the feet that are doing extra duty getting you around. When you get back to your room, elevate your legs to give them a rest. And even if you are a confirmed shower-taker at home, you'll find that a soak in the tub does wonders for a travel-weary body.

PLAYING SAFE

Another concern when you are alone, especially for women, is safety in hotel rooms. Ask for a room near the elevator; don't accept a room at the end of a long corridor. In a large hotel, someone from the front desk should always escort you to your room when you check in. The employee should unlock the room door, check to be sure no one is in the bathroom and pull back curtains over any sliding glass doors. Sliding doors should have a secure lock, preferably in the floor track. If not, ask for some type of rod to put into the track. The hall door should have a chain as well as a bolt lock and a peephole so that you can see who is there. If someone you are not expecting knocks for entry, it's a good idea to call housekeeping or maintenance to ask whether they have actually sent someone.

Never hang the "Make Up My Room" sign on the door; it announces to the world that the room is unoccupied. To discourage intruders, do the opposite—when you are not expecting the maid, hang out the "Do Not Disturb" sign as you leave the room.

It's also wise to check the location of the fire exit nearest to your room—just in case. A helpful booklet published by the federal government, "A Safe Trip Abroad," suggests that a room between the second and seventh floors is the best bet, high enough to prevent easy entry from outside but low enough for fire equipment to reach.

Chances are that nothing will happen to spoil your trip, but you'll sleep easier away from home if you take intelligent precautions.

WORRY INSURANCE

One final matter to think about before you travel is insurance. Many tour companies and several independent companies now offer trip cancellation insurance. The average cost is low and can prove a worthwhile investment whenever you plan far ahead for a very expensive trip. Cruises, for example, offer sizable discounts for early booking, but if it's necessary for you to cancel your plans at the last minute, you can lose your entire payment.

Insurance also includes coverage for any costs that may occur due to travel delays en route.

Your U.S. health insurance probably will not cover you outside the United States, but travel insurance is available. Access America, Inc., 600 Third Ave., New York, NY 10163; 800-284-8300 is one organization providing this service. Travel agents and tour operators can supply names of other groups who will supply coverage.

Holders of Gold Visa, MasterCard, and American Express cards also may be entitled to many travel benefits, from life insurance to car rental discounts to a help-line abroad with an English-speaking operator who can advise on medical or legal problems. It pays to check what your card offers, as it may be worth upgrading if you travel often.

BE READY FOR THE BLUES

Many of us have the fantasy that vacations will be happy and exciting from beginning to end. That is not reality, whether you travel alone or with a companion.

Leaving familiar surroundings creates stress—pleasant stress, yes, but it is a strain learning your way around a new place, nonetheless. You may not sleep as soundly in a strange bed. Add the fatigue of unaccustomed exercise and it's easy to understand why vacation emotions tend to be uneven, sometimes shooting from exuberant high to lonesome low. There will inevitably be moments when you wish there were someone close to share a beautiful sunset or a wonderful experience.

The best way to cope when those feelings arise is to let your feelings out in writing—write to a friend back home or in your journal, the solo traveler's best friend. It's okay to talk about your blues, but make a point of writing about the better side of the trip, as well. It really helps to put the good and bad in perspective.

One other suggestion: In addition to guidebooks, take along the most engrossing books you can find about your destination, either nonfiction or novels set in the locale you are visiting. You'll be learning and building excitement for the next day's outings even while you are distracting yourself from loneliness.

13

HAVE A SINGULAR TRIP

THE DICTIONARY GIVES A NUMBER OF DEFINItions for the word *singular*. The first reads, "a separate person, an individual." The next category reads "distinguished by superiority, exceptional, of unusual quality."

The best solo vacations are a combination of these two. They are uniquely yours, individual. They are superior because they have been tailored to your own interests and personality.

Surely, somewhere in these pages there must be trips that are of special interest to you, excursions that might not suit even your favorite companions. Maybe you are an amateur archaeologist at heart, or you've always yearned to go on safari or to see South America or sail the Caribbean. Or maybe you'd rather strike out on your own to explore the pleasures of Paris or Madrid.

Whatever your pleasure, sign up. Take the challenge and take off. Don't let fear of the unknown keep you at home. Instead of worrying about misfortunes that might occur, think of all the wonderful possibilities—the chances to broaden your experience and your self-esteem.

Vacations serve a great many important functions. They are our best chance to rest from routine and revive the spirit, to be introduced to new places and people, to hone old skills and acquire new ones. All of these experiences can be even more meaningful when on your own, for solo travel offers a big bonus. With the knowledge and confidence gained as a successful traveler, you will be a more aware person—and you'll never feel quite as fearful or dependent on others again.

Probably none of us would choose to spend all of our vacations alone, but that does not mean that we cannot reap the special pleasures and rewards that can come with singular travel. With the right preparation and an optimistic outlook, single can be a singular way to go!

TRAVEL INFORMATION RESOURCES

TRAVEL BOOK SOURCES (ALL TAKE MAIL ORDERS)

THE COMPLETE TRAVELLER, 199 Madison Ave., New York, NY 10016; 212-685-9007.

TRAVELLERS BOOK STORE, 22 W. 52d St., New York, NY 10022; 212-664-0995.

BOOK PASSAGE, 51 Tamal Vista Blvd., Corte Madera, CA 94925; 800-321-9785.

LONELY PLANET PUBLICATIONS, Embarcadero West, 112 Linden St., Oakland, CA 94607; 800-322-7333. (Best publishers of books on travel off the beaten path.)

Helpful booklets for travelers from the federal government include:

A SAFE TRIP ABROAD
TIPS FOR TRAVELERS TO THE CARIBBEAN
TIPS FOR TRAVELERS TO MEXICO
TIPS FOR TRAVELERS TO EASTERN EUROPE AND YUGOSLAVIA
TIPS FOR TRAVELERS TO THE MIDDLE EAST AND NORTH AFRICA
TIPS FOR TRAVELERS TO THE PEOPLE'S REPUBLIC OF CHINA
TRAVEL TIPS FOR SENIOR CITIZENS

Each is $1 and may be ordered from the Superintendent of Documents, Government Printing Office, Washington, D.C. 20402; 202-783-3238.

EUROPEAN TOURISM OFFICES

For names and addresses of U.S. offices of 23 European countries, write to U.S. European Travel Commission, Suite 565, New York,

NY 10111; 212-307-1200. Include a stamped self-addressed envelope and they will also send a list of major events in Europe for the current year.

U.S. STATE OFFICES OF TOURISM

They can supply addresses for specific cities in the state.

ALABAMA BUREAU OF TOURISM AND TRAVEL, 532 S. Perry St., Montgomery, AL 36104; 800-252-2262; in state, 800-392-8096.

ALASKA DIVISION OF TOURISM, Box E, Juneau, Alaska 99811; 907-465-2010.

ARIZONA DIVISION OF TOURISM, 1100 W. Washington St., Phoenix, AZ 85007; 602-542-8687.

ARKANSAS DEPARTMENT OF PARKS AND TOURISM, 1 Capitol Mall, Little Rock, AR 72201; 800-643-8383; in state, 800-482-8999.

CALIFORNIA OFFICE OF TOURISM, 1121 L St., Suite 600, Sacramento, CA 95814; 800-862-2543.

COLORADO TOURISM BOARD, 1625 Broadway, Suite 1700, Denver, CO 80202; 800-433-2656.

CONNECTICUT DEPARTMENT OF ECONOMIC DEVELOPMENT, 210 Washington St., Hartford, CT 06106; 800-243-1685; in state, 800-842-7492.

DELAWARE TOURISM OFFICE, 99 Kings Highway, Box 1401, Dover, DE 19903; 800-441-8846; in state, 800-282-8667.

DISTRICT OF COLUMBIA VISITORS ASSOCIATION, 1575 Eye St. NW, Washington, D.C. 20005; 202-789-7000.

FLORIDA TOURIST DIVISION, 126 Van Buren St., Tallahassee, FL 32301; 904-487-1462.

GEORGIA TOURIST DIVISION, Box 1776, Atlanta, GA 30301; 800-847-4842.

HAWAII VISITORS BUREAU, 2270 Kalakaua Ave., Suite 801, Honolulu, Hawaii 96815; 808-923-1811.

IDAHO TRAVEL COUNCIL, 700 W. State St., Boise, ID 83720; 800-635-7820.

ILLINOIS TOURIST INFORMATION, 310 S. Michigan Ave., Chicago, IL 60604; 800-223-0121.

INDIANA TOURISM DEVELOPMENT, 1 N. Capitol, Suite 700, Indianapolis, IN 46204; 800-292-6337.

IOWA TOURISM OFFICE, 200 E. Grand Avenue, Des Moines, IA 50309; 800-345-4692.

KANSAS TRAVEL AND TOURISM DIVISION, 400 W. 8th St., Suite 500, Topeka, KS 66603; 913-296-2009; in state, 800-252-6727.

KENTUCKY DEPARTMENT OF TRAVEL DEVELOPMENT, Capital Plaza Tower, 22d floor, Frankfort, KY 40601; 800-225-8747.

LOUISIANA OFFICE OF TOURISM, Box 94291, Baton Rouge, LA 70804; 800-334-8626; in state, 504-342-8119.

MAINE PUBLICITY BUREAU, 97 Winthrop St., Box 23000, Hallowell, ME 04347; 800-533-9595.

MARYLAND OFFICE OF TOURISM DEVELOPMENT, 217 E. Redwood St., Ninth floor, Baltimore, MD 21202; 800-331-1750.

MASSACHUSETTS OFFICE OF TRAVEL AND TOURISM, 100 Cambridge St., Boston, MA 02202; 800-533-6277.

MICHIGAN TRAVEL BUREAU, Box 30226, Lansing, MI 48909; 800-543-2937.

MINNESOTA OFFICE OF TOURISM, 375 Jackson St., 250 Skyway Level, St. Paul, MN 55101; 800-328-1461; in state, 800-652-9747.

MISSISSIPPI DEPARTMENT OF TOURISM, Box 22825, Jackson, MS 39205; 800-647-2290.

MISSOURI DIVISION OF TOURISM, Box 1055, Jefferson City, MO 65102; 314-751-4133.

MONTANA PROMOTION DIVISION, 1424 Ninth Ave., Helena, MT 59620; 800-541-1447; in state, 406-444-2654.

NEBRASKA DIVISION OF TRAVEL AND TOURISM, 301 Centennial Mall S, Box 94666, Lincoln, NB 68509; 800-228-4307; in state, 800-742-7595.

NEVADA COMMISSION ON TOURISM, 600 E. Williams St., Suite 207, Carson City, NV 89710; 800-638-2328.

NEW HAMPSHIRE OFFICE OF VACATION TRAVEL, Box 856, Concord, NH 03301; 603-271-2666.

NEW JERSEY DIVISION OF TRAVEL AND TOURISM, C.N. 826, Trenton, NJ 98625; 800-537-7397.

NEW MEXICO TOURISM AND TRAVEL DIVISION, 100 St. Francis Dr., Santa Fe, NM 87503; 800-545-2040; in state, 505-827-0291.

NEW YORK DEPARTMENT OF ECONOMIC DEVELOPMENT, 1 Commerce Plaza, Albany, NY 12245; 800-225-5697.

NORTH CAROLINA DIVISION OF TRAVEL AND TOURISM, 430 N. Salisbury St., Raleigh, NC 27611; 800-847-4862.

NORTH DAKOTA TOURISM PROMOTION, Capitol Grounds, Bismarck, ND 58505; 800-437-2077; in state, 800-472-2100.

OHIO DIVISION OF TRAVEL AND TOURISM, Box 1001, Columbus, OH 43266; 800-282-5393.

OKLAHOMA TOURISM AND RECREATION DEPARTMENT, 215 N.E. 28th St., Oklahoma City, OK 73105; 800-652-6552.

OREGON TOURISM DIVISION, 595 Cottage St. NE, Salem, OR 97310; 800-547-7842; in state, 800-233-3306.

PENNSYLVANIA DIVISION OF TRAVEL MARKETING, 439 Forum Building, Harrisburg, PA 17120; 800-847-4872.

RHODE ISLAND DEPARTMENT OF ECONOMIC DEVELOPMENT, 7 Jackson Walkway, Providence, RI 02903; 800-556-2484.

SOUTH CAROLINA DIVISION OF TOURISM, Box 71, Columbia, SC 29202; 803-734-0122.

SOUTH DAKOTA DEPARTMENT OF TOURISM, 711 Wells Ave., Pierre, SD 57501; 800-843-1930; in state, 800-952-2217.

TENNESSEE TOURISM DEVELOPMENT, Box 23170, Nashville, TN 37202; 615-741-2158.

TEXAS TOURISM DIVISION, Box 12008, Austin, TX 78711; 800-888-8839 or 512-462-9191.

UTAH TRAVEL COUNCIL, Council Hall, Capital Hill, Salt Lake City, UT 84114; 801-538-1030.

VERMONT TRAVEL DIVISION, 134 State St., Montpelier, VT 05602; 802-828-3236.

VIRGINIA DIVISION OF TOURISM, 1021 E. Cary Street, Richmond, VA 23219; 800-847-4884.

WASHINGTON STATE DEPARTMENT OF TRADE AND ECONOMIC DEVELOPMENT, 101 General Administration Building, Olympia, WA 98504; 206-586-2088.

WEST VIRGINIA TOURISM DIVISION, 2101 Washington St., Charleston, WV 25305; 800-225-5982.

WISCONSIN DIVISION OF TOURISM DEVELOPMENT, 123 W. Washington Ave., Box 7970, Madison, WI 53707; 800-432-8747; in state or neighboring states, 800-372-2737.

WYOMING TRAVEL COMMISSION, I-25 and College Dr., Cheyenne, WY 82002; 800-225-5996; in state, 307-777-7777.

INDEX